Essentials of
International
Management

To Tilley
And what should they know of
England who only England know?

Rudyard Kipling,
The English Flag

David C. Thomas

E s s e n t i a l s   o f
International
Management

A Cross-Cultural Perspective

Sage Publications
International Educational and Professional Publisher
Thousand Oaks ▪ London ▪ New Delhi

For information:

 Sage Publications, Inc.
2455 Teller Road
Thousand Oaks, California 91320
E-mail: order@sagepub.com

Sage Publications Ltd.
6 Bonhill Street
London EC2A 4PU
United Kingdom

Sage Publications India Pvt. Ltd.
M-32 Market
Greater Kailash I
New Delhi 110 048 India

Printed in the United States of America

Library of Congress Cataloging-in-Publication Data

Thomas, David C. (David Clinton), 1947-
  Essentials of international management: A cross-cultural perspective
/ By David C. Thomas.
    p. cm.
Includes bibliographical references and index.
  ISBN 0-7619-2468-X (c) — ISBN 0-7619-2181-8 (p)
  1. International business enterprises—Management. 2. International
business enterprises—Management—Cross-cultural studies.
3. Intercultural communication. I. Title.
  HD62.4 .T488 2001
  658'.049—dc21   2001001626

02   03   04   05   06   07   10   9   8   7   6   5   4   3   2   1

Acquiring Editor:	Marquita Flemming
Editorial Assistant:	MaryAnn Vail
Production Editor:	Denise Santoyo
Editorial Assistant:	Cindy Bear
Typesetter/Designer:	Denyse Dunn
Cover Designer:	Ravi Balasuriya

Contents

SECTION II: ROLES OF THE INTERNATIONAL MANAGER

SECTION III: INTERNATIONAL MANAGEMENT CHALLENGES

SECTION IV: INTERNATIONAL MANAGEMENT RESEARCH

List of Tables and Figures

TABLES

FIGURES

Preface

As globalization shapes the role of managers, international responsibilities become the norm rather than the exception, and contact with other cultures becomes commonplace. The need for scholars and managers equally to understand the influence of culture on management practice has never been greater.

This book extracts key concepts on international management from a cross-cultural perspective and condenses them into a concise volume. The amount of description and number of examples given for a particular concept are limited. However, the complexity of cross-cultural management is not glossed over but is presented in all its ragged detail. Consistent with this approach, care has been taken not to speculate when evidence supporting a particular concept or relationship is limited. Rather, the book is extensively referenced and indexed so that the interested reader has ready access to the source of the material presented and can easily follow up on areas of most interest.

This book owes its existence, in part, to dissatisfaction with the available material with which to teach an advanced course in international (cross-cultural) management. Designed as an "essentials" volume that presents key issues in international management in a concise way, this book allows a number of options for its use in the classroom. It can be used in combination with complementary readings and cases as the core text for an advanced course in international management with a micro focus, or if combined with more experiential exercises, it can form the basis of short courses for students with some background in organizational behavior or international business. The book may also be a useful supplement in courses with a macro approach to international manage-ment. In addition, my hope is that scholars, particularly those without a deep background in cross-cultural management, will find it a concise reference to key issues and ideas in the field. Moreover, I believe that managers who invest the effort required to go beyond a superficial knowledge of cross-cultural issues will find it a useful guide.

Similar to any book that purports to be an "essentials" volume, choices were made concerning the domain of the topic area and the par-ticular perspective that informed the organization of the material pre-sented. In this book, I examine cross-cultural management issues from a predominantly psychological perspective. As opposed to being country specific, this book's view of culture focuses on the interactions of people from different cultures in organizational settings. That is, the approach used is to understand the effect of culture in a way that can then be ap-plied to a wide variety of cross-cultural interactions in a number of or-ganizational contexts. Students of organizational behavior, industrial and organizational psychology, and social psychology will find many of the topic areas familiar. However, the focus of this book is on applica-tion of these concepts to international management.

Section I presents four chapters that provide an essential basis for un-derstanding the influence of culture on international management. In Chapter 1, I describe the role of the international manager and present the context in which the international manager must function. I briefly explore the major facets of the international management environment (legal, political, economic, and cultural), with the cultural aspect pre-sented as, in many ways, the most challenging dimension. In Chapter 2, I demystify and define culture in practical terms that can used to explain and predict. That is, I suggest that culture shapes, at the most funda-mental level, the way individuals' cognitions are structured. I discuss the reasons that cultures form and persist and compare and contrast the influence of culture to the influence of human nature and personality. I also present the central debates surrounding the culture construct. Chapter 3 is devoted to the major frameworks that have been used to describe the systematic variation in cultures. The goal of the chapter is to convey the idea that cultural variation is not random but systematic, and can, therefore, be used to explain and predict behavior. In Chapter 4, I apply the basics of social cognition to the context of cross-cultural inter-action. Among the concepts discussed are selective perception, stereo-typing, ethnocentrism, differential attributions, behavioral scripts, and cultural differences in motivation. The message in this chapter is that culture affects managerial behavior through identifiable psychological mechanisms.

Section II contains three chapters that focus on the roles of decision maker, negotiator, and leader that dominate the activities of international managers. In Chapter 5, I review the process of decision making and explore the opportunity for cultural variation in the ways that managers simplify the complex international decision-making environment. In addition, I discuss the ethical dilemmas presented by decision making in an international context. In Chapter 6, I discuss, in terms of the application of cross-cultural communication, the process and behavioral aspects of negotiation. I present the basics of communication, concepts that transfer meaning across cultures, as grounding for understanding negotiation across cultures. In Chapter 7, I explore the difficult task of motivating and leading individuals from different cultures. I contrast Western theories of leadership with theories indigenous to other cultures and present a cross-cultural model of leadership.

Section III is devoted to some of the challenges that face international managers, which can be informed by a better understanding of intercultural interactions. Chapter 8 presents the first of these challenges that involves multicultural work groups and teams. I identify the fundamental factors affecting performance of all work groups and describe culture as influencing these groups through three interrelated, yet distinct, mechanisms. I also discuss key organizational factors that influence the performance of multicultural work groups. In Chapter 9, I discuss international organizations both in terms of a universal logic to organizing and the influence of culture on organizational structure. I describe the basic dimensions of organizational structure and design and discuss different schools of thought with regard to explaining organizational structure. I present the influence of culture and examples of cross-national variation in organizational forms. A discussion of the multinational corporation as a unique organizational form leads to consideration of its influence on managerial roles and the relationship of culturally different individuals to the firm. Chapter 10 looks at the challenges associated with the assignment of individuals overseas from both the perspective on the firm and that of the individual expatriate. A significant volume of research has tried to explain the success or failure of overseas employees by examining individual, organizational, and environmental factors. A review of this literature points to contradictions and paradoxes, which suggest that an overseas assignment can be a double-edged sword.

Chapter 11 recognizes that our understanding of international management is only in its infancy and addresses the challenge of continued learning. In this chapter, I outline general issues concerning the limitations of current management theory to explaining international management. Then, I classify studies of international management regarding the types of questions that they can answer. Finally, I present key methodological issues regarding cross-national and cross-cultural research.

The globalization of the business environment that is being driven by technological and economic factors is resulting in an ever-increasing number of cross-cultural interactions in the workplace. Understanding the influence of culture on interpersonal interactions in organizational settings is now a fundamental requirement of effective international management. I hope that this book will be an aid to that understanding.

As I continue to try to improve my own cultural sensitivity, I recognize that my own background influences my ability to be objective. I would be more than pleased to hear from readers who think my cultural orientation (I'm a naturalized New Zealander, now living in Canada, but born and educated in the United States) may have caused me to miss or misrepresent things that are obvious to them.

DAVID C. THOMAS

Acknowledgments

This book is the product of the assistance and support of a number of people and environments. Their contributions both direct and indirect are sincerely appreciated.

My thanks go to Richard Brislin who was kind enough to introduce the idea for the book and me to Sage Publications. Marquita Flemming at Sage helped to refine the concept of the book and has been supportive and encouraging throughout the process. I am also grateful to the many other staff members at Sage, particularly Denise Santoyo, MaryAnn Vail, and Anna Howland, who have had a hand in bringing the book to life. I am especially grateful to Denise McIntyre for her careful but enthusiastic editing job. My research assistants Yong Xu and Rong Ou also helped with many of the details of manuscript preparation.

Several people took the time to read all or portions of the manuscript, including Allan Bird, Kerr Inkson, and Tatiana Kostova. Their critical insights and helpful comments were very welcome and greatly improved the final product. Any errors or omissions are of course my responsibility alone.

I owe an intellectual debt to *Social Psychology Across Cultures,* written by Peter B. Smith and Michael Bond. Their book proved to me that a rigorous treatment of a nebulous concept such as "culture" was possible.

Finally, three beautiful natural environments contributed to my ability to produce this book. Parts of the manuscript were written at our home in Henderson Valley, New Zealand; at Bob and Saili Doktor's house in Honolulu; and finally, in my office in Vancouver, British Columbia, where financial support was also provided by a President's Research Grant from Simon Fraser University. As you see, and to quote the Kava Boys, "We're not too specific, we just love the Pacific."

Section I
Management
and Culture

One

Introduction

The Challenging Role of the International Manager

*It is generally agreed that planning, organizing, coordinating and control-
ling are basic activities of management.*
                                    Henri Fayol (1916, as cited in Gray, 1987)

*Globalization represents a new stage of world development—a development
process that is having a profound effect on business activities.*
                                    Barbara Parker (1998)

The world of international management is no longer limited to
jet-setting corporate troubleshooters or seasoned expatriate managers. Virtually all business conducted today is global business. It
is difficult to identify a product or service that is not somehow influenced by a cross-border transaction of some kind. Likewise, international responsibilities and contact with other cultures are commonplace and might not even involve leaving the office. Dramatic shifts in

economics, politics, and technology shape the role of the international manager. These shifts are often encapsulated in *globalization*.

This chapter explores the context in which international managers must function in terms of its economic, legal, political, and cultural elements by examining the changes that define globalization. Each of these environmental factors is influential; however, the most difficult to understand and the most often neglected can be the influence of culture. This becomes clear when international management is defined by the structure and content of managerial roles as opposed to the functions of management. The roles that managers play share certain features across cultures but are best understood within their cultural context. By focusing on these roles, the importance of the manager's interactions with individuals from different cultures becomes apparent. Although economics, politics, and technology can define the playing field of international management, it is a game of cross-cultural interactions being played.

Globalization

Globalization has been described as the absence of borders and barriers to trade (Ohmae, 1995), the "crystallization of the world as a single place" (Robertson, 1995, p. 38), or the overlapping of the interests of business and society (Renesch, 1992). Parker (1998) provides a useful general definition when she describes globalization as an increase in the permeability of traditional boundaries, including physical borders, such as nation-states and economies, industries and organizations, and less tangible borders, such as cultural norms or assumptions. This increase in permeability is the result of shifts that have taken place in technological, political, and economic spheres. The following five categories of change illustrate the process of globalization.

Disappearing Boundaries

Traditional economic boundaries between countries are dramatically reduced with the advent of free-trade areas. These regional integration agreements became increasingly prominent in the 1990s. At the dawn of the 21st century, the number of regional trade agreements was more than 100 up from about 45 a decade earlier (World Trade Organization, 1999). The three largest trade groups, the European Union (EU), the North American Free Trade Agreement (NAFTA), and the Asia-Pacific Economic Cooperation (APEC), account for about one-half of the world's trade (WTO, 1999). In addition, the World Trade Organization (WTO), formed in 1995 as a result of the Uruguay round of the General Agreement on Tariffs and Trade (GATT), now has 136 member-nations with the goal of reducing tariffs and liberalizing trade across the board. The result of these agreements is to create a greater degree of interconnectedness among the world's economies. Therefore, local economic conditions are no longer the result of purely domestic influence. The worldwide effect of the financial crisis in Asia in 1997 provides a dramatic example of this interrelatedness.

Organizational boundaries are also affected by globalization. In modern multinational corporations (MNCs), production, sales and marketing, and distribution might all be located in different countries to capitalize on certain location-specific advantages. Moreover, conventional organizational forms are giving way to networks of less hierarchical relationships (Kogut, 1989) and cooperative strategic alliances with other firms (Jarillo, 1988). An additional aspect of changing organizational boundaries is the emergence of virtual organizations in which employees do not meet face to face but are linked by computer technology (Erez & Earley, 1993).

Dynamic Work Environment

Related to the increased permeability of economic and organizational boundaries are changes that affect the stability of the work environment within organizations. These include downsizing, privatization, and movement toward team-based management. For example, globalization means that layoffs can occur in Milan or Seattle because of cheaper labor in Mexico or Malaysia. Increased rates of mergers and acquisitions, because of efforts to remain competitive in a more difficult environment, result in workforce reductions. These workforce changes have an effect on those who remain in the company, as well as on those who leave (Offerman & Gowing, 1990).

A second factor influencing the work environment in many firms is privatization. Governments in both developed and developing countries are selling state-owned business to private investors at an increasing rate ("Privatisation," 1997). Privatization enables formerly government-controlled enterprises to be available for purchase by foreign firms, thus reducing boundaries. In addition, because these enterprises have often been noncompetitive, privatization has a dramatic effect on the worklife and management in these firms. Major changes in technology, workforce size, and management are often required to meet global standards of quality and efficiency. The privatization of government-run enterprise in the former Soviet Union, where over 12,000 state-owned companies were sold ("Russia's State Sell Off," 1994), is perhaps just the most obvious example of this worldwide trend (e.g., Sanderson & Hayes, 1990).

Finally, organizations around the globe are increasingly looking toward the formation of teams of workers as a solution to productivity problems (Hoerr, 1989). Concurrently, demographic shifts in the workforce are occurring in many countries. These demographic changes include increasing cultural diversity because of ease of movement of workers of all skill levels across borders, the rising average age of employees, and the addition of more women to the workforce (Johnston, 1991). Introducing teams in these increasingly multicultural workplaces is a complex affair involving changing work methods, compensation systems, level of employee involvement, and the role of the first-line supervisor (Thomas, Ravlin, & Barry, 2000). These changes, resulting from downsizing, privatization, and team-based management, contribute to create a more complex and dynamic work environment for firms around the world.

Information Technology

The most significant force toward globalization, the one with the most potential to shape the international management landscape, might be the dramatic advances in information technology (Naisbitt, 1994). The rate of change in communications and computing technology is staggering. Multinational firms can now communicate all types of information (e.g., voice, data, text, graphics) throughout their geographically dispersed enterprise instantaneously. In addition, access to information, resources, products, and markets is influenced by improved information technology. With a computer, a modem, and a telephone line, it is now possible to establish a business that is almost entirely unconcerned with traditional boundaries and barriers, including barriers with regard to economies of scale and scope (Parker, 1998). The decreasing price and increased sophistication of computing systems has placed in the hands of small business capabilities that only a few years ago were available only to large multinationals. Information technology breakthroughs that affect almost all areas of human endeavor seem to be occurring on an almost daily basis. Some authors warn that this technological change will render physical place irrelevant for so-called virtual firms and ultimately be the undoing of the nation-state (e.g., Knoke, 1996). At a minimum, the likely effect is that the work roles of employees and managers will need to be adjusted to reflect an increasingly information-driven environment.

Increased Trade and Investment

Despite the negative effects of the 1997 Asian financial crisis, world trade among countries has grown at an average rate of over 5% since 1990 and exceeded $13.6 trillion in 1998 (WTO, 1999). The so-called triad of United States, Japan, and the European Union combine to account for a major portion of world trade. However, as shown in Table 1.1, trade is growing rapidly in developing economies in Asia, such as China, Korea, and Malaysia.

TABLE 1.1 Selected Leading Exporting Countries

Rank	Country	Value US$ (billions)	Percentage Change 1990-98
1	United States	682.5	7.11
2	Germany	539.7	3.2
3	Japan	387.9	3.8
7	Canada	214.3	6.7
9	China	183.8	14.5
12	Korea	132.3	9.3
13	Mexico	117.5	14.1
14	Singapore	109.9	9.6
15	Chinese Taipei	109.9	6.3
20	Malaysia	73.3	12.1
	World Average		5.8

SOURCE: World Trade Organization, 1999. Reprinted with permission.

The overall increase in trade is consistent with the globalization of products and markets. In addition, although the developed world continues to trade at approximately the world average, trade in other economies, mainly in Asia, is developing rapidly. The result is a shift in the economic center of the universe toward Asia with potentially dramatic effects on the economic backdrop of international management (Parker, 1998).

In addition to increased trade, the level of foreign direct investment (FDI) also has a globalizing effect. FDI, as a percentage of world gross domestic product (GDP), doubled between 1985 and 1994 (United Nations Conference on Trade and Development, 1999). The world's 100 largest nonfinancial MNCs held $1.8 trillion in 1997 and employed approximately 6 million people in their foreign affiliates (UNCTAD, 1999). Most

FDI comes from developed countries, and as nations become more affluent, they pursue FDI in geographic regions with economic growth potential. In 1998, only 2 of the top 100 firms, in terms of FDI, were from developing countries (UNCTAD, 1999). These were Petreleos de Venezuela and Daewoo Corporation (Korea). Moreover, geographic proximity can be declining as a significant factor in determining the location of FDI. For example, the United States led all other countries in FDI in 1998, investing over $990 billion overseas, whereas the leading developing countries that received FDI were China and Indonesia (UNCTAD, 1999). The top 10 firms in terms of FDI are listed in Table 1.2.

Two fundamental implications are drawn from these trends. First, multinational firms now manufacture and sell on a global basis on an unprecedented scale. Over 500,000 foreign affiliates established by almost 60,000 parent companies are in operation worldwide (UNCTAD, 1999). The expansion of international production continues to gather momentum. Second, despite the financial setback of 1997, Asia continues to grow in terms of economic power and competitiveness. For example, over 200,000 of the foreign affiliates just mentioned were located in Asia, and almost all of the increase in foreign direct investment in developing countries in 1998 occurred in China.

New Actors on the International Stage

Some authors suggest that globalization, as defined by economic integration, is nothing new (see Parker, 1998). This view stems from the fact that trade in terms of a percentage of gross world product is only slightly higher at the end of the 20th century than it was before 1914 (Farnham, 1994). From this perspective, it is possible to argue that globalization is just business as usual. However, it seems impossible to ignore the numbers of new entrants to the international business arena in recent years.

Although international commerce might have existed as early as 3000 B.C. (Mendenhall, Punnett, & Ricks, 1995), the most rapid expansion of international business occurred in the latter half of the 20th century. The actors on the international business stage were originally the firm and its foreign constituency but were soon joined by home- and host-country governments, and more recently, by special interest groups, international agencies, and economic alliances (Robinson, 1984). In addition, the characteristics of these actors have changed over time.

U.S. multinational firms dominated the postwar period, but in 1999, as shown in Table 1.3, only a little over one-third of *Fortune* magazine's Global 500 was U.S. based.

TABLE 1.2 Top Ten Firms in FDI (1998)

Rank	Company	Headquarters	Foreign Sales US$ (billions)	Foreign Assets US$ (billions)
1	General Electric	United States	28.7	128.6
2	General Motors	United States	49.9	73.1
3	Royal Dutch/Shell Group	Neth/UK	50.0	67.0
4	Ford Motor Company	United States	43.8	N/A
5	Exxon	United States	92.7	50.1
6	Toyota	Japan	55.2	44.9
7	IBM	United States	46.4	43.6
8	BMP Amoco	United Kingdom	48.6	40.5
9	Daimler-Benz	Germany	125.4	36.7
10	Nestlé SA	Switzerland	51.2	35.6

SOURCE: Adapted from United Nations Conference on Trade and Development, 2000.

As noted earlier, technology is facilitating the entry of small business into the international arena. For example, in the mid 1990s, 25% of all exporting firms had fewer than 100 employees (Aharoni, 1994). In 1996, small and medium-size enterprises accounted for 80% of all the MNCs in Sweden, 60% of these firms in Italy, and over 50% of the new foreign affiliates established by Japanese firms in that year (UNCTAD, 1999). In addition, the service sector of the global economy is increasing rapidly with as much as 70% of advanced economies contained in this sector, and with trade in services now about 25% of world exports (Parker, 1998). A growing percentage of international mangers are involved in industries such as travel, transportation, entertainment, advertising, and telecommunications.

Often omitted from discussions of actors on the international stage are international gangs. Global gangs based in Russia, China, Hong Kong, Japan, Columbia, Italy, and the United States manufacture and transport illegal drugs around the world, trade in human cargo, and use the international banking system to launder billions of dollars (Parker, 1998). Worldwide trade in human beings is valued in the billions of dollars, and INTERPOL estimates that illegal drug sales account for about $400 billion annually.

TABLE 1.3 Distribution of the 1999 *Fortune* Global 500

Country	Number of Firms
United States	179
Japan	105
France	37
Britain	37
Germany	36
Netherlands*	11
Switzerland	11
South Korea	11
Canada	11
Italy	8
All others	54

SOURCE: *Fortune,* July 24, 2000. Reprinted with permission of *Fortune* magazine.
NOTE: * Includes dual headquarters.

In summary, the actors encountered on the global stage are now more likely to include firms headquartered outside of the United States. Increasingly, they could be small to medium-size businesses and are more likely then ever to be a part of the service sector. Finally, international managers must recognize that the increased permeability of boundaries associated with globalization also applies to illegal activities.

Some might argue that globalization has a single cause, such as technology or trade liberalization. I suggest that it is sometimes difficult to disentangle the causes of globalization from its effects. What seems clear is that the environment of international business is undergoing changes that influence traditional boundaries. One key result of globalization is that international managers face an external environment more complex, more dynamic, more uncertain, and more competitive than ever before.

Environment of International Management

The elements of the international manager's environment can be divided into four categories: economic, legal, political, and cultural. In the following section, an overview of the management issues associated with the first three categories is presented. Consistent with the focus of this book, the cultural environment is discussed in more detail in subsequent chapters.

Economic Environment

Making managerial decisions on a global basis requires an understanding of the economic strategies of countries in (or with) which one is conducting business. Economic systems are usually classified as market, command (centrally planned), or mixed. In market economies, resources are allocated and controlled by consumers who decide on this allocation by buying goods. In these systems, most property is privately owned. In command economies, resources are allocated and controlled by the decisions of government and property is publicly owned. Mixed economies combine elements of both fundamental types. In reality, no country has a purely command or purely market economy, and all are mixed to some extent. For example, even in a market economy like the United States, there is some government control and ownership of resources. By considering each of these two dimensions separately, a more realistic classification scheme emerges. Table 1.4 shows the interrelationship between control of economic activity and ownership of production.

Although the most logical combinations of ownership and control are in Sector A and Sector I, most countries in the world have economies with a variety of combinations of ownership and control. For example, China is probably best located in block I but, as discussed ahead, might soon be in block E, B, or H, and the United States probably lies in the upper part of block D (Daniels & Radebaugh, 1998).

The last two decades of the 20th century witnessed a decline in centrally planned economies in favor of more market-based approaches with the implied economic freedom. The attraction of market-based economies is not surprising when one considers that nations with the greatest economic freedom also have the highest standard of living, and those with the least economic freedom have the lowest standard of living (Parker, 1998). The shift from centrally planned to market economies resulted in a number of countries whose economic systems can be regarded as in transition. Particularly evident is the transition resulting from the fall of communism in Russia and eastern Europe. However, similar shifts are also occurring in Africa, Latin America, and China. The transition has taken different forms in different countries because of their different histories, resources, and cultures. However, the steps in the transition typically involve (a) deregulation, (b) privatization, and (c) the creation of a legal system that protects property rights (Hill, 2001). Deregulation involves the removal of legal restrictions to market activity, the establishment of

TABLE 1.4 Interrelationships Between Control and Ownership

	Ownership		
Control	Private	Mixed	Public
Market	A	B	C
Mixed	D	E	F
Command	G	H	I

SOURCE: Adapted from Daniels & Radebaugh, 1998.

private enterprise, and changes to the way in which private enterprise is allowed to compete. Privatization transfers the ownership of property from the state to private individuals and often involves the sale of state assets. Moreover, for a market economy to function effectively, a legal system must exist that protects the rights of owners. Otherwise, the incentives to engage in economic activity are diminished. The implications of these transition economies for managers are immense, because these shifts have the effect of potentially doubling the size of the world market (Hill, 2001). However, along with this potential comes risk.

The level of economic development of a country is generally related to its economic stability (Daniels & Radebaugh, 1998). Therefore, a country's level of economic development is a key indicator of risk for international managers. The economic performance of a country can be calculated in a number of ways: gross national product (GNP), gross domestic product (GDP), and per capita income calculations. The World Bank uses per capita GNP to determine the economic health of countries in its analyses and operations. The range of per capita GNP is enormous: Luxembourg at $45,100 having the highest income and Ethiopia at $100 the lowest (World Bank, 2000). An examination of the classification of countries by the World Bank regarding income shows an interesting pattern. That is, all the high-income countries (per capita GNP of $8,956 or more in 1997), except for Australia and New Zealand, are in the Northern Hemisphere (Daniels & Radebaugh, 1998). Most of the world's wealth (about 80%) is in these Northern Hemisphere high-income countries, which represent only about 15% of the world's population (World Bank, 2000). A stark example of the gap between rich and poor is given in the fact that the 200 richest people in the world have assets in excess of the combined income of 41% of the world's people ("The world's richest people," 1998).

Although per capita GNP is an important way of gauging the economic well-being of a country, two other measures can be of particular interest to international managers: indexes of purchasing power parity (PPP) and a measure of quality of life called the human development index (HDI). The basic idea of PPP is to calculate the amount of a country's currency required to purchase the same market basket of goods and services as some baseline (typically the dollar in the United States). Table 1.5 presents a comparison of selected countries in terms of per capita GNP and PPP.

TABLE 1.5 1998 Per Capita Income for Selected Countries

Ranking GNP per capita	Country	GNP per capita*	PPP International $
1	Luxembourg	45,100	36,703
7	Japan	32,350	23,592
10	United States	29,240	29,240
26	Canada	19,170	22,814
36	New Zealand	14,600	16,084
75	Mexico	3,840	7,450
97	Russia	2,260	6,180
145	China	750	3,051
149	Indonesia	640	2,407
173	Vietnam	350	1,689
206	Ethiopia	100	566

SOURCE: Adapted from World Bank, 2000.
NOTE: * Atlas methodology (US dollars).

For example, as shown in Table 1.5, although the per capita GNP of China is US$750, this buys the equivalent of goods and services costing US$3,051 in the United States. Therefore, PPP is a measure of economic well-being more indicative of the purchasing power of the country's currency.

The HDI is a broader indicator of the well-being of a country's people that takes into account life expectancy, educational attainment, and income. In 1999, the United Nation's *Human Development Report* listed the top five countries:

1. Canada

2. Norway

3. United States

4. Japan

5. Belgium

Of the 174 countries surveyed, Hong Kong (classified as high-quality-of-life country) ranked 24th, China (a medium-quality-of-life country) ranked 98th, and Nigeria (a low-quality-of-life country) ranked 146th (UN Development Program, 2000). Although these analytical approaches do not indicate the extent to which a country's population is satisfied with its quality of life, they do provide an important comparative indicator of level of development.

In summary, although economic boundaries are fading, distinctive economic systems continue to exist. More important, perhaps, is the wide variation that exists regarding the level of economic development and quality of life throughout the world. These differences present the international manager with a variety of challenges in terms of assessing both market and investment potential. In addition, the economic environment in a country affects labor-force issues, such as the demographics and quality of the labor force, hours worked, working conditions, and compensation (Parker, 1998).

Legal Environment

Some of the complexity of international management arises from the variety of laws and regulations that exist throughout the world. Basic features of laws in any society exist to (a) preserve the social order, (b) provide a basic model of conduct, (c) establish the nature of property and other rights, and (d) mediate the views of different segments of society into a set of enforceable rules (Sundaram & Black, 1995). There are three fundamental bases for legal systems. *Common law* is the foundation of the legal system in England and 26 other countries influenced by the English legal system, including the United States. In this system, previous court decisions and common custom act as precedents for legal interpretations. In comparison, *civil law* is based on a comprehensive set of statutes organized into a code, which leaves less room for interpretation and is the basis for the legal system in approximately 70 countries including much of Europe, Latin America, and the Far East (Japan, South Korea, Taiwan) and the state of Louisiana in the United States. *Islamic law* is derived from the teachings of the Prophet Mohammed as found in the *Qur'an* and includes aspects of civil law (Sundaram & Black, 1995) and is the basis for the legal system in approximately 27 Islamic countries predominantly in the Middle East and central Asia and covers all aspects of life (Litka, 1988).

Although MNCs might think of their economic activities as transcending national borders, the legal environment of international business is composed of over 200 different nations all of which have equal sovereignty under international law. International law contains unwritten, as well as more formal, understandings resulting from the repeated interactions among these nations. Compared with domestic law, international law is less coherent because it incorporates not only the laws of individual nation-states but also any treaties (multilateral, bilateral, or universal) and conventions such as the Geneva Convention on Human Rights or the Vienna Convention of Diplomatic Security (Sundaram & Black, 1995). The principles of international law can be divided into six broad categories:

1. sovereignty and sovereign immunity,
2. international jurisdiction,
3. doctrine of comity,
4. act of state doctrine,
5. treatment and rights of aliens, and
6. the appropriate forum for hearing disputes.

Box 1.1 provides a description of each of these basic principles.

The international manager should recognize that international law leaves considerable room for ambiguity with respect to transactions that involve causes and effects in more than one country. That is, situations can arise in which the manager can be caught in a void that exists at the intersection of sovereign boundaries. The particular areas of concern are the following:

1. international antitrust issues;
2. multinational bankruptcy;
3. product, process, and environmental liability across borders;
4. trade disputes;
5. protection of intellectual property; and
6. tradeoffs between business in the host country and national security or foreign policy issues (Sundaram & Black, 1995).

BOX 1.1

Basic Principles of International Law

Sovereignty and Sovereign Immunity—The principle of sovereignty under-lies all international law and states that in times of peace every state has the sovereign right to existence, legal equality, jurisdiction over territory, own-ership of property, and diplomatic relations with other states. In turn, this implies that one country's court system cannot be used to rectify injustices or impose penalties on another unless that country agrees.

International Jurisdiction—Three types of jurisdiction are specified by inter-national law. The *nationality principle* holds that every country has jurisdic-tion over its citizens no matter where they are located. The *territoriality principle* holds that every nation has the right of jurisdiction within its legal territory. Finally, the *protective principle* holds that every country has juris-diction over behavior that adversely affects its national security even if the conduct occurred outside that country.

Doctrine of Comity—The doctrine of comity, although not part of interna-tional law, is a custom of mutual respect for the laws, institutions, and governments of other countries in the matter of jurisdiction over their own citizens.

Act of State Doctrine—Under this principle, all acts of other governments in their own territory are considered to be valid by U.S. courts even if such acts are illegal or inappropriate under U.S. law.

Treatment and Rights of Aliens—Countries have the right to admit foreign citizens and can impose special restrictions on their conduct (such as the right of travel, where they can stay, and what business they can conduct), and can also deport aliens. Special laws can be set up for the treatment of aliens and there is no presumed equality in international law between natives and aliens.

Appropriate Forum for Hearing and Settling Disputes—A U.S. principle that applies to international law, it allows U.S. courts to dismiss cases brought before them by foreigners, but requires them to examine issues, such as where the plaintiffs are located, what evidence must be gathered, and where the property to be used in restitutions is located.

SOURCE: Adapted from Sundaram & Black, 1995.

In summary, both the inconsistencies of laws around the world as well as the gray areas of international law present the international manager with a significant challenge.

Political Environment

Political systems are the structures and processes by which a nation integrates the parts of society into a functioning unit. There are numerous varieties of political systems. However, they can be roughly classified along a continuum that represents the degree that citizens participate in decision making. The two extremes are the pure democracy advocated in Ancient Greece at one end and totalitarianism at the other. Modern democracies represent only an approximation of the Greek ideal. The following features are representative of modern democratic systems:

- Freedom of opinion, expression, the press, and freedom to organize

- Elections in which voters decide who is to represent them

- An independent and fair court system

- A relatively nonpolitical bureaucracy and defense infrastructure

- A relatively accessible decision-making process (Almond & Powell, 1984)

On the other end of the spectrum, totalitarianism typically takes one of two forms, theocratic or secular. In theocratic totalitarianism, religious leaders are also the political leaders, as in Islamic countries in the Middle East, such as Iran and Saudi Arabia. Secular totalitarianism includes socialism and communism, where ideological as opposed to religious concepts form the basis of the political system and leaders rely on bureaucratic power, military power, or both.

As indicated by the preceding comparison, key elements of democracy are the freedom of political rights and civil liberties. Each year, countries are ranked, by a U.S.-based monitoring organization, according to the extent to which these freedoms exist. Based on this ranking for 1999, Table 1.6 indicates the percentage of the 192 countries surveyed that were "free," "partly free," or "not free."

The number of countries classified as "free" in 1999 is a dramatic increase from just a few years before. This is the result of many of the emerging or less stable economies (e.g., El Salvador, Honduras, India, Mali, Nicaragua, Philippines, Romania, Thailand, Venezuela) being classified as "partly free" previously.

TABLE 1.6 Percentage of Countries Classified as "Free," "Partly Free," or "Not Free"

	1998-99
Free	45.8%
Partly Free	28.1%
Not Free	26.0%

SOURCE: Freedom House, 1999. Reprinted with permission.

The classification of countries along these lines might be somewhat helpful in understanding the type of government interventions that a manager can expect. However, the stated ideology of a country might not always reflect the actual interactions between managers and government. China, for example, is currently implementing some characteristics of market economy while still maintaining a political hard line.

In addition to understanding the probable nature of a government's involvement in business affairs, international managers must be concerned with the likelihood that a government will undergo changes negatively affecting business activity—"political risk." Two categories of political risk are typically defined. *Macro* political risk is activity of government likely to affect all business conducted in a country, whereas *micro* political risk is limited to specific sectors of the economy or specific foreign businesses. Factors contributing to the overall level of political risk in a country include the stability of government, the amount of internal and external conflict, the level of corruption, law and order, and the role of religion and the military in politics. The level of political risk can vary considerably across countries and can take a number of forms. Three basic categories of political risk can be identified.

- *Transfer risks*—Government policies limiting the transfer of capital, payments, production, people, or technology in or out of the country.

- *Operational risks*—Government policies and procedures directly constraining management and performance of local operations.

- *Ownership control risks*—Government policies or actions inhibiting ownership or control of local operations (Schmidt, 1986).

Research suggests the degree of political risk faced by a firm is a function of both the country in which it operates and the characteristics of the company's operations (Kobrin, 1979; Kobrin, Basek, Blank, & LaPalombra, 1980). The challenge for international managers is to assess the probability of each type of risk in relationship to their involvement in the country and then to formulate an appropriate response. Managers can employ a variety of integrative, protective, and defensive techniques to manage political risk depending on characteristics of their firm (Gregory, 1989).

These three aspects of the international business environment (economic, legal, and political) provide the backdrop against which international managers must function. In the remainder of this book, although recognizing the importance of these aspects of the environment, the focus is on the effect of culture on management. Culture is singled out as uniquely important to international management for three reasons. First, to a great extent, the economic, legal, and political characteristics of a country are a manifestation of a nation's culture. That is, these systems are derived from a country's culture and history. Even in cases where a single person or a small number of people dictates these systems and maintains them through force, history and culture can contribute to their development. As discussed in more detail in Chapter 2, culture stems from the fundamental ways in which a society learns to interact with its environment. The economic, legal, and political systems that have developed over time are the visible elements of a more fundamental set of shared meanings. Culture affects the goals of the institutions of society, the way the institutions operate, and the attributions their members make for policies and behavior (Schwartz, 1992).

Second, unlike economic, legal, and political aspects of a country, which are observable, culture is largely invisible. That is, the influence of culture is difficult to detect and managers therefore often overlook it. Although culture might or might not be the most important influence on the practice of management, it is the aspect of the management context most often neglected. Finally, as argued in the next section, the practice of management largely focuses on interpersonal interactions. One of the distinct characteristics of international management is that these interactions occur with individuals who are culturally different. For many "international" managers, the global nature of their environment can consist largely of working with a multicultural workforce in their own country. This perspective on international management, that management is what managers do as compared to what functions they serve, emphasizes the importance of interpersonal interactions across cultures.

What International Managers Do

Most management textbooks describe management in terms of some derivation of Henri Fayol's 1916 definition that "to manage is to plan, organize, coordinate, command, and control" (as cited in Gray, 1987, p. 13). However, these functions of management are difficult to observe; they do not operate in any sequential way, and there are some managerial activities that do not fit neatly into any of these categories. Dissatisfaction with this description of management has led a number of scholars to seek alternative ways to describe what managers do. The best known of these studies was conducted by Henry Mintzberg in the late 1960s (Mintzberg, 1973). He suggested that managers have formal authority over their organizational unit, and that this status divides their activities into interpersonal, informational, and decisional role categories. Contrary to earlier beliefs that managerial work was systematic and rational, Mintzberg demonstrated that it was more accurately characterized by brevity, variety, and fragmentation, with a high degree of interpersonal interaction (1973). A review of 30 studies of managerial work conducted by Hales (1986) summarized the features presented in Box 1.2. These 10 features are largely consistent with Mintzberg's description. Notable is the extent to which what managers do involves interactions with other people.

Efforts to categorize managerial work into identifiable roles have been less consistent. This is perhaps because of the wide variety of jobs that are classified as "managerial" (Stewart, 1976). Mintzberg's (1973) framework of 10 roles aggregated into three role categories (interpersonal, informational, and decisional) was derived from the direct observation of the daily activities of five chief executive officers. Subsequent survey research (McCall & Segrist, 1980), conducted with 2,609 managers, found some support for the idea that managerial jobs have some similarity across levels and functions. Support was found for 6 of Mintzberg's 10 role classifications. Only the leadership role seemed to differ according to level and function. Another test of these role categories (Shapira & Dunbar, 1980), conducted with both MBA students and managers, found that the 10 roles could be meaningfully divided into two categories: One category dealt with the generation and processing of information, whereas the other category dealt with roles that involved decisions. The resultant framework focused on an input-output formulation of managerial work, with interpersonal roles, particularly leadership, seen as being integrated into other aspects of the manager's job. Others also argue that interpersonal roles, such as leadership, are actually a part of the other managerial roles (Weick, 1974). Table 1.7 presents a comparison of these three classifications of managerial roles.

These findings, to some extent, underlie the organization of subsequent chapters of this book around the leadership, decision-making, and communication and negotiation roles that form the key components of

BOX 1.2

Characteristics of Managerial Work

It combines a specialist (professional) and a managerial element.

The substantive elements involve liaison and management and responsibility for work process, within which are contained more detailed work elements.

The character of work elements varies by duration, time span, recurrence, unexpectedness, and source.

Much time is spent in day-to-day troubleshooting and ad hoc problems of organization and regulation.

Much managerial activity consists of asking or persuading others to do things, involving the manager in face-to-face verbal communication of limited duration.

Patterns of communication vary in terms of what the communication is about and with whom the communication is made.

Little time is spent on any one particular activity and, in particular, on the conscious systematic formulation of plans.

Planning and decision making tend to take place in the course of other activity.

Managers spend a great deal of time accounting for and explaining what they do, in informal relationships and in political activity.

Managerial activities are rife with contradictions, cross-pressures, and conflicts. Much managerial work involves coping with and resolving social and technical conflict.

There is considerable choice in terms of what is done and how. Part of managerial work is setting the boundaries of and negotiating the work itself.

SOURCE: Adapted from Hales, 1986.

TABLE 1.7 Comparison of Studies of Managerial Role Categories

Mintzberg, 1973	McCall & Segrist, 1980	Shapira & Dunbar, 1980
Interpersonal	*Interpersonal*	
Figurehead		
Leader	Leader	
Liaison	Liaison	
Informational	*Informational*	*Informational*
Monitor	Monitor	Figurehead
Disseminator		Disseminator
Spokesman	Spokesman	Spokesman
		Liaison
Decisional	*Decisional*	*Decisional*
Entrepreneur	Entrepreneur	Entrepreneur
Disturbance Handler		Disturbance Handler
Resource Allocator	Resource Allocator	Resource Allocator
Negotiator		Negotiator
		Leader
		Monitor

the international manager's job. Regardless of the labels given to the categories, there seems to be at least some moderate agreement about the common behaviors associated with managerial work. Clearly, however, interpersonal interactions are at the core of management.

Organizational Context, Culture, and Managerial Roles

Despite the emphasis on describing the similarities among managers, some research has tried to systematically account for differences in the work of managers (e.g., Stewart, 1976). Of particular interest is the extent to which the global context of international management might affect the manager's role. In an attempt to identify both the generalizations that can be made about managerial work and to account for the differences that exist among managerial jobs, Stewart (1982) presents a model that is helpful in understanding how the role of international managers might vary. The model, shown in Figure 1.1 pictures two different jobs, each

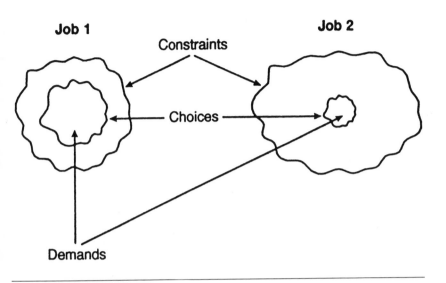

Figure 1.1. Differences in Demands, Constraints, and Choices in Two Jobs
SOURCE: Stewart, R. (1991). *Managing Today and Tomorrow.* Reprinted with permission of Macmillian Press Ltd.

consisting of an inner core of demands, an outer boundary on constraints, and in between an area of choices.

These factors change over time according to the legal, political, economic, and organizational context and can also be influenced by the jobholder. In Figure 1.1, Job 1 shows tighter job constraints, higher job demands, and, therefore, somewhat less choice than Job 2. *Demands* are what anyone in the managerial job must do. These are such things as meeting minimum performance criteria and doing certain kinds of work, for example, attending required meetings or filing a particular report. *Constraints* are the factors, both internal and external to the organization, that limit what managers can do. These include limitations with regard to resources, technology, geography, legal, trade unions, and any organizational restrictions placed on the manager. *Choices* are the activities that the manager can elect to do. These involve choosing what work is done and how it is done. It includes choices that are common to all managerial jobs and can also be thought of, in Mintzberg's (1973) terms, as emphasizing different managerial roles.

From the previous discussion of the environment faced by international managers, it is clear that they face demands and constraints that are both quantitatively and qualitatively distinct. Although empirical research generally found more similarities than differences in managerial roles (Hales, 1986), some studies demonstrate the effect of contextual factors, such as environmental and technological complexity (Gibbs, 1994), the size of the firm (Choran, 1969), the amount of uncertainty in the environment (Leifer & Huber, 1977), and the organization's structure (Aldrich & Herker, 1977; Hales & Tamangani, 1996) on managerial roles. For example, in one study, environmental complexity increased the frequency of informational roles, whereas complexity and dynamism increased the frequency of decisional roles (Gibbs, 1994). In another, managers in more centralized organizations spent more time in downward communication in contrast to those in decentralized organizations who emphasized upward communication (Hales & Tamangani, 1996). In summary, the manager's role relates directly to the constraints and demands of the national and organizational environment and involves choices in which roles are emphasized.

Consistent with the choices that managers have in their roles, research finds that managers can have jobs with similar demands and constraints and still differ in what roles they choose to emphasize (Graen, 1976; Stewart, 1982). One very apparent difference involves the choices that managers from different cultures make about their roles. For example, differences in the activities that managers emphasize have been found for Germans as compared with British managers (Stewart, Barsoux, Kieser, Ganter, & Walgenbach, 1994), and among Chinese, Japanese, Korean, and U.S. managers (Doktor, 1990). Therefore, the roles and work behaviors of managers are the result of both the national and organizational context, which establishes demands and constraints on the choices they make, which is influenced by national culture.

The effect of culture on management is the focus of much of the remainder of this book. However, it is important to emphasize that culture affects the roles and behavior of managers indirectly, as well as directly, such as in the choice of a particular role emphasis. The direct effect of culture is taken up, in some detail, in subsequent chapters. However, culture also influences managerial roles indirectly by shaping the context in which managers must perform. For example, in a study of Chinese managers, Boisot and Xing (1992) found that although Chinese managers share many behavioral characteristics with their U.S. counterparts, they do so in an institutional setting that places different demands and constraints on their behavior. Specifically, because of the strong hierarchical organization, Chinese managers spent about the same amount of time in downward communication as U.S. managers, but about four times as much time in communication with superiors and only about one-half as much time in communicating with outsiders and peers. Similarly, Stewart et al. (1994) found differences in German and British firms that gave rise to specific differences in roles for managers. For example, German organizations were flatter and more integrated, and placed a greater emphasis on technical as opposed to interpersonal controls than did British firms. This resulted in German managerial jobs that involved less concern over gaining cooperation, less awareness of organizational constraints, less choice over job roles, more involvement in the technical aspects of tasks, less direct supervision, fewer meetings and networking, but more desk work than the jobs of British managers. In these cases, national cultural differences influenced managerial jobs indirectly. That is, culture shapes the context of managerial work, which in turn influences managerial roles.

Summary

The environment of international management is changing. Globalization is affecting the traditional boundaries in a wide range of areas. Rapid change is occurring with regard to economic alliances, the work environment, trade and investment, and the players on the international stage. And all of this change is being facilitated by a revolution in information technology. Therefore, international managers face an environment that is more complex, more dynamic, more uncertain, and more competitive than ever before.

The environment of international management can be divided into economic, legal, political, and cultural factors. Although traditional economic boundaries are fading, distinctive economic systems continue to be influential. In addition, the wide variety in the level of economic development around the world presents numerous challenges to the international manager. Although international managers might view their economic activities as global, the legal environment of international business still relies on the concept of national sovereignty as fundamental, which presents the international manager with many inconsistencies. Also, international managers must understand the probable nature of a government's involvement in business affairs, and the degree of risk associated with the likelihood that a government could undergo changes. The challenges presented by these economic, legal, and political aspects of the international business environment are formidable. However, it is the influence of culture on management that can be the most difficult to deal with. This is because culture has a broad influence on behavior and on other environmental factors. In addition, cultural effects are difficult to observe.

Management can be defined both in terms of what managers do and what functions they perform. Focusing on what managers do emphasizes the importance of the interpersonal aspects of the manager's job. Managers around the world share a significant degree of similarity in the roles they perform. In subsequent chapters of this book, the leadership, communications and negotiation, and decision-making roles of international managers are explored in detail. However, managers around the world also differ in important aspects of their roles and behavior. These differences are the result of both a direct effect of culture on behavior and a more indirect effect of culture on organizational context. Thus, by defining management in terms of managerial roles, which must be played out in a dynamic global environment, the pervasive effect of culture on management is revealed.

Two

Describing Culture

What It Is and
Where It Comes From

Deep cultural undercurrents structure life in subtle but highly consistent ways that are not consciously formulated. Like the invisible jet streams in the skies that determine the course of a storm, these currents shape our lives; yet, their influence is only beginning to be identified.

Edward T. Hall (1976)

Chapter 1 suggests that culture has a broad influence on what international managers do. To understand more specifically how culture affects the practice of management, we first need a clear definition of culture. Although culture is a widely recognized word, defining the concept of culture is challenging. Anthropologists Kroeber and Kluckhohn (1952) identify over 160 different definitions of the term *culture.* Clyde Kluckhohn (1962) presents a widely accepted definition, which integrates many of these perspectives: "Culture consists of patterned ways of thinking, feeling and reacting, acquired and transmitted mainly by symbols, constituting the distinctive achievement of human groups, including their embodiment in artifacts; the essential core of culture consists of traditional (i.e., historically derived and selected) ideas and especially their attached values" (p. 73). From a more psychological perspective, Triandis (1972) presents culture as the subjective perception of the human-made part of the environment. This includes the categorization of social stimuli, associations, beliefs, attitudes, roles, and values that individuals share. A complimentary view is that of Hofstede (1980), who suggests that culture consists of shared mental programs that control individuals' response to their environment.

Features of Culture

Each of the definitions just presented has limitations. However, many of the concepts presented in these definitions have implications for understanding the relationship between cultural issues and international management. The following elements are of particular significance.

Culture as Shared

Culture is something shared by members of a particular group. Hofstede (1991) makes this point well when he describes culture as mental programming that lies between human nature on one side and personality on the other. As shown in Figure 2.1, individuals carry in their mind three levels of programming about how they interact with their environment. At the broadest level, all human beings share certain biological reactions. We eat when we are hungry, for example. At the narrowest level are the personality characteristics that are unique to each of us as individuals. Culture occurs at an intermediate level and is a collective phenomenon that is about elements of our mental programming that we share with certain others.

Culture as Learned

A second feature of culture present in many definitions is that culture is transmitted through the process of learning and interacting with the environment. Over time, the people in a society develop patterned ways of interacting with their environment. That is, language, systems of government, forms of marriage, and religious systems are all functioning when we are born into a society. These patterns are transmitted to the new entrants as they learn the various responses to each environmental

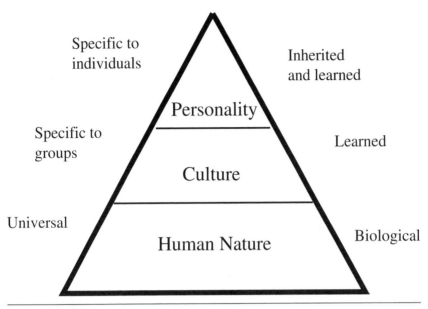

Figure 2.1. Three Levels of Mental Programming
SOURCE: Adapted from Hofstede, 1980. © G. Hofstede. Used with permission.

contingency. For example, guidance about behavior that is considered appropriate in a particular culture is often contained in the stories that parents tell their children (Howard, 1991). This implies, of course, that it is possible to learn the cultural patterns of another society.

Culture as Systematic and Organized

A third defining element is that cultures are integrated coherent logical systems, the parts of which are interrelated. That is, culture is more than a random assortment of customs. It is an organized system of values, attitudes, beliefs, and behavioral meanings related to each other and to the environmental context. To understand a particular facet of a culture, it is necessary to understand the cultural context. Ferraro (1994) provides a good example of this point. Most U.S. citizens have difficulty identifying with the marital practice of polygamy. A number of contextual factors support this general lack of comfort with the practice in U.S. culture. First, it is illegal. Second, it is counterproductive in a cash economy in which more wives mean more money to support them and their children. However, for the Kikuyu of East Africa, polygamy is a viable marital alternative. Kikuyu society is based on subsistence agriculture, and more wives and children enhance the economic well-being of the household. Moreover, however, social status is based on the size of one's household and particularly on the number of male kinspeople in one's social unit. More wives mean more sons. In addition, because Kikuyu religion is fundamentally ancestor worship, larger families mean a bigger religious following. Therefore, not only are cultural beliefs about polygamy not immoral, they are very logical when considered in cultural context.

The following statement synthesizes, at the most general level, a working definition that is useful in considering the effects of culture on international management practice. That is, culture consists of systems of values, attitudes, beliefs, and behavioral meanings that are shared by members of a social group (society) and that are learned from previous generations. This definition does not clearly distinguish between social systems and culture, as some would suggest (Rohner, 1984), because in practice, these concepts "shade into one another" (Smith & Bond, 1999, 39). That is, some values, attitudes, and beliefs will be shared more widely than will others. It is important to note that although culture is neither genetic nor about individual behavior, it is contained within the knowledge systems of individuals. These knowledge systems are formed during childhood and reinforced throughout life (Triandis, 1995). Therefore, they are pervasive but often not immediately apparent to society members.

Consistent with this perspective, Schein (1985) describes three levels of culture: artifacts and creations, values, and basic assumptions. His model, like most definitions, differentiates between superficial or obvious elements of culture and more deeply held aspects. Figure 2.2 depicts the relationship among the three levels of culture, which can be likened to an iceberg with only a small percentage being visible above the surface of the water.

Figure 2.2 shows that above the surface are cultural artifacts, which include all the visible features of a culture, such as the architecture of its physical environment, language, technology, clothing, manners, dress, and so on. Just below the surface are the espoused values of the culture. These consciously held values relate directly to the observed artifactual level. Deep below the surface are the basic underlying assumptions shared by the culture, which are the ultimate source of values and action. These beliefs, perceptions, thoughts, and feelings operate at an unconscious level and are taken for granted by members of a cultural group. As pointed out in Chapter 1, because of this characteristic, international managers often overlook the influence of culture.

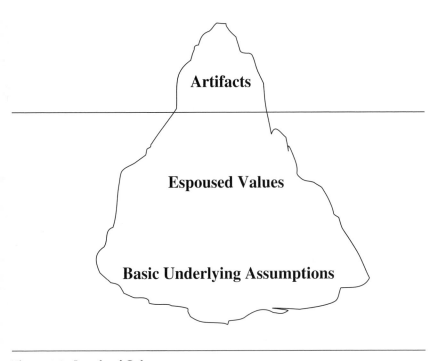

Figure 2.2. Levels of Culture
SOURCE: Adapted from Schein, 1985.

Why Cultures Differ and Persist

Armed with a working definition that defines culture as a shared set of knowledge structures, it is now possible to examine elements of the environmental context that give rise to and reinforce cultural differences. It is not possible to evaluate all possible contributors to cultural variation. However, anthropologists have derived a set of assumptions about how cultures interact with the environment. These assumptions, which relate to how societies confront and solve the common problems of existence, are summarized in Box 2.1.

Based on these assumptions, elements of culture evolve in terms of different solutions to common problems. Understanding how cultural elements might have developed or are reinforced can help locate a particular characteristic in its context.

BOX 2.1

Assumptions About a Society's Interactions With the Environment

There are a limited number of common human problems for which all peoples at all times must find solutions. (For example, every society must decide on how to feed, clothe, house, and educate its people.)

There are a limited number of alternatives that exist for dealing with these problems.

All alternatives are present in a society at all times, but some are preferred over others.

Each society has a dominant profile or values orientation, but in addition has numerous variations or alternative profiles.

In both the dominant profile and the variations there is a rank order preference for alternatives.

In societies undergoing change, the ordering of preferences may not be clear.

SOURCE: Adapted from Kluckhohn & Strodtbeck, 1961, as presented in Adler, 1997.

Survival

Many cultural characteristics originally developed to aid the survival of groups in their environment. For example, many Western cultures shake hands with their right hand as a form of greeting. Initially, this was probably an indication that no weapon was being held or about to be drawn with the dominant right hand. Similarly, the Maori of New Zealand have an elaborate challenge ceremony or "wero," which is now reserved for greeting dignitaries (Barlow, 1991). Originally, this challenge, which involves the sending forth of warriors who challenge the visiting party by prancing about and brandishing fighting weapons followed by the presentation of a token on the ground to their leader, was to determine the intentions of visitors. If they come in peace the leader will pick up the token and the warriors will lead the visitors onto the Marae (community meeting place). Having determined the intent of a visitor, there was no need in this culture to display an empty right hand as a form of friendly greeting. As a sign of peace, the Maori greeting among individuals is the act of pressing noses or "hongi" (Barlow, 1991). As another example, people in different climates seem to have different attitudes toward time.

For example, the lack of urgency often observed in tropical climates might have originally reflected the lack of seasonality related to agriculture. That is, because crops can be grown year-round, there is no need to plant and harvest at certain times and therefore little regard for deadlines.

Children learn such concepts in term of beliefs about right or wrong, good or bad, ugly or beautiful, and so on. Therefore, cultural concepts that have their foundation in ancient beliefs about survival or fundamental beliefs about right and wrong are likely "programmed" at a very deep level of consciousness (Hofstede, 1991; Schein, 1985). Their meaning might not be apparent to the outsider and can even be obscured to members of the cultural group.

Language

Language plays a particularly prominent role in the way culture is transmitted (Hall, 1966). One long-standing view is that because people encode things in memory in terms of a particular language, language defines the way they view the world (Whorf, 1956). That is, language determines the content of a society's mental representation of their environment. Although language is influenced by the environment and reflects the concerns of society, some disagreement exists among linguists about the degree of control that language exerts over perceptions, attitudes, and behavior (Bonvillian, 1993). For example, the Inuit language of the indigenous people of the northern part of North America contains numerous words describing snow. Apparently, however, the existence of many more terms for snow does not necessarily indicate the ability to distinguish types of snow any better than with fewer terms (Pinker, 1994). That is, language does not constrain thought. For example, when we do not have a word for something, we invent or borrow one. However, because we use language for interaction with others, it has a powerful role in shaping behavior and in perpetuating beliefs and habitual patterns of interaction (Berger & Luckman, 1966), hence, culture. Language, therefore, is an artifact of culture that helps to perpetuate its values, attitudes, beliefs, and behavioral routines. The fierce protection of the French language by francophone Canadians is an example of the recognition of the powerful effect of language in perpetuating culture.

Religion

Religion reflects beliefs and behaviors shared by groups of people that cannot be verified by empirical tests (Terpstra & David, 1985). Therefore, religious values are closely related to cultural values. The extent to which religion influences the cultural profile of a society depends on the extent to which a particular religion is dominant or state sanctioned, the importance that society places on religion, the degree of religious homogeneity in the society, and the degree of tolerance for religious diversity that exits in the society (Mendenhall et al., 1995). In addition, some evidence suggests that devoutly religious individuals are more likely to endorse the dominant cultural profile of a society (Burris, Branscombe, & Jackson, 2000).

Although Christianity is currently the dominant religion worldwide, its percentage of followers is projected to be relatively stable in the near future with Islamic religions and Hindus representing an increasing percentage of the world population (Barrett, 1982). Table 2.1 shows the geographic distribution of the major religions around the world as of the middle of 1998.

Of course, religions are not evenly distributed across the planet with some religions concentrated in specific geographic regions. For example, Islam is largely concentrated in Asia and Africa, and Shinto exists almost exclusively in Japan. Obviously, therefore, religion has a greater influence in some cultures than in others.

Debates Surrounding the Concept of Culture

In part, because of the ambiguity of the culture concept, a number of debates emerge regarding culture in the literature. The issues raised are important because they influence the utility of the concept of culture in explaining and predicting behavior in organizations. These issues are the concept of a national culture, the convergence or divergence of cultures, the concept of an organizational culture, and the effects of acculturation.

National Culture

A key question to identifying culture, so that its effect on management can be assessed, is the extent to which a nation has a distinctive culture. The term *nation* is often used as a synonym for culture without any further conceptual grounding (Bhagat & McQuaid, 1982). In fact, much of the research in this book reports little more than the nation in which respondents lived. It should be apparent that based on the definition of culture presented previously, this could be misleading. That is, multiple cultures can exist within national borders and the same cultural group can span many nations. For example, Canada is the home to both Anglophones and Francophones, each having distinctive cultures. The

TABLE 2.1 Distribution of Religions Around the World (thousands of adherents)

Religion	Africa	Asia	Europe	Latin America	North America	Oceania	World
Baha'i	2,263	3,260	126	825	753	105	6,764
Buddhist	138	348,806	1,517	622	2,445	266	353,794
Chinese folk religions	33	377,795	250	184	839	61	379,162
Christian	356,277	283,734	558,729	462,965	256,882	24,452	1,943,038
Confucianist	0	6,207	11	0	0	23	6,241
Ethnic religions	97,200	148,189	1,262	1,231	424	259	248,565
Hindu	2,411	755,500	1,382	785	1,266	345	761,689
Jewish	230	4,139	2,530	1,121	5,996	95	14,111
Muslim	315,000	812,000	31,401	1,624	4,349	248	1,164,622
Shinto	0	2,727	0	7	55	0	2,789
Sikh	53	21,531	236	0	498	14	22,332
Other religions	164	102,718	517	12,197	1,502	67	117,164
Nonreligious	4,863	600,822	108,000	15,300	27,500	3,170	759,655
Atheists	420	121,451	23,444	2,673	1,569	356	149,913

SOURCE: Compiled from the *World Almanac and Book of Facts,* 2000.

First Nations peoples of North America span the borders of the United States and Canada, and any major North American city will have pockets of many distinct cultures that also exist elsewhere. However, the 20th century saw the emergence of nation-states that, at least initially in many cases, were a political expression of cultural similarity. These two perspectives raise the question of the appropriateness of the concept of a national culture.

Hofstede (1983) makes a powerful argument in favor of national culture. He argues that because nations are political entities, they vary in their institutions, forms of government, legal systems, educational systems, labor, and employment relations systems. These factors influence the way in which people interact with their environment and each other and thereby condition the way they think—their "mental programming." In addition, he suggests that nationality has a symbolic value to citizens that influences how we perceive ourselves. That is, we all derive our self-identity, in part, from our nationality. For managers, the activities of firms are governed by national sovereignty. Therefore, from an international business perspective, national culture is probably the most logical level of analysis from which to begin to understand the cultural environment.

If, for practical purposes, the concept of national culture is adopted, two major issues must be recognized (Smith & Bond, 1999). First, by comparing national cultures, the large number of subcultures that exist within some nations is at risk of being ignored. We must remember that differences of the magnitude observed between any two countries might also be found between selected subcultures within a country. Within any country, cultural differences that are not obvious to the outside observer are often much more apparent to local nationals. Second, we risk ignoring the variation, conflict, and dissent that exits within national cultures. That is, each individual has unique life experiences that contribute to diversity within the culture. Both of these issues can be managed if we focus on characterizations of values, beliefs, and behaviors that individuals within a culture share as opposed to drawing on broader generalizations of national character (Hofstede, 1983; Smith & Bond, 1999). However, finding agreement on the defining elements of a complex concept, such as culture, is not easy. The search for a common language to describe cultural variation is discussed in Chapter 3.

Convergence or Divergence

An additional consideration to identifying culture is the extent to which cultures around the world are becoming more similar or more different. The fact that national culture is related to other societal factors, such as political, legal, educational, and labor relations systems, leads some authors to suggest that the rapid technological and economic development around the world (characteristic of globalization) will have a homogenizing effect on culture (Dunphy, 1987; Webber, 1969). Others, however, argue that cultural diversity will persist, or even expand, as people with different cultural orientations respond to this rapid development (Cole, 1973; Lincoln, Olson, & Hanada, 1978).

The argument for convergence of cultures hinges on the fact that nations are not static entities but develop over time. This development of nations is evident in changes, such as the expansion of education, increased occupational diversity, urban intensification, and development of mass communication (Yang, 1988). Proponents of the convergence perspective suggest that this modernization results from a common economic orientation (Eisenhardt, 1973) and eventually leads to a common society where differences in ideology (values) will cease to exist (Kerr, Dunlop, Harbison, & Myers, 1960). That is, given enough time, cultures will converge to the point that no difference in values, attitudes, beliefs, and behavior exists. Furthermore, because, until recently, economic development was equated with Western capitalistic economic orientations, convergence suggests adopting the ideological values of the "West" (Ralston, Holt, Terpstra, & Yu, 1997).

Some support for the convergence hypothesis is provided by Inglehart's (1977, 1990) survey of values in Europe. He identified two value orientations (materialist and postmaterialist) related to a country's wealth. As wealth increased, so did endorsement of postmaterialist values. A steady year-by-year increase in the endorsement of postmaterialist values was found in Europe over a period of 15 years (Inglehart, 1990). This sort of empirical finding supports the notion that as wealth gradually increases in a country, cultural differences diminish and people become more similar. In addition, sociologists suggest that to participate effectively in a modern society, people must possess a core set of psychological characteristics (Kahl, 1968). Yang (1988), in a review of the literature on modernization, found a high degree of agreement on the characteristic of a modern person regardless of culture. These are summarized in Box 2.2. This profile of a modern person is conceptually similar to key concepts in descriptions of "Western" culture.

Smith and Bond (1999) point out an interesting reaction in developing countries to the idea of cultural convergence. That is, as arguments for cultural convergence are popularized, many developing countries take action to distinguish themselves from the West and assert their cultural uniqueness. Political leaders in these countries are often concerned with the growth in self-centeredness and erosion of civil harmony associated with Western-style modernization (Smith & Bond, 1999).

In addition to technological and economic pressures, an additional force toward cultural homogeneity is an increasing awareness of the interdependence of humanity (Smith & Bond, 1999). That is, humankind's pursuit of personal and national wealth leads to the depletion of energy resources, overharvesting of the oceans, erosion of the atmosphere, destruction of rain forests, and depletion of agricultural land. This results in a common dilemma (Dawes, 1980) of the maintenance of the systems that support life on earth. One result of this common threat is the development of "world mindedness" or internationalism, which implies a common set of attitudes and behaviors toward people of different races, nations, and cultures. Although this is a relatively new concept, some preliminary empirical support for a growth in internationalism (or what might be termed by some as globalization) around the world has been found (Der-Karabetian, 1992). The long-term effect, of course, would be to reduce variability of differences among national cultures.

BOX 2.2

The Profile of a Modern Person

- A sense of personal efficacy (antifatalism)
- Low social integration with relatives
- Egalitarian attitudes toward others
- Openness to innovation and change
- A belief in sex equality
- High achievement motivation
- Independence or self-reliance
- Active participation in social organizations
- Tolerance of and respect for others
- Cognitive and behavioral flexibility
- Strong future orientation
- Empathetic capacity
- A high need for information
- The propensity to take risks in life
- Secularization in religious belief
- A preference for urban life
- An individualistic orientation toward others
- Psychological differentiation
- A nonlocal orientation

SOURCE: Yang, 1988. Reprinted with permission of Sage Publications, Inc.

Despite the logic of arguments in favor of cultural convergence, upon close examination they are somewhat less compelling. Although Inglehart (1990) found a shift toward postmaterialist values related to economic development in Europe, this finding does not hold for other elements of culture. That is, culture is more than just holding postmaterialist values, and other variations in national culture that have nothing to do with modernization are probably related to social behavior in much the same way (Smith & Bond, 1999). Moreover, modernization is probably not the linear uniform process that it is sometimes presented to be. Studies of modernization reveal that countries can modernize in different ways, at different rates, and with different outcomes (Sack, 1973). Smith and Bond (1999) argue that because of the unique origins and complexity of cultures, cultures will evolve in different and unpredictable ways making the idea of convergence toward some common end point highly unlikely. In addition, cultural systems might be able to combine traditional and modern elements in unique ways. For example, Hong Kong Chinese seem to be able to retain their traditional respect for authority while rejecting its fatalism and adopting modern competitiveness but rejecting modern views toward sexual promiscuity (Bond & King, 1985).

At the level of organizations, the convergence argument centers on convergence toward common organizational practices in different countries because of technological determinism. This was a popular line of thinking, particularly regarding the economic resurgence of Japanese industry, during the late 1970s and early 1980s (Ouchi, 1981). However, research results indicate that similar general technology could be operated differently by different social systems (Dunphy, 1987). For example, although Japan adopted Western technology, distinctive practices that related to national culture persisted (Whitehill & Takezawa, 1978). That is, despite technological changes toward "American" methods over a 15-year period, Japanese workers maintained many traditional attitudes toward their work environment, such as the commitment to the company and its productivity goals, and a norm for workplace harmony.

The debate over cultural convergence versus divergence has resulted in a number of compromise proposals concerning organizations. Child (1981), in a review of organizational studies, suggested that cultural-convergence-divergence was a matter of level of analysis. His study concludes that studies of macrolevel issues of organizational structure and technology often indicate cultural convergence, whereas research concluding divergence was typically involved with the more microlevel issues of the behavior of individuals within organizations. Yang (1988) suggests convergence in only those cultural characteristics that relate specifically to functioning more easily in a technological environment. That is, certain behaviors and attitudes are necessary to adapt to the imperatives of an industrial society, but others have no functional relationship to industrialization. They are, therefore, not influenced by modernization. Ralston and colleagues (Ralston, 1993; Ralston et al.,

1997) attempted to accommodate the middle ground by coining the term *crossvergence* to refer to the incorporation by individuals of influences from both national culture and economic ideology.

None of these compromise approaches is likely to be entirely satisfactory to proponents of extreme convergence or divergence perspectives. However, they offer the opportunity to understand existing cultural variability while also allowing for growth and change within cultures.

Organizational Culture

Since the early 1980s, managers were made aware of the sociocultural dynamics that develop within organizations called organizational culture (Smircich & Calas, 1986). The notion of the existence of an organizational culture raises two questions about the conceptualization of culture and its influence. First, how are national culture and organizational culture related? How are they similar or different? Second, to what extent does an organizational culture moderate or negate the effect of national culture?

The term *organizational culture* was imported into the management literature from anthropology. However, the definition of culture is not synonymous in the two fields (Smircich, 1983). Following the introduction of the term to the literature by Pettigrew (1979), the concept of organizational culture was popularized in management literature in the early 1980s (e.g., Deal & Kennedy, 1982; Peters & Waterman, 1982). Although there is no consensus as to the definition of the term, many authors describe it as an internal attribute of the organization that is socially constructed, historically determined, holistic, and difficult to change (Hofstede, Neuijen, Ohayv, & Sanders, 1990).

Schein's (1985) conceptualization of levels of culture presented earlier in this chapter was originally applied to organizational culture (although it can be applied to any cultural group). Much of the literature on organizational culture focuses on what Schein describes as the consciously held values of the culture. For an organization, these are its strategies, goals, and philosophies. That is, the core of corporate culture was seen as the values that organization members shared (Ott, 1989; Peters & Waterman, 1982). However, these studies typically failed to distinguish between the values of the founder or top managers and those shared by the majority of organization members. Subsequent research has had a tendency to focus on the behavior of organization members as an indicator of corporate culture (Kotter & Heskitt, 1992). Hofstede et al. (1990) have made perhaps the clearest distinction between the constructs of corporate and national culture. They provide evidence that organizational culture and national culture are composed of different elements. That is, although the culture (values) of founders and key leaders shape organizational cultures, the way these cultures affect organizational members is through the routinized practices of the organization. It is primarily these practices that are passed on from one generation of organization members to the next and form the culture of the organization. The reason proposed for this distinction is that people enter organizations after their national cultural values, attitudes, and fundamental beliefs are well-developed, whereas organizational practices are learned through workplace socialization (Hofstede et al., 1990). That is, organization members adopt an organizational culture through selection and socialization (Feldman, 1976), whereas people are born into their national culture. This focus on behavioral norms as the fundamental element of organizational culture amplifies the distinction between organizational culture and societal culture. That is, norms tell people how they should behave in a particular situation, whereas culture tells them the inherent meaning of the situation (D'Andrade, 1989).

This perspective causes some scholars (Erez & Earley, 1993) to go so far as to call the study of organizational culture "misguided" in that organizations do not really have cultures but are themselves the product of societal culture. Regardless of the terminology, however, organizations might have some effect on an individual's values, fundamental attitudes, and beliefs. This effect is probably very weak in comparison to national culture and has limited lasting impact (Triandis, 1995). For example, Hofstede's (1980) classic study, discussed in more detail in Chapter 3, found striking cultural differences within a single MNC that is often described as having a "strong" corporate culture. In addition, Laurent (1983) found that managers working for a single MNC maintained, or even enhanced, their national cultural distinctiveness when compared to managers working for different firms in their native countries. This effect is consistent with the idea that individuals are only partly involved with their organizations although they are totally immersed in their national culture. That is, membership in the organization is conditional and based on an exchange relationship between the individual and the firm, whereas membership in a national culture is unconditional. Table 2.2 outlines the characteristic differences in national and organizational culture.

Another avenue for the possible effect of organizational culture is in its compatibility with national culture. Research suggests that national- or societal-level culture influences the relationship of organizational culture to organizational outcomes (England, 1983). For example, studies found that matching societal and organizational cultures resulted in higher job satisfaction (Lincoln et al., 1978), more effective quality circles (Ferris & Wagner, 1985), and better decision making (Misumi, 1984). A

TABLE 2.2 Comparison of Organizational and National Culture

National Culture	Organizational Culture
• Shared meanings	• Shared behaviors
• Unconditional relationship	• Conditional relationship
• Born into it	• Socialized into it
• Totally immersed	• Partly involved

more complete discussion of this compatibility issue is presented in Chapter 9, in which organization structure is discussed. However, it is important to note that organizational norms, rules, and procedures might need to be evaluated in terms of their consistency with societal culture.

In summary, organizational culture might be a somewhat different construct and composed of different elements from that of national culture. In addition, entry to and transmittal of organizational culture occur in different ways and at different times from national culture. Moreover, individuals are only partly involved with an organizational culture as compared to totally immersed in their national culture. However, the influence of organizational norms must be considered in understanding causes of behavior in organizations.

Acculturation

The concept of culture, as presented in this book, suggests that culture is resistant to change from such forces as socialization in an organization. However, this is not meant to suggest that cultures are static. One way that cultures change is through the process of acculturation. Acculturation concerns the psychological and behavioral changes that occur in people because of contact with people from different cultures. Most often, it is used to describe the changes in people who relocate from one culture to another. Acculturation can be either individual or collective. In collective acculturation, the whole group, as opposed to the individual, changes and achieves a special status in the new society (Triandis, 1995). For example, observation of Chinese immigrants to western Canada suggests that they often adopted a collective acculturation strategy because of their appearance differences to the local population. European migrants to the same area were seen to acculturate on an individual basis.

The gradual process of psychological acculturation that occurs during immigration results in changes in individual behavior, identity, values, and attitudes (Berry, 1990). For example, in a study of Italian and Greek immigrants to Canada, first-generation immigrants exhibited a stronger ethnic identification than did their children (Lalonde & Cameron, 1993). That is, over time the identification of people with their new country becomes stronger. However, some evidence exists to suggest that these changes might be quite slow. Boski (1991), in a study of two generations of Polish immigrants to Canada, found that after two generations, participants' values were still more closely allied to prototypical Polish than to Canadian value profiles.

Culture and Social Groups

A key aspect of culture presented in this chapter is that culture is associated with a specific group of people. Identifying ourselves with a particular social group places boundaries around our group (in-group) and defines nonmembers as an out-group. The in-group–out-group distinction is useful in describing attitudes and behavior both within and across cultural-group boundaries.

The identification of social groups serves no purpose if no one is excluded. That is, groups are about differentiation. For example, anthropologists report that those cultural groups that exist in isolation do not have characteristics (e.g., tribal name or unique symbols) that indicate a strong group identity (Mead, 1937). Treating culture as associated with social groups further illuminates two important considerations of cultural groups. First, the characteristics of groups can change as members come and go. Second, our membership in a cultural group helps to determine how we perceive ourselves—our self-identity—as well as how others perceive us. That is, the mere categorization of individuals into different groups results in a number of assumptions about both the in-group and out-group members.

The assumptions about group members that arise from categorizing ourselves and others as members of certain groups can lead to different beliefs about, attitudes toward, and behavior directed at different cultural groups. When categorized as a group, individuals are thought to be relatively more similar in their beliefs and behavior, their behavior is thought to convey less information about them as individuals, and the group is believed to be a more important cause of their behavior than individual characteristics (Wilder, 1986). The in-group–out-group boundary that results from categorization has several implications for the way individuals select, structure, and process social information. The way in which social categorization influences the process of culture's influence on management behavior is developed more fully in Chapter 4. In brief, however, this categorization results in a comparison of our own group with other cultural groups resulting in intergroup bias. Intergroup bias can be either positive or negative but most often favors our own group.

In-Group Bias and Prejudice

The universal bias toward our own group is related to the role of our cultural group in defining who we are. That is, we derive our sense of self, in part, from our identification with the groups to which we belong, including our cultural group (Tajfel, 1981). To maintain our self-image, we favorably compare the attributes of our own group with out-groups (Tajfel & Turner, 1986). Therefore, we consistently discriminate in favor of the group(s) with which we identify.

Prejudicial judgments about members of out-groups relate to beliefs about the character of these groups. These, often negative, attitudes toward out-group members are based solely on their membership in a particular group. Prejudice translates to discrimination when action is taken for, or more frequently against, members of this out-group. The extent to which prejudicial attitudes result in discriminatory behavior depends on both personal and cultural factors (Smith & Bond, 1999). However, in-group favoritism is a consistent consequence of social categorization that occurs across gender, age, and nationalities (Wilder, 1986). Numerous, management-related examples of this bias exist, including reports of the so-called country-of-origin effect (Peterson & Jolibert, 1995). That is, products described as coming from a person's own country are consistently rated higher in quality than the same products coming from another country.

Ethnocentrism

In much of the cross-cultural management literature, the attitudes that reflect the categorization of cultural groups is encapsulated under the term *ethnocentrism*. Ethnocentrism is described as an attitude that one's own cultural group is the center of everything and all other groups are evaluated with reference to it (Sumner, 1940). Although related to a narrow or provincial perspective often labeled "parochialism," ethnocentrism is a universal tendency resulting from social categorization that has broad implications. Triandis (1994) identifies the following characteristic of ethnocentrism:

- What goes on in our culture is seen as "natural and correct," and what goes on in other cultures is perceived as "unnatural and incorrect."
- We perceive our own in-group customs as universally valid.
- We unquestionably think that in-group norms, roles, and values are correct.
- We believe that it is natural to help and cooperate with members of our in-group, to favor our in-group, to feel proud of our in-group, and to be distrustful of and even hostile toward out-group members (pp. 251-252).

Examples of ethnocentric attitudes in management include beliefs that the way business is conducted in one's own country is the only way to be effective, that people of one's own culture are naturally better suited to almost any management job, and the role of women in management is only correct as it exists at home.

Summary

This chapter presented the concept of culture as a set of shared mental representations that, in the most fundamental way, shape the way in which managers interact with their world. Therefore, it is responsible for the way in which management is conceptualized and the way in which managers enact their various roles. Culture is not inherited but is developed over time by the way societies interact with their environment. It is learned by each new generation. Culture is presented as a characteristic that can be associated with any social group. Thinking of culture in this way places boundaries around our cultural group and differentiates us from other groups. This perspective provides a basis in social cognition for understanding the influence of culture.

In addition, the concept of a national culture is presented as an appropriate starting place for the understanding of cultural influences in international management. International managers are concerned with the legal and political characteristics of countries, which are derived from its history and culture. Culture can be thought of as the most fundamental characteristics of a society even though some aspects of culture will be more widely shared than others. National culture can be seen as distinct from organizational culture both in terms of its constituent elements and its influence on behavior. Although national cultures are relatively stable, they do change over time, and individuals can identify with a new culture through the process of acculturation.

Arguments can be presented for both the convergence and divergence of national cultures. However, the reality probably occupies some middle ground. That is, some aspects of cultures could be converging because of globalization, but other aspects of culture are unaffected by this technological and economic change.

↳ which ones?

Three

Comparing Cultures

Systematically Describing Cultural Differences

All people are the same. It is only their habits that are so different.

Confucius

Culture can be best expressed in the complex interactions of values, attitudes, and behavioral assumptions of a society. However, for culture to be a useful concept in management studies, we must be able to "unpackage" the culture concept (Schwartz, 1994). Although alternative definitions and theoretical perspectives are as numerous as the disciplines that use culture as a fundamental concept, much of our understanding of cultural variation has been achieved by reducing our analysis to the study of values. That is, the essence of culture is described by the content and structure of the basic mental representations that members of particular social groups share. As noted in Chapter 2,

47

these value differences arise from the solutions that different social groups have devised for dealing with the finite number of problems with which all people must deal. Because there are a limited number of ways in which a society can manage these problems (Kluckhohn & Strodtbeck, 1961), it is possible to develop a system that categorizes and compares societies on this basis. By examining the choices that social groups make, we can infer their preferences for such fundamental human issues as their relationships to their environment and to each other. This provides the ability to categorize a social group according to these shared assumptions about the way things ought to be or the way one should behave.

This chapter reviews the major frameworks that have been devised for categorizing and comparing cultures, as is the concept of cultural distance. Despite being conducted at widely different times and using different methods, they have resulted in very similar descriptions of cultural dimensions. This similarity leads to a more in-depth description of the concepts of individualism and collectivism and their relationship to other elements of the sociocultural system. Finally, I examine the uses to which the systematic descriptions of culture are put.

Kluckhohn and Strodtbeck Framework

Early work in comparative anthropology produced a framework with a good theoretical basis that has influenced the way the management literature has conceptualized cultural variation (Maznevski, DiStefano, & Nason, 1993). This categorization identified six dimensions along which a society can be categorized (Kluckhohn & Strodtbeck, 1961). These variations in value orientations concern the following issues:

- *Relationships to nature*—People have a need-duty to control or master nature (domination), to submit to nature (subjugation), or to work together with nature to maintain harmony and balance (harmony).

- *Beliefs about human nature*—People are inherently good, evil, or a mixture of good and evil.

- *Relationships among people*—The greatest concern and responsibility is for one's self and immediate family (individualist), for one's own group that is defined in different ways (collateral), or for one's groups that are arranged in a rigid hierarchy (hierarchical).

- *Nature of human activity*—People should concentrate on living for the moment (being), striving for goals (achieving), or reflecting (thinking).

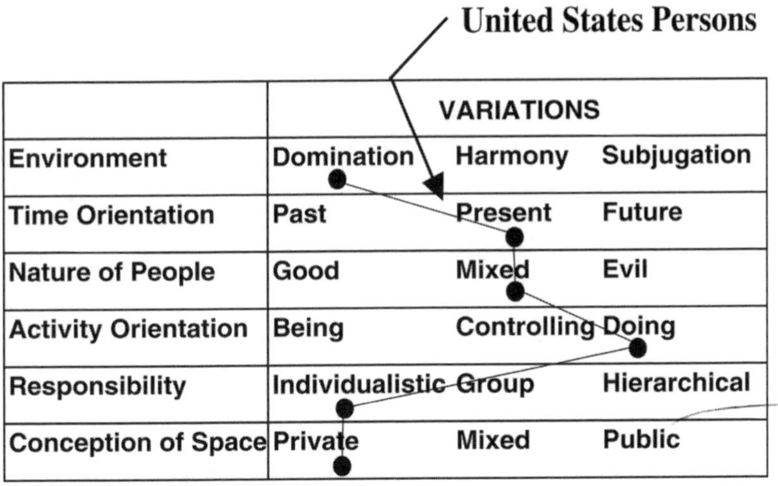

United States Persons

	VARIATIONS		
Environment	Domination	Harmony	Subjugation
Time Orientation	Past	Present	Future
Nature of People	Good	Mixed	Evil
Activity Orientation	Being	Controlling Doing	
Responsibility	Individualistic Group		Hierarchical
Conception of Space	Private	Mixed	Public

Figure 3.1. Cultural Variation in Value Orientations
SOURCE: Adapted from Kluckhohn & Strodtbeck, 1961.

- *Conception of space*—The physical space we use is private, or public, or a mixture of public and private.

- *Orientation to time*—People should make decisions with respect to traditions or events in the past, events in the present, or events in the future.

Figure 3.1 shows the variations in the assumptions that people exhibited across cultures on these six dimensions. Because many readers will be familiar with the U.S. culture, this preference pattern is highlighted in the figure.

In this conceptualization of cultural variation, the six value orientations are not bipolar dimensions. That is, a high preference for one assumption does not necessarily imply a low preference for the other two assumptions in the same value orientation. All preferences can be represented in a society, but with a rank order of the preferred alternatives. For example, people from the United States might exhibit a preference for a present-time orientation, but a future orientation might be a close second choice.

Despite the validity of this framework, which was demonstrated in extensive field research (Kluckhohn & Strodtbeck, 1961), and the obvious management behavior implications for a particular preference (e.g., a *doing* orientation suggests that employees would be motivated to achieve goals, whereas a *being* orientation suggests that employees would only work as much as needed to support their lifestyle), very few management studies have used this theoretical orientation. This is probably because of the lack of a psychometric instrument that measured these dimensions in a fashion applicable to the managerial context. Recent efforts at scale development (Maznevski et al., 1993) confirm the validity of the dimensions and show promise as a useful tool to describe cultural variation in a way that will be useful to management researchers.

Hofstede's Study

A framework that has received a great deal of research attention is Hofstede's (1980) now-classic study of work values. Based on attitude surveys of 117,000 employees of a large U.S. multinational corporation (later identified as IBM), Hofstede extracted four dimensions with which he could classify the 40 different countries represented. These dimensions were named *individualism-collectivism, power distance, uncertainty avoidance,* and *masculinity-femininity.* The questionnaire items that were most strongly represented in each dimension are shown in Table 3.1.

Individualism-collectivism is the extent to which one's self-identity is defined according to individual characteristics or by the characteristics of the groups to which the individual belongs on a permanent basis, and the extent to which individual or group interests dominate. Power distance refers to the extent that power differences are accepted and sanctioned in a society. Uncertainty avoidance is the extent to which societies focus on ways to reduce uncertainty and create stability. Masculinity-femininity refers to the extent to which "traditional" male orientations of ambition and achievement are emphasized over "traditional" female orientations of nurturance and interpersonal harmony. By giving each of the 40 countries a score, ranging from 0 to 100 on each of the four dimensions, Hofstede derived a classification of national cultures. The original sample was later expanded to include 50 countries. The scores given to the countries are shown in Table 3.2.

It is particularly important to point out that Hofstede's scores were the average score for all participants in each country. Therefore, it is not appropriate to infer that because two nations differ on a particular value dimension that any two individuals from those countries will differ in the same way. That is, within each nation, there might be variation on a particular dimension, such that a particular individual will not be at all representative of the mean score. For example, Figure 3.2 shows the

TABLE 3.1 Hofstede's Four Dimensions of Culture-Related Values

Value	Questionnaire Item	Response
Power distance	How frequently, in your experience, does the following problem occur: employees being afraid to express their disagreement with their managers?	(Frequently)
Uncertainty avoidance	Company rules should not be broken, even if the employee thinks it is in the company's best interest.	(Strongly agree)
	How long do you think you will continue working for this company?	(Until I retire)
Individualism	How important is it to you to have a job that leaves you sufficient time for your personal or family life?	(Very)
	How important is it to you to have considerable freedom to adapt your own approach to the job?	(Very)
Femininity	How important is it to you to have a good working relationship with your manager?	(Very)
	How important is it to you to work with people who cooperate well with one another?	(Very)
Masculinity	How important is it to you to have an opportunity for high earnings?	(Very)
	How important is it to you to get the recognition you deserve when you do a good job?	(Very)

SOURCE: P. B. Smith & M. H. Bond, *Social Psychology Across Cultures*. Copyright ©1999, Allyn & Bacon. Reprinted by permission.

hypothetical distribution of individual scores on individualism-collectivism between a collectivist country (Malaysia) and an individualist country (New Zealand).

As shown in Figure 3.2, it is entirely possible to find an individual in New Zealand who scores lower on individualism than someone in Malaysia. Hofstede (1980) called making the mistake of applying the scores at the country level to individuals the "ecological fallacy."

TABLE 3.2   Hofstede's Rankings

Country	Power Distance	Individualism	Masculinity	Uncertainty Avoidance
Argentina	49	46	56	86
Australia	36	90	61	51
Austria	11	55	79	70
Belgium	65	75	54	94
Brazil	69	38	49	76
Canada	39	80	52	48
Chile	63	23	28	86
Colombia	67	13	64	80
Costa Rica	35	15	21	86
Denmark	18	74	16	23
Equador	78	8	63	67
Finland	33	63	26	59
France	68	71	43	86
Germany (F.R.)	35	67	66	65
Great Britain	35	89	66	35
Greece	60	35	57	112
Guatemala	95	6	37	101
Hong Kong	68	25	57	29
Indonesia	78	14	46	48
India	77	48	56	40
Iran	58	41	43	59
Ireland	28	70	68	35
Israel	13	54	47	81
Italy	50	76	70	75
Jamaica	45	39	68	13
Japan	54	46	95	92
Korea (S)	60	187	39	85
Malaysia	104	26	50	36
Mexico	81	30	69	82
Netherlands	38	80	14	53
Norway	31	69	8	50
New Zealand	22	79	58	49
Pakistan	55	14	50	70
Panama	95	11	44	86
Peru	64	16	42	87
Philippines	94	32	64	44
Portugal	63	27	31	104
South Africa	49	65	63	49
Salvador	66	19	40	94
Singapore	74	20	48	8
Spain	57	51	42	86
Sweden	31	71	5	29
Switzerland	34	68	70	58
Taiwan	58	17	45	69
Thailand	64	20	34	64
Turkey	66	37	45	85
Uruguay	61	36	38	100
United States	40	91	62	46
Venezuela	81	12	73	76
Yugoslavia	76	27	21	88
Regions:				
East Africa	64	27	41	52
West Africa	77	20	46	54
Arab countries	80	38	53	68

SOURCE: Adapted from Hofstede, 1991.

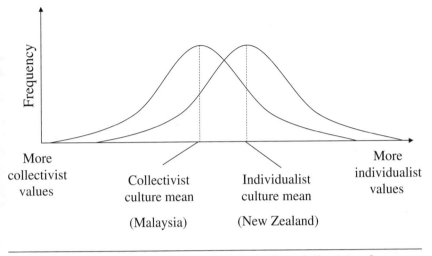

Figure 3.2. Hypothetical Distribution of Indivdualism-Collectivism Scores

Consistent with the individual variation noted previously, it is also increasingly clear that the level of agreement among individuals in a society concerning the importance of a particular value dimension can vary systematically. That is, there could be differing degrees of consensus on any particular value orientation. Recently, researchers have measured this intranational consensus, as the opposite of variation, by examining differences in the standard deviation in measures of value orientations across cultures (e.g., Au, 1999; Schwartz & Sagie, 2000). Although systematic differences in consensus seem to exist, the implications for the degree of consensus in a society either overall or on specific value orientations are only beginning to be understood. However, some evidence suggests that value consensus is related to socioeconomic development and democratization of societies (Schwartz & Sagie, 2000), and implications are proposed for organizational behavior similar to those found for other types of heterogeneity (Au, 1999).

Confucian-Dynamism

In an effort to investigate the possibility that Hofstede's study (1980) might contain cultural bias, because it was developed in the West, a group of researchers conducted a subsequent study based on Chinese values (Chinese Culture Connection, 1987). This survey was conducted in 23 countries and in a similar way to Hofstede's original study. The factors were then compared to those obtained by Hofstede in the same countries. This study also indicated four underlying dimensions of cultural-value orientations. These were labeled as the following: *integration*, examples of which included tolerance, harmony, and solidarity with others; non-competitiveness, trustworthiness, and contentedness; *human heartedness*, including kindness, patience, courtesy, and a sense of righteousness; *Confucian work dynamism*, including order, thrift, persistence, and sense of shame; and *moral discipline*, including moderation, being disinterested and pure, and having few desires. Even though the studies used measures based in very different cultures and were conducted with different samples, substantial similarity was found for three of the four dimensions. In addition, a new dimension, Confucian work dynamism (later called long- versus short-term orientation by Hofstede, 1991) was found to be important in the Chinese culture. Table 3.3 shows the relationship (correlations) between the dimensions found in the Chinese Culture Connection (1987) study with those in the original Hofstede study.

As shown in Table 3.3, the dimensions of individualism-collectivism, masculinity-femininity, and power distance describe cultural variations that hold up under this additional analysis. That is, they are correlated with dimensions found in the Chinese Culture Connection study (1987). However, because the dimensions of uncertainty avoidance and Confucian dynamism do not correlate as highly with dimensions derived in the other culture, they might be less universally applicable.

Cultural Distance

One of the benefits of quantitative measures of cultural dimensions, such as those described earlier, is the ability to construct indexes of "cultural distance" between countries. That is, it is possible to address the question of how different overall national cultures are from each other based on the value orientations measured. For example, by using Hofstede's four cultural dimensions, a measure of national cultural distance was developed (Kogut & Singh, 1988). The measure is an index, which is corrected for differences in the variances of each dimension and then arithmetically averaged.

The algebraic formula for the index is as follows:

$$\text{Cultural Distance} = \sum_{i=1}^{4} [(I_{ij} - I_{iu})^2 / V_i]/4$$

I_{ij} = index for the ith cultural dimension for the jth country
I_{iu} = index for the ith cultural dimension for the uth country
V_i = variance for the ith cultural dimension

TABLE 3.3 Correlations Between Hofstede Dimensions and Chinese Culture Connection Dimensions

Hofstede	Chinese Culture Connection			
	Integration	Human Heartedness	Confucian Work Dynamism	Moral Discipline
Individualism	0.65	−0.05	−0.32	−0.54
Masculinity	0.11	0.67	0.08	0.22
Power Distance	−0.58	0.13	0.23	0.55
Uncertainty Avoidance	0.06	−0.04	0.22	0.36

SOURCE: Adapted from Chinese Culture Connection, 1987.

This index represents the relative distance of nations from each other in the multidimensional space defined by the four cultural dimensions. As such, it transcends the specific value orientations of the cultures represented to indicate the overall degree of similarity-dissimilarity between different nationalities. For example, using this index, the cultural distance between the United States and Japan is 2.6325, whereas the cultural distance between the United States and Canada is 0.247.

Although indexes such as this can have some use in assessing the overall similarity or dissimilarity of nations regarding the dimensions measured, care must be taken in their interpretation. They are only meaningful as a very broad comparison at the national level and thus are subject to all the caveats associated with equating nation and culture, as expressed in Chapter 2. In addition, it is important to treat such indexes with caution because they are far removed from and depend on the accuracy of measurement of the mental representations from which they were derived (see Usunier, 1998).

Criticism of Hofstede's Study

Hofstede's conceptualization of culture as a finite number of dimensions has found favor with management researchers and has led to numerous studies utilizing one or more of the dimensions to explain observed differences across nations. However, it is not without critics (e.g., Dorfman & Howell, 1988; Roberts & Boyacigiller, 1984). Hofstede's arguments about the existence of dimensions of cultural variation were consistent with other conceptions of cultural variation. However, problems with the work focus on how he operationalized these constructs (Dorfman & Howell, 1988). For example, Hofstede's framework was developed from two surveys conducted in 1968 and 1972 inside IBM that restricts the ability to generalize to other organizations whose members might be systematically different. More serious, perhaps, is that the items in the survey were not developed from any theoretical base but extracted from a broader survey designed to assess employee satisfaction, perception of work, and personal beliefs and goals (Hofstede, 1991).

Other methodological criticisms associated with the approach used include the following: (a) a technical issue associated with the mathematics of the factor analysis in that there were too few data points for the number of questionnaire items, (b) that two of the Hofstede dimensions were separated arbitrarily, (c) that on the face of them, many of the items within dimensions seem to be unrelated to each other, and (d) that many of the items related to several of the dimensions (Dorfman & Howell, 1988; Maznevski et al., 1993). Notwithstanding the criticism of Hofstede's study, the four cultural dimensions seem to make sense and have been validated in subsequent work.

Schwartz Value Survey

Since Hofstede's study (1980), two additional large-scale surveys of values have been conducted. Each of these studies adds something new to our understanding of cultural differences. The first of these is the Schwartz Value Survey. Based on a review of previous theory and research, Shalom Schwartz and his colleagues (Sagiv & Schwartz, 1995; Schwartz, 1992, 1994; Schwartz & Bilsky, 1990) conducted a series of studies on the content and structure of human values. The content of values refers to the various criteria that people use to evaluate events and select courses of action. Structure refers to the organization of these values based on their similarities and differences.

Initially, Schwartz and his colleagues (Sagiv & Schwartz, 1995; Schwartz, 1992, 1994; Schwartz & Bilsky, 1990) identified three universal human requirements. The first issue was the nature of the relationship between the individual and the group. The second issue is the preservation of the society itself, and the final problem related to the relationship of people to the natural world. From these requirements that all societies share, they derived 56 values that reflected various ways of satisfying these needs. Respondents in 20 (later an additional 40) countries were asked the extent to which each value was a guiding principle in their lives. The results were mapped separately for each country by using a statistical procedure called smallest space analysis. This analysis showed which items clustered together. With some exceptions (e.g., China and Zimbabwe), the resulting maps were very similar across countries. A typical map for a student sample is shown in Figure 3.3.

As shown in Figure 3.3, the values clustered into 10 groups called *value types*. Of the 56 original values, 45 were determined to have meanings that were consistent across cultures. That is, they appeared in the same cluster in all cultures. The results of this study strongly suggest that the structure of values is consistent across cultures. That is, there is a similar relationship among values in all cultures. On close examination, these 10 value types can be seen as a refinement to Hofstede's earlier work (Smith & Bond, 1999). On the left side of Figure 3.3 are value types that are consistent with collectivism such as tradition, security, and conformity, whereas on the right are value types of achievement, self-direction, and hedonism representative of individualism. In addition, Hofstede's notion of power distance is captured in the two opposing value types of power and universalism; and masculinity-femininity is represented as achievement versus benevolence. This framework does not indicate which value dimensions are most important in each culture. However, it captures a broad range of value dimensions that are important in all cultures and establishes that the meanings of these values are consistent across cultures.

To define cultural dimensions at the level of national culture, Schwartz and colleagues (Sagiv & Schwartz, 1995; Schwartz, 1992, 1994; Schwartz & Bilsky, 1990) performed a multidimensional scaling analysis on the correlations between the average ratings of the 45 universal values (shown previously) in a number of different samples in 63 countries (Sagiv & Schwartz, 2000). This analysis yielded seven value types that were labeled as the following:

1. *egalitarianism*, recognition of people as moral equals;

2. *harmony*, fitting in harmoniously with the environment;

3. *embeddedness*, people as embedded in the collective;

4. *hierarchy*, unequal distribution of power is legitimate;

5. *mastery*, exploitation of the natural or social environment;

6. *affective autonomy*, pursuit of positive experiences; and

7. *intellectual autonomy*, independent pursuit of own ideas.

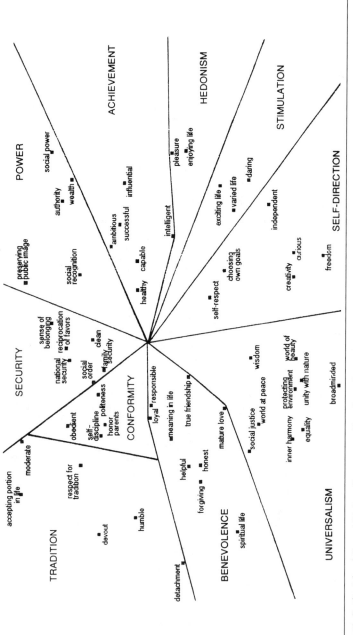

Figure 3.3. Individual Level Value Structure (Student Sample)

SOURCE: Schwartz, 1992. Reprinted with permission of Academic Press.

Although this process used the same measures of values described earlier, it is important to emphasize that the analysis is at the national culture level. Having defined these dimensions of national culture, they went on to compare samples from 57 countries on this profile of values. Then, using a technique called a co-plot, they constructed a profile of differences between all pairs of countries in the sample. This procedure generates a two-dimensional graphic representation of the relationship of countries to each other on all seven dimensions simultaneously (see Sagiv & Schwartz, 2000). An example of a comparison of samples of teachers is shown in Figure 3.4.

As shown in Figure 3.4, the location of country samples along the seven value vectors indicates their relationship to each other. The direction of the vector indicates the increasing importance of the value type in relationship to the center of the diagram marked by the X. For example, the line drawn on Figure 3.4 indicates the importance that each sample attributes to *intellectual autonomy*. To locate a country sample on this dimension, a perpendicular is drawn from the position of the country to the vector. The lines drawn on the figure indicate that this dimension is very important in France, less so in Norway, India, and Singapore, and very unimportant in Ghana. Because the co-plot summarizes the position of countries on seven value types on only two dimensions, the graphic location of each country is not perfect. Overall, however, it generally provides an accurate representation of the relationship of countries to each other (Sagiv & Schwartz, 2000), and studies with other samples have shown very similar patterns of relationships (Schwartz, 1992).

Trompenaars's Dimensions

Another, recent broad-based study of value orientations was conducted by Fons Trompenaars. During a 10-year period, he administered a values questionnaire to over 15,000 managers in 28 countries. Subsequently, it was used in a much larger number of countries (Trompenaars, 1993) and includes a number of former Soviet-bloc countries not included in previous studies of values. His seven value dimensions were derived primarily from the prior work of North American sociologists and anthropologists (Kluckhohn & Strodtbeck, 1961; Parsons & Shils, 1951). The first five of these dimensions concerned relationships among people.

- *Universalism-Particularism:* Universalism is a belief that what is true and good can be discovered and applied universally, whereas particularism is a belief that unique circumstances determine what is right or good.

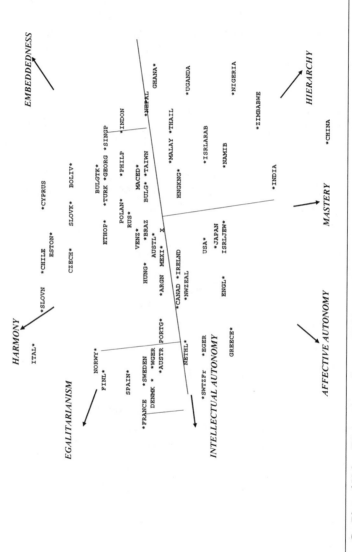

Figure 3.4. Co-Plot of Value Dimensions Across 57 National Cultures

SOURCE: Sagiv & Schwartz, 2000. Reprinted with permission of Sage Publications, Inc.

- *Individualism-Collectivism:* Similar to Hofstede's definition, this dimension concerns the extent to which people plan their actions with reference to individual benefits versus those of the group.

- *Neutral-Affective:* In neutral cultures, emotion should be held in check, and maintaining an appearance of self-control is important, whereas in affective cultures, it is natural to express emotions.

- *Specific-Diffuse:* This dimension refers to the extent to which individuals are willing to allow access to their inner selves to others. In specific cultures, people separate the private part of their lives from the public, whereas in diffuse cultures, these aspects of the individual overlap.

- *Achievement-Ascription:* This dimension is about how status and power are determined in a society. In an ascription society, status is based on who a person is, whereas in an achievement society, status is based on what a person does.

The final two dimensions are similar to Kluckhohn and Strodtbeck's (1961) categorization and are about orientations toward time and the environment:

- *Time:* This dimension is about past versus future orientations, but also with the extent to which time is viewed as linear versus holistic and integrative with past and present together with future possibilities.

- *Environment:* This dimension refers to the extent to which individuals feel that they themselves are the primary influence on their lives. Alternatively, the environment is seen as more powerful than they and people should strive to achieve harmony with it.

A recent analysis of Trompenaars's data yielded two main dimensions of cultural variation at the national level (Smith, Dugan, & Trompenaars, 1996). These were the following:

- *Loyal involvement-Utilitarian involvement,* representing varying orientations toward group members, and

- *Conservatism-Egalitarian commitment,* representing orientations toward obligations of social relationships.

These can be seen as extensions and refinements of Hofstede's (1980) individualism-collectivism and power-distance dimensions, respectively. This refinement is also consistent with the relationship found between the Schwartz Value Survey (SVS) and Hofstede's dimensions. That is, the most important relationships that exist between the SVS value types and the Hofstede dimensions are for the dimensions of individualism-collectivism and power distance (Schwartz, 1994).

As discussed, the results of the three major studies of national variation in value orientations have some remarkable similarity, despite being conducted at widely different times, with different samples, and using different methods. This consistency of findings lends validity to this approach to describing cultural variation. In addition, however, because they appear in some form in all of the frameworks, individualism-collectivism and power distance are perhaps more important to understanding cultural variation. Indeed, these dimensions relate to two of the three fundamental issues that Schwartz and colleagues (Sagiv & Schwartz, 1995; Schwartz, 1992, 1994; Schwartz & Bilsky, 1990) identified as being common among societies. The first has to do with boundaries between individuals and groups and the second with the preservation of order in society.

Individualism and Collectivism

Individualism and collectivism are perhaps the most useful and powerful dimensions of cultural variation in explaining a diverse array of social behavior (Triandis, 1995). Individualism refers to the tendency to view one's self as independent of others and to be more concerned about the consequences for one's self of a particular behavior. Alternatively, collectivism refers to the tendency to view one's self as interdependent with selected others and to be concerned about the consequences of behavior for one's reference group, and to be more willing to sacrifice personal interests for the good of this group. However, individualism-collectivism should not be depicted as simply a dichotomy of self-interest and group interest. That is, collectivism does not equate with socialism. For example, collectivists can pursue self-interests as well as group interests as long as priority is given to the group (Erez & Earley, 1993), and self-interests can be instrumental in attaining group interests. In addition, as noted in Chapter 2, individualists and collectivists both derive their sense of self, in part, from the groups with which they identify, their in-groups. Although individualists and collectivists probably behave similarly toward members of their in-group, they differ in the way in which they designate who is a member of this group. That is, collectivists form very few of these groups, but the groups are broad in scope encompassing many interrelated relationships. By contrast, individualists have many groups with which they identify, but their relationships within these groups are superficial.

A significant amount of research on a wide array of organizational topics has relied on the individualism-collectivism dimension. In fact, so much comparative management research has used this conception of cultural variation that some authors have suggested that other dimensions of culture could have been inappropriately ignored (Earley & Gibson, 1998). In addition to an overreliance on this concept of culture, its relationship to other cultural factors is often ignored. The following sections describe some refinements in the individualism-collectivism construct.

Tightness and Complexity

The cultural patterns represented by individualism and collectivism might be affected by a number of different influences. However, the degree of cultural tightness and complexity are, according to Triandis (1995), major influences on the degree of individualism or collectivism in a society. Individualism is a result of looseness and complexity, whereas collectivism is a result of tightness and simplicity.

Tightness refers to the extent to which members of a culture agree about what is correct behavior, believe they must behave exactly according to cultural norms, and believe they will receive or should give severe criticism for even small deviations from cultural norms (Pelto, 1968). Japan is an example of a tight culture, whereas the United Sates is a loose culture. Tightness is also associated with homogeneous cultures that often have high population density. Alternatively, loose cultures often have multiple and sometimes conflicting norms about appropriate behavior. Although a culture might be characterized as tight or loose overall, both tightness and looseness can occur in a society in different contexts (Triandis, 1995). For example, a culture can be tight in its political orientation but loose in terms of religion.

Cultural complexity refers to the amount of differentiation in the various domains of individuals' lives. The numbers of different roles available to individuals, the size of communities, and the GNP per capita of a country are suggested as measures of cultural complexity. For example, hunter-gatherer societies are less complex than modern societies that have thousands of different possible roles represented. In support of this idea, Hofstede (1980) found a high positive correlation between GNP and individualism with wealthier countries being more individualistic.

The proposed relationships between tightness, complexity, and individualism- collectivism are presented in Figure 3.5. As suggested in Figure 3.5, collectivism is maximized in tight simple cultures such as might be found in the subcultures of the kibbutz in Israel and the Amish of North America, whereas individualism is maximized in loose complex

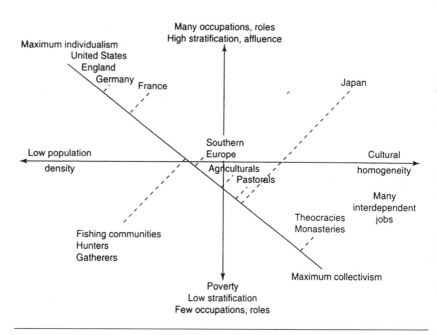

Many occupations, roles
High stratification, affluence

Maximum individualism
United States
England
Germany
France

Japan

Low population
density

Southern
Europe
Agriculturals
Pastorals

Cultural
homogeneity

Many
interdependent
jobs

Theocracies
Monasteries

Fishing communities
Hunters
Gatherers

Maximum collectivism

Poverty
Low stratification
Few occupations, roles

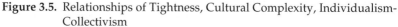

Figure 3.5. Relationships of Tightness, Cultural Complexity, Individualism-
Collectivism

SOURCE: H. C. Triandis, *Culture and Social Behavior.* Copyright ©1994, McGraw-Hill. Reproduced with
permission.

cultures like metropolitan France and the United States. Although the
relationships suggested in Figure 3.5 have yet to be validated by empirical tests, they offer an additional and richer perspective that might help
to understand the cultural variation that we observe.

Vertical and Horizontal Dimensions

In addition to the differences in motives and in the specification of reference group members noted earlier, a number of other refinements of
the individualism-collectivism concept have been suggested (Earley &
Gibson, 1998). For example, Triandis (1995) identified more than 60 different culture-specific characteristics that differentiate between different
kinds of individualism and collectivism. Significant among these is the
concept of vertical and horizontal dimensions that relate to the way in
which people view their status relationship with others. This concept is
conceptually similar to Hofstede's (1980) power-distance dimension

and relates to the SVS (Schwartz, 1992) value orientations of hierarchy and harmony and Trompenaars's (1993) achievement-ascription dimension. In combination with individualism and collectivism, these dimensions correspond to the four types of self, independent or interdependent (Markus & Kitayama, 1991) and same or different (Triandis, 1995).

Table 3.4 indicates how these different combinations of vertical and horizontal individualism and collectivism correspond to how people define themselves, their value orientations on the Rokeach (1973) dimensions, their dominant political systems, and their typical patterns of social behavior as defined by Fiske (1990).

As shown in Table 3.4, this distinction between vertical and horizontal individualism and collectivism results in four different cultural profiles or syndromes. However, the correlation between power distance and collectivism (at $r = .67$ according to Hofstede, 1980) suggests that vertical collectivism and horizontal individualism might be the dominant cultural profiles around the world (Triandis, 1995). Triandis (1995) offers the following defining attributes of these cultural syndromes.

Vertical collectivists see themselves as an aspect of an in-group, but members of the in-group are different in terms of status. These cultures are characterized by patterns of social relationships that emphasize communal sharing according to need and authority ranking, or the distribution of resources according to rank (Fiske, 1990). They typically have social systems that do not reflect the values of individual freedom or equity (Rokeach, 1973). Inequality is the accepted norm, and serving and sacrificing for the in-group feature prominently.

In horizontal individualism, the self is autonomous and people are generally equal. These cultures are characterized by patterns of social behavior that emphasize equity in resource sharing according to contribution and distribution of resources equally among members (Fiske, 1990). They have social systems that emphasize both the values of equality and individual freedom (Rokeach, 1973).

What these two dominant syndromes suggest is that verticality serves to reinforce collectivism, and horizontalness reinforces individualism. For example, although the United States might be more vertical than, say, New Zealand or Canada, all individualistic cultures relative to collectivist cultures are horizontal.

The previous discussion has identified the main attempts that have been made to identify dimensions along which cultures could be systematically described and compared. Each is deficient in some regard, but taken as a whole, they begin to paint a reasonably clear picture that cultural variability is systematic and that cultural characteristics can be identified and described. Of the dimensions identified, the concepts of

TABLE 3.4 Culture, Self, Orientation, and Politics

	Vertical		Horizontal	
	Collectivism	Individualism	Collectivism	Individualism
Kind of self	Interdependent Different from others	Independent Different from others	Independent Same as others	Independent Same as others
Fiske orientation	Communal sharing Authority ranking	Communal sharing Authority ranking	Communal sharing Equality matching	Communal sharing Equality matching
Rokeach values	Low equality Low freedom	Low equality High freedom	High equality Low freedom	High equality High freedom
Political system	Communalism (e.g., Indian village)	Market democracy (e.g., U.S., France)	Communal living (e.g., Israeli kibbutz)	Democratic socialism (e.g., Sweden, British Labor party)

SOURCE: From *Individualism and Collectivism,* by Harry C. Triandis. Copyright ©1995 Westview Press, a member of Perseus Books, L.L.C.

individualism and collectivism appear to be especially important in describing and comparing social behavior.

Use of the Frameworks

The significance of being able to systematically define cultural variations is that it then provides a basis for explaining and predicting behavior on a comparative basis. However, the ability to profile national cultures along a limited number of dimensions also opens up the possibility for a dramatic oversimplification of the effect of culture.

One of the ways that these cultural frameworks have been used is to attempt to construct profiles of the consequences of each cultural pattern, for example, individualism versus collectivism. To be accurate about these consequences, it would be necessary to randomly sample all the world's cultures, assign them to individualist or collectivist groups, and examine differences on every outcome that we are interested in. However, it is virtually impossible to collect a truly random sample of cultures, and time and resource constraints limit the number of outcomes that can be examined. Therefore, we can really only speculate about the general consequences of particular cultural patterns based on more limited samples.

Because of the limitations mentioned, much cross-cultural management research relies on overly simplistic models of the effect of culture. This oversimplification results in stating that people from this particular type of culture behave this way, whereas those from that other type of culture behave like that. Often, this is done by referring to an existing typology of attributes of national culture, very typically Hofestede's (1980) now almost 30-year-old numeric ratings. In effect, by suggesting that culture works in this way, we have substituted "sophisticated stereotypes" of a culture for the complex reality that exists (Osland & Bird, 2000). Therefore, instead of explaining cultural effects, it can have the opposite effect of constraining the way in which people regard members of another culture. For example, we run the risk of thinking of all Japanese people as high on "masculinity," and "uncertainty avoidance," low on "individualism," and moderate on "power distance." The fallacy of this approach is apparent to anyone who has encountered behavior in members of another culture inconsistent with the picture painted by the profile. These seeming paradoxes can usually be explained when the situational context or cultural history of a particular country is considered (Osland & Bird, 2000). Subsequent chapters of this book present a more sophisticated way of thinking about cultural influence that accounts for such factors.

However, these problems do not render the systematic description of cultural variation useless. On the contrary, as described in Chapter 11, they can be valuable in selecting national cultures to compare when trying to assess the degree of similarity or difference on responses to particular management questions. In addition, they are useful tools, both for researchers and managers, as long as their limitations are understood. The following conditions are a concise summary of the care that should be taken when using descriptions of cultures based on a limited number of dimensions, so-called cultural stereotypes. They should be

- They should be consciously held, that is, we recognize that we are dealing with limited information;

- They should be limited to describing members of the other cultural group and not contain an evaluative component;

- They should provide an accurate description of the behavioral norm of the cultural group;

- They should be used as a first best guess about the behavior of a cultural group prior to developing direct information about individuals in the group; and

- They should be modified based on additional information gained about the group through observation or experience (Adler, 1997).

The underlying rationale for these simple "rules of thumb" becomes more apparent as a more sophisticated understanding of the influence of culture is developed. This is the subject of the next chapter.

Summary

This chapter presents the main attempts at systematically describing variations in national culture. Our understanding of cultural differences is influenced largely by studies of national differences in values, and a high degree of consistency is found in the structure of values across cultures. Each of the frameworks presented in this chapter offers useful ways to systematically describe the ways that national cultures might differ. Of the dimensions of cultural variation described to date, the most powerful in terms of explaining and predicting behavior is individualism-collectivism. Refinements of this dimension, such as consideration of vertical and horizontal elements, might make it more useful in defining the dominant cultural profiles in the world. Our ability to systematically describe cultural variation is a necessary but limited first step in understanding the effect of culture on management behavior.

Four

How Culture Works:

Fundamentals of Cross-Cultural Interaction

"What kind of bird are you, if you can't sing?" chirped the bird.
"What kind of bird are you, if you can't swim?" quacked the duck.
Prokofiev in "Peter and the Wolf"

As described in Chapter 3, much of the written work on international management is content to identify variations in national culture and then describe the implications of this cultural variation for a wide range of behaviors and organizational issues. This identification of cultural variation is important, but it is only a first step. This approach alone does not do justice to the influence of culture because it fails to identify precisely how these cultural differences affect management behavior in organizations. This book suggests that culture manifests its influence through a number of intermediate mechanisms or conduits. These mechanisms concern how managers think about, evaluate, and respond to people who are culturally different.

As noted in Chapter 1, interpersonal interactions are at the core of the manager's job. The most fundamental issue in international management is the interpersonal interaction among people who are culturally different. This chapter explores the mechanisms for the influence of culture by examining the basics of social cognition in the context of cross-cultural interactions. These concepts are then summarized in a general model of cultural influence on management behavior. In addition, this chapter examines the influence of the motives that culturally different individuals might have. The goal of the chapter is to outline a framework for cultural influence that can then be applied to understanding a range of cross-cultural management issues.

Social Cognition

Our understanding of how culture influences behavior in organizations is grounded in social cognition. Social cognition, in general, is concerned with the role that our mental representations have in how we process information about people or social events. It is relevant to the study of cross-cultural interactions when these mental representations are about members of a cultural group and how these representations affect the processing of information about members of that group.

Individuals have a wide array of mental representations on which to draw. Stored in these mental representations are the specific features that define an object, event, or situation and the rules defining their interrelationships (Markus & Zajonc, 1985). These structures are called "schemas" when they define a category, or "scripts" when they contain a behavioral sequence. For example, the term *fish* defines a category that contains the features "scales," "gills," and "swims." These cognitive structures are derived from our past experiences and are simple representations of the complex concepts that they represent. They help us reduce the complexity of our environment to a manageable number of categories. For example, "fish" defines the category that contains "salmon" but it is does not perfectly describe a salmon. Once formed, these categories are used in future information processing. That is, we "chunk" information in order to facilitate later recall (Miller, 1956). For example, our knowledge of the features of the category *fish* can be used to infer information about all kinds of fish.

In international management, we are most concerned with the effect of the categorization of persons, particularly regarding their culture. The categorization of persons operates in the same way as the categorization of other aspects of the environment and occurs because of our inability to process all the complexity presented by our surroundings (Wilder, 1978). Box 4.1 provides an example of the basic categorization process.

BOX 4.1

Basis Categorization Process

People develop cognitive structures that help them organize and process information efficiently. These structures consist of categories (referred to as schemas) that develop slowly over time through repeated experiences with objects, persons, situations, or all. Schemas are like pigeonholes into which mail is sorted in a nonautomated post office. Each hole might be labeled with the last three digits of a postal code. As letters are sorted, the post office worker does not have to read the name or street address on the letter, or even look at the city of the address. The sorter need only glance at the last three digits of the code and the letter can be sorted into an appropriate pigeonhole. The information processing demands on the sorters are greatly reduced and letters can be sorted more quickly. Letters that do not have postal codes or whose last three digits don't match any of the pigeonhole labels are likely to be thrown into the "dead letter" bin or placed into a special location where they are dealt with later.

SOURCE: Adapted from Shaw, 1990.

Like the post office example, we often sort others into groups, which separate them from nonmembers. Likewise, we categorize ourselves according to our membership within or outside of the social groups in our environment (Turner, 1987). This categorization includes information about the relevant attitudes and behaviors associated with these groups. The total of these social identifications used by people to describe themselves is their social identity. People differ in the relative importance of the different components involved in their social identity. As noted in Chapter 3, individualists and collectivists can differ in the way in which they designate who is a member of their group. However, for all of us, one of the groups that forms part of our social identity is our cultural group.

We also categorize others in terms of the characteristics that they share, such as physical appearance, religion, political views, lifestyle, and country of origin. Through the assignment of a set of characteristics to a particular national culture label, we create a schema for that nationality. To the extent that culture is consistent with these more directly observable characteristics, we are also categorizing them according to their cultural group. The systematic description of national cultures described in Chapter 3 is one such form of categorization. However, the most important aspect of categorizing others can be whether they belong to our own cultural group.

This categorization of others and ourselves results in a sense of who we are and how we should act toward others (Tajfel, 1981). It is this categorization of our social environment into "them and us" that underlies much of the discussion in this chapter.

Cultural Norms and Scripts

One result of identifying with a particular cultural group is the adoption of its norms. Cultural norms, like other norms, are acceptable standards of behavior that are shared by members of our cultural group. They tell us what is expected of us in certain situations. Although individuals can vary in the extent to which they adopt them, the norms of groups with which we identify are a powerful influence on our behavior (Asch, 1951). In fact, continued acceptance as a member in our cultural group often requires that we exhibit certain behavior. For example, the somewhat derogatory terms *oreo* or *banana* are sometimes used by blacks or Asians to describe a person as black or yellow on the outside but white on the inside. This reflects a belief that these people hold attitudes or exhibit behavior inconsistent with the norms of their ethnic group and therefore do not really belong.

As discussed in Chapter 3, cultures vary along identifiable dimensions that reflect the value orientations of society. Likewise, the norms for behavior in a society differ systematically. Recognizing these differences is a first step in understanding the influence of culture. However, just understanding the norms of a society is insufficient to explain and predict cross-cultural interactions. Not all societal norms are enforced in all situations. Social groups only enforce norms if they perform one of the following functions:

(a) *facilitate the group's survival,* for example, by protecting them from other groups;

(b) *increase the predictability of group member's behavior;*

(c) *reduce embarrassment for group members;* or

(d) *express the central values of the group, that is, clarify the group's identity* (Goodman, Ravlin, & Schminke, 1987).

Therefore, an individual's behavior is influenced by the cultural norms of society, but only to the extent that a norm exists for a particular situation and for which societal sanctions for noncompliance exist. It is important to consider that societal norms derived from different sources can be applied in different situations. For example, the very high level of charitable giving characteristic of people in the United States seems inconsistent with their norm for self-reliance. Although self-reliance might be a central value, the cultural history of the United States as a pioneer society also suggests a norm for helping others in community projects and emergencies (see Osland & Bird, 2000). In addition, as discussed later in more detail, norms can be more important predictors of behavior in collectivist than in individualist cultures.

Related to normative behavior are culturally based *scripts*. Scripts are mental representations that we have about ourselves in a given situation (Abelson, 1981; Gioa & Poole, 1984). They differ from schemas in that they are concerned with actions and a sequence of events (Markus & Zajonc, 1985). These scripts, once developed, are used in interaction situations based on situational cues. Scripts exist, for example, for how people interact with other members of their organization under certain conditions. They consist of a particular action plan or behavioral sequence indicated for familiar situations. When individuals find themselves in these familiar situations, they do not actively think about how they should behave in detail. They react more or less automatically. People rely on scripts to guide behavior when cues about a situation match a particular script. For example, people in the U.S. culture might have a script for attending a business meeting that includes arriving on time (or a little early), engaging in brief pleasantries with others before rapidly getting down to business, pressing one's point of view during the meeting, and arriving at a decision. Attending a business meeting invokes this behavioral sequence without much active thought.

We should expect cultural differences in the content of behavioral scripts for a particular situation because they can be guided by cultural norms (Miller, 1994). Because scripts are learned, members of one's cultural group can pass them on and reinforce them. An example of a culturally based normative script is that most Chinese are strongly influenced to be respectful and obedient to superiors if they are present or even indirectly involved in a work situation (Liu, 1986). That is, the situational cue of the involvement of superiors automatically invokes respectful and obedient behavior. As this example suggests, scripts not only aid in interpreting behavior, they guide the planning and execution of activities (Lord & Kernan, 1987). Evidence of the existence of culturally based scripts has been found in work-group interactions (Thomas, Ravlin, & Wallace, 1996) and negotiator behavior (Brett & Okumura, 1998). In addition, managers are likely to have scripts for a range of familiar interactions in business settings such as meetings, sales presentations, and employee interviews. Therefore, much of our behavior and the behavior that we observe in others is a semireflexive response to the situation influenced by cultural norms. How we respond to this behavior depends, in part, on our ability to perceive it.

Selective Perception

Perception is the process by which individuals interpret the messages received from their senses and thereby give meaning to their environment. As suggested previously, at any one time, the environment presents us with more information than we can effectively deal with. Therefore, we screen out much of what is presented to us by our senses. Differences in perceptions are influenced by the characteristics of the perceiver, the person (or object) being perceived, and the situation. Research on perception has consistently found that different people can be presented with the same stimulus and perceive it differently (e.g., Dearborn & Simon, 1958).

Of particular importance to international management are differences in the way people from different cultures perceive events and each other. That is, does culture influence which stimulus receives attention and which does not? Different priorities for what stimuli we should attend to are formed by the gradual internalization of prevailing cultural patterns (Markus & Kitayama, 1991; Miller, Bersoff, & Harwood, 1990). That is, as we are socialized into a particular cultural group, we learn how to perceive. We share certain expectations and understandings of situations. For example, Mexican and U.S. children, when presented simultaneously (using a tachioscope) with pictures of a bullfight and a baseball game, perceived the event differently. The Mexican children recalled only the bullfight, whereas the U.S. children recalled only the baseball game (Bagby, 1957). That is, these two cultural groups had "learned" to attend to particular stimuli. Anyone observing a nonfamiliar sporting event for the first time can attest to selective perception. Unless you are Australian, Aussie Rules football is probably a mystery to you, and people from other than the United States have more difficulty picking out the many subtleties of a baseball game.

When we perceive people as opposed to objects or events, a key element of our perception is whether a person is categorized as a member of our in-group or an out-group member. A number of factors seem to influence the extent to which we categorize others as a member of our group or not (Smith & Bond, 1999).

- First, certain category indicators, such as race and gender, may be universal indicators of group membership.

- Second, the distinctiveness of the category indicator against the social field may be a primary categorization factor if, for example, the number of distinctively different others is small. For example, Anglo-Europeans are obvious in rural Japan.

- Third, the extent to which a person is prototypical of a particular group influences categorization into that group. Atypical persons are harder to categorize.

- Fourth, deviations from normal speech in terms of accent, syntax, or grammar are particularly salient cues for group membership. The most dramatic speech difference is, of course, the use of a foreign language.

- Finally, a history of interactions with another group will enhance the ability to categorize them. For example, our attention is heightened with groups with whom we have had a history of conflict.

An important effect of categorization of others as out-group members is that once categorized they are subsequently perceived as being more similar to each other than in-group members (Linville, Fischer, & Salovey, 1989). That is, we see the individual variation that occurs in our own cultural group but perceive other cultures as homogeneous. For example, to non-Japanese, all Japanese people might seem very similar in appearance and behavior.

Selective perception also depends on the characteristics of what is being perceived. We tend to pay more attention to information that is distinctive (Rubin, 1915), or somehow inconsistent with our expectations (McGuire & Padawer-Singer, 1976). That is, behavior somehow "out of place" or uncharacteristic of the other culture will be recalled more accurately. Still another way in which information presented by our environment is filtered is through *selective avoidance.* When confronted with information contrary to our existing views, we "tune it out" by diverting our attention elsewhere (Kavanaugh, 1991).

Therefore, as discussed earlier, cultural differences can influence perception in several ways. First, we are socialized by our culture to perceive things in a particular way. Second, we tend to have better recall of information inconsistent with our culturally based expectations but also tend to filter out this information if it is incompatible with our views. Finally, we perceive members of other cultures to be more similar to each other than members of our own cultural group.

Perceived Similarity and Attraction

The perceptual bias about our own versus other cultural groups, noted previously, has an additional implication for cross-cultural interactions. This is, perceptions of similarity lead to interpersonal attraction (Byrne, 1971). Essentially, we are attracted to people whom we perceive to be similar to us, because this similarity validates our view of the world and the way it should be. That is, we look to others to obtain what is called consensual validation (Festinger, 1957). When someone agrees with us, this agreement validates our view and provides "evidence" that we are correct. Disagreement has just the opposite effect. Several decades of research supports the idea that similarity, particularly attitude and status similarity, leads to interpersonal attraction.

Other aspects of similarity, such as religion and race (Kandel, 1978), national culture (Thomas & Ravlin, 1995), age (Ellis, Rogoff, & Cramer, 1981), and even the preference for particular activities (Lydon, Jamieson, & Zanna, 1988), can also predict interpersonal attraction. In fact, we might be biologically programmed to respond positively to similarity of all kinds (Rushton, 1989).

Similarity can also influence other aspects of interpersonal interaction. For example, demographic similarity is related to increased frequency of communication and friendship ties (Lincoln & Miller, 1979) and frequency of technical communication (Zenger & Lawrence, 1989). Therefore, regardless of our other perceptual biases, the extent to which other individuals are perceived as similar to us influences our attitudes and behavior toward them. Essentially, other things being equal, perceptions of similarity predict more positive interactions.

The mechanisms that lead to selectively perceiving others are based on learning to perceive in a certain way because of socialization in a culture. However, these mechanisms also rely on some expectation of how people outside our own culture will behave. As discussed in the following section, these expectations about culturally different others are often based on very limited information.

Stereotypic Expectations

Stereotypes are a categorization of the characteristics and behavior of a set of individuals (Ashmore & Del Boca, 1981). That is, stereotypic expectations of a cultural group are a result of the natural cognitive process of social categorization described earlier. These expectations are based on simplifying the plethora of information provided by our environment.

Stereotypes need not be negative or noxious, although the term *stereotype* often conjures up negative images because of its linkage to prejudice (Allport, 1954) and the fact that stereotypes invariably include feelings about the cultural group as well as expected behavior.

National Stereotypes

Early research on stereotypes indicated that people could hold intense stereotypes about other national cultures even though they had never met a person from that culture (Katz & Braly, 1933). However, these cultural stereotypes are often associated with other groups with which one's culture has had a long history (often a negative history) of association. One has only to observe the fans at a soccer match between England and Scotland or at a rugby game between New Zealand and Australia to get a sense of the intensity of feelings associated with national stereotypes. The rest of the world might see Australia and New Zealand or Scotland and England as similar to each other. However, nationals of those countries will be quick to point out significant differences.

The suggestion, made in previous chapters, that we can categorize cultures based on a limited number of dimensions is a form of national stereotyping. This presents us with a simple, some would say overly simple, representation of a cultural group. However, as noted at the conclusion of the Chapter 3, these "on average" cultural expectations can be useful if we are aware of the influence of stereotyping.

Stereotypes are based on very limited information about others. That is, we use very basic physical or social evidence (i.e., skin tone or country of birth) to categorize people and to organize information about them (Taylor, 1981). For example, if I have had little or no contact with Japanese people, my stereotype might consist almost entirely of information gained from secondary sources such as films or television. The opportunity for inaccuracy in my expectation of typical Japanese behavior is obvious.

Resistance to New Information

Once we categorize an individual as a member of a category, such as a culture, the associated information about the category is applied to them. Once formed, these stereotypic expectations of others tend to become self-perpetuating (Snyder, 1981). That is, we reconstruct information about the social category (culture) to be consistent with our stereotype and behave toward members of the culture in ways that confirm our expectations. New information about a member of the culture is often discounted as not representative, thereby maintaining the stereotype (Hamilton, 1979). For example, when confronted with a Japanese businessperson who exhibits a very Western behavior of using an informal greeting, we discount this individual as being atypical and still maintain our stereotypic expectation that Japanese businesspeople are formal.

Stereotype Complexity and Evaluation

Because stereotypes are learned, we tend to have more complex (more and better-organized information) stereotypes about social categories with which we have more familiarity (Fiske & Taylor, 1984). Therefore, we have more complex mental pictures of our own culture than we do of other cultures. This leads to the expectation of more variability in behavior in our own culture than in others, as previously noted. However, it also results in differences in our evaluation of new information about that culture. That is, new information about a social group for which we have a very simple stereotype (e.g., another culture) is evaluated more extremely (more positively if the information is positive, and more negatively if the information is negative) than for groups for which we have a more complex picture. For example, in a study of identically qualified law students of two different ethnic groups, members of the evaluator's own ethnic group were evaluated less extremely (Linville & Jones, 1980). Therefore, the more information we have about a cultural group, the more likely we are to accept (evaluate accurately) new information about them.

Social Dominance

National stereotypes might also ascribe to what is called social dominance theory (Sidanius, 1993; Smith & Bond, 1999). That is, there might be a generally accepted hierarchy of nationalities based on status. High status can be attached to a particular nation because of economic dominance or other desirable characteristics. According to the theory, the extent to which my national group is high status will influence the attitude of others toward it and my attachment to it. For example, nationals of less developed countries might hold U.S. nationals in high esteem because of the level of economic development of the United States.

As discussed earlier, the usefulness of stereotypic expectations about members of another culture is thus limited by the following:

1. the extent to which these mental pictures contain accurate information,

2. our recognition that either positive or negative feelings about the cultural group are invariably attached to the stereotype, and

3. our ability to adjust our expectations based on new information about the group.

An example of an effective use of a stereotype in international business is presented in Box 4.2.

In this example, accurate stereotypes were helpful but not sufficient to achieve an effective intercultural interaction. It was also important to understand why the cultural groups behaved as they did. That is, they needed to make a judgment as to the cause of the behavior. Social categorization of cultural groups also influences the way in which the causes of behavior are evaluated.

Differential Attributions

Attribution helps us to understand and react to our environment by linking the observation of an event to its causes. The search for and assignment of cause for behavior seems to be a mental process that operates in much the same way across cultures (Schuster, Fosterlung, & Weiner, 1989). Any number of causes might be assigned to behavior we observe. However, the central distinction is between factors that are internal to the individual (personality, culture) and factors external to the individual (Trope, 1986). Internally caused behaviors are those under the control of the individual, and externally controlled behaviors are forced on the person by the situation. In order to attribute behavior, we rely on cues from the situation that indicate the extent to which individuals are in control, such as whether or not the behavior is distinctive to a situation, consistent over time, and if the same behavior is displayed in similar situations (Kelley, 1972).

Inconclusive Information

Sometimes, however, the situational cues that we rely on to make attributions are inconclusive. That is, not all behavior is unambiguous about its cause. In cases in which our observations do not clearly indicate to us the cause of behavior, we rely on information we already have about the individual to make a judgment (Darley & Fazio, 1980). In cross-cultural interactions, we might rely on our stereotypic expectations of another culture to fill in the gaps (e.g., people from the United States will behave in their own self-interest). In other cases, we can project our

---

BOX 4.2

Use of Cultural Stereotypes

In meetings between U.S. and Mexican businessmen, each had an accurate stereotypic expectation about the other's orientation toward time. Both agreed that Mexicans were "polychronic" or had a "manãna" orientation, with a flexible perspective on time. Both also agreed that Americans were "monochronic" (take time constraints and deadlines seriously). This agreement allowed the groups to reach a compromise on how to manage time, but only after they understood why each group held the expectation that they did.

SOURCE: Y.-T. Lee & G. Duenas, Stereotype Accuracy in Multicultural Business, in *Stereotype accuracy: Toward Appreciating Group Differences.* Copyright © 1995, American Psychological Association. Reprinted with permission of the American Psychological Association.

---

own behavior on the situation (e.g., what would cause *me* to behave that way). In either case, cultural differences influence the process. In the first case, our cultural-based expectations of an out-group member influence our attribution. In the second, our own culturally based behavioral norms or scripts influence our judgment of causality. Box 4.3 provides an example of making an inappropriate attribution for the behavior of a member of another culture.

In this case, Helen has made an attribution (to his character) for Hideo's behavior based on information she held in memory because the situation did not clearly indicate to her the cause of his behavior.

Attribution Error

Attribution of the cause of behavior is also influenced by whether or not the behavior is being exhibited by a member of our own cultural group. Again, the social categorization of our environment is at work. Because we derive part of our self-identity from our association with our cultural group, we are favorably biased toward that group. Therefore, we are more likely to attribute desirable behaviors by members of our in-group to internal causes, but more likely to attribute desirable behaviors of out-group members to transient external causes (Hewstone, 1990). That is, if members of our cultural group exhibit positive behavior (perform well on a task), we are more likely to attribute that behavior to their ability or effort. In contrast, when we observe the same behavior by members of another cultural group, we are more likely to attribute it to

---

BOX 4.3

Attribution to Internal Cause

Helen Conner had been working in a Japanese company involved in marketing cameras for 2 years and was well respected by her colleagues. In fact, she was so respected that she was often asked to work with new employees of the firm as these younger employees learned the ropes. Recently, one young employee, Hideo Tanaka, was assigned to develop a marketing scheme for a new model camera. He worked quite hard on it, but the scheme was not accepted by his superiors because of industry-wide economic conditions. Helen and Hideo happened to be working at desks near each other when the company executive transmitted the news of the scheme's nonacceptance. Hideo said very little at that point. That evening, however, Helen and Hideo happened to be at the same bar. Hideo had been drinking, and he vigorously criticized his superiors at work. Helen concluded that Hideo was a very aggressive Japanese male and that she would have difficulty working with him again in the future.

SOURCE: Cushner & Brislin, 1996. Reprinted with permission of Sage Publications, Inc.

---

luck or other favorable circumstances. Research with several different cultural groups has supported this group-serving bias in attributions (e.g., Al-Zahrani & Kaplowitz, 1993; Taylor & Jaggi, 1974), which is called "the ultimate attribution error" (Pettigrew, 1979). Biased belief systems about members of one's own national culture are pervasive and extend, for example, to favoritism for products coming from one's own country, the so-called country-of-origin effect (Peterson & Jolibert, 1995) mentioned in Chapter 2.

Cultural Differences in Attribution Bias

Despite the strong evidence in support of a universal in-group bias effect, some variation across cultures may exist. For example, it is possible that in some cases, it might not be possible for a group to find a positive basis on which to compare itself with others (Tajfel, 1981). Also, in cultures characterized by vertical collectivism, disadvantaged groups might accept as legitimate the higher status of other groups (Smith & Bond, 1999). In addition, individualists and collectivists may not engage in intergroup comparisons to the same degree (Hinkle & Brown, 1990). Collectivists might not be as interested in comparing themselves with out-groups and instead focus on their in-group (Triandis, 1994). Individualists, by contrast, might make more comparisons but also make a distinction between groups with which they do and do not compare themselves (Smith & Bond, 1999).

As outlined previously, our interactions with culturally different others depend, in part, on how we attribute the cause of their behavior. Cultural differences influence this attribution through the meaning that we give to the situational cues presented and the expectations that we have for behavior in the other culture. In most cases, we can expect bias in the attributions for the behavior of members of our own culture versus members of other cultures.

Cross-Cultural Interaction Model

In the preceding section, several mechanisms were identified through which culture can be seen to influence behavior. To suggest more specifically how this influence occurs, it is helpful to examine the actions and reactions that comprise a cross-cultural encounter. The following interaction sequence is typical of those that occur regularly in international management contexts. It highlights the effect of cultural differences on an interpersonal interaction. Inferences about the processes through which culture influences behavior can be made at each step of the interaction sequence.

The interaction presented in Figure 4.1 assumes as a starting point some behavior of a person from another culture. The person might behave according to some culturally based script for the situation or, because of some expectation about how this person's behavior will be perceived, adjusts the behavior. There are an almost infinite number of situations in which a cross-cultural interaction might take place. However, many situations in business settings will be familiar. Situational cues determine the extent to which the situation evokes a preexisting behavioral sequence, a script. If a script does not exist for the situation, the individual will give more thought as to how to behave and how such behavior might be perceived.

Next, the person perceiving the behavior interprets the meaning of these actions. This interpretation consists of two stages. The first is the identification of the behavior. This identification can, as discussed in this chapter, be influenced by culturally biased selective perception. An important part of the identification is categorizing the other person as a member of another culture (out-group). This categorization is influenced by the extent to which the behavior being exhibited matches a preexisting expectation. Behavior consistent with expectations will result in an

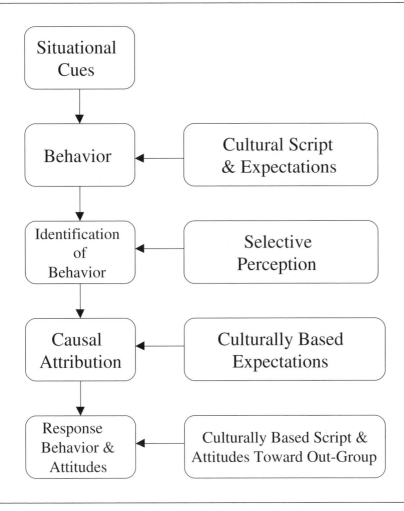

Figure 4.1. Cross-Cultural Interaction
SOURCE: Based on Shaw, 1990, & Thomas, 1992.

automatic categorization, whereas inconsistent information must be processed more thoroughly.

The second part of the function is attributing the behavior to a cause. This attribution is influenced by the culturally based expectations that the perceiver has for members of the other culture. The extent to which situational cues about the cause of the behavior exist and the relative development of the perceiver's mental representation of the other culture both influence the accuracy of the attribution. Individuals with very well-developed prior conceptions of another culture are likely to be less extreme and more accurate in their evaluation of behavior. In situations where the cues are ambiguous or provide little information, individuals will rely more heavily on information they already have to make a judgment. That is, they must rely on stereotypic expectations of the other culture.

Finally, the perceiver's attitudes and behavioral response depend on how the behavior is attributed. To the extent that the attributions made are attributed to a familiar cause, the response behavior itself can be scripted. If, however, the behavior does not fit an existing category, the person might be unable to use an existing script to guide behavior and invent a new one. The reactive behavior starts another interaction sequence. The ability of people to adjust old scripts or create new ones is a significant part of having a successful cross-cultural encounter (Shaw, 1990).

This behavioral sequence plays itself out day after day in international organizations between coworkers, between managers and subordinates, between negotiators, and among work-group members. The situational context and the status of the participants vary, but the fundamentals of the interaction remain the same. Box 4.4 provides an example of how such a cross-cultural interaction sequence might proceed in an encounter between a manager and subordinate.

The interaction in Box 4.4 is an example of misattributions by both parties and a subsequent escalation of the problem as one behavior sequence builds on the previous one. Todd's first mistake was in relying on a U.S.-based behavioral script for dealing with a Korean employee. Chungmin considered being reprimanded in public very rude and attributed this behavior to Todd's thoughtlessness. She responds by relying on a Korean script for expressing her displeasure through subtle cues. Todd fails to perceive these cues accurately (because he lacks a well-developed schema for Korean culture) and has difficulty making an attribution for Chungmin's behavior. He tries to solve the problem by having an open and frank discussion with Chungmin, another Western script that is not well-received. Chungmin responds with more subtle cues.

The model presented in Figure 4.1 is, of course, a simplification that does not take into account important aspects of an interpersonal interaction, such as the motives of the participants involved and other information-processing demands of the situation. This simplification allows the effect of culture through social cognition to be demonstrated.

Box 4.4

Cross-Cultural Interaction Sequence

Todd works for an American company in Korea. Sometimes he wonders why he ever accepted a position overseas—there seems to be so much that he just doesn't understand. One incident in particular occurred the previous Friday when his secretary, Chugmin, made a mistake and forgot to type a letter. Todd considered this a small error, but made sure to mention it when he saw her during lunch in the company cafeteria. Ever since then, Chugmin has been acting a bit strange and distant. When she walks out of his office, she closes the door more loudly than usual. She will not even look him in the eye, and she has been acting very moody. She even took a few days of sick leave, which she has not done in many years. Todd has no idea how to understand her behavior. Perhaps she really is ill or feels a bit overworked.

When Chungmin returns to work the following Wednesday, Todd calls her into his office. "Is there a problem?" he asks. "Because if there is, we need to talk about it. It's affecting your performance. Is something wrong? Why don't you tell me, it's okay."

At this, Chungmin looks quite distressed. She admits the problem has something to do with her mistake the previous Friday, and Todd explains that it was no big deal. "Forget it," he says, feeling satisfied with himself for working this out. "In the future, just make sure to tell me if something is wrong." But over the next few weeks, Chungmin takes 6 more sick days and does not speak to Todd once.

SOURCE: Cushner & Brislin, 1996. Reprinted with permission of Sage Publications, Inc.

Motivation Across Cultures

Motivation involves the reasons that people take or persist in a particular action. Western explanations of motivation (e.g., equity theory, Adams, 1965; expectancy theory, Vroom, 1964) depend on the assumption that people will act in their own self-interest. However, culture guides choices by giving meaning and ascribing value to motivational variables. That is, cultural values reflect individuals' needs but also prescribe the behavior required to satisfy those needs (Erez & Earley, 1993). Therefore, we should expect that members of different cultures would respond to different motivating factors in their intercultural interactions. For example, for people from the United States, differentiation and individual rewards might be central motivating factors, whereas these would have a negative effect in a culture that values equality and cooperation. Central to understanding the nature of motivation in different cultures is the way in which people define themselves, their self-concept.

Cultural Variation in Self-Concept

People in all cultures develop an understanding of themselves as physically distinct and separate from others (Hallowell, 1955). However, beyond the physical self, individuals have an inner or private self that consists of thoughts and feelings that cannot be directly known by others (Markus & Kitayama, 1991). Some aspects of the inner self are probably universal (e.g., I am hungry), but others can be specific to different cultures (e.g., my soul will be reincarnated) because of a shared understanding of what it means to be human (Triandis, 1989). A key cultural distinction in the definition of the inner self is the extent to which people regard themselves as *separate* from others or as *connected* with others (Markus & Kitayama, 1991).

An independent self-concept is characteristic of Western cultures in which the self is an autonomous individual with unique attributes whose behavior is organized and made meaningful by reference to one's own internal thoughts and feelings. As noted in Chapter 3, this concept of self is a key characteristic of the cultural dimension of individualism (Triandis, 1995). In contrast, in the interdependent self, the individual is less differentiated and more connected to others. In this conceptualization, behavior is determined, contingent on, and, to a large extent, organized by a perception of the thoughts, feelings, and actions of others in the larger social unit (Markus & Kitayama, 1991). An interdependent self-concept is characteristic of collectivist cultures. For example, the word for self in Japanese, *jibun,* refers to one's share of the life space (Hamaguchi, 1985). Although a number of culturally specific conceptions of self can exist, as with definitions of cultural-value orientations, it is a convenient simplification to think in terms of two types of self-concept: independent and interdependent.

Motivational Implications of Differing Self-Concepts

There are several motivational implications of these two types of self-concept. First, those with independent self-concepts will be motivated to express internal needs, rights, and the capacity to withstand undue social pressure (Janis & Mann, 1977). In contrast, those with interdependent self-concepts will be motivated to be receptive to others, to adjust to their needs, and to restrain their inner needs or desires (Markus & Kitayama, 1991). Moreover, people with interdependent self-concepts report that they are more influenced in their behavior by contextual factors including norms (Singelis & Brown, 1995; Trafimow & Finlay, 1996). Consistent with this finding, social norms are found to be a more important determinant of behavior for collectivists than for individualists (Triandis, 1995).

One study of the motives of Chinese people (collectivists) found high levels for the need to comply, socially oriented achievement, change, endurance, nurturance, and order; moderate levels for autonomy, deference, and dominance; and low levels of individually oriented achievement, aggression, exhibition, and power (Bond & Hwang, 1986). That is, the interdependent self-concepts of the Chinese were reflected in the needs that were expressed.

It can also be argued that differences in the self-concept lead to differences in the extent to which the reduction of cognitive conflict or dissonance is a motivator. Dissonance occurs when one says or acts one way in public but feels quite differently in private (Festinger, 1957). If, as is the case for people with an interdependent self, one's internal attitudes and opinions are not a significant defining aspect of the self, there is little need to make these internal attitudes consistent with external behavior. Furthermore, as noted above, these internal feelings should be regulated as required by the situation.

Finally, motives linked to the self, such as self-enhancement or self-verification, can assume a different form depending on the concept of self being enhanced or verified (Markus & Kitayama, 1991). The motive to maintain a positive self-image is probably universal. However, what constitutes a positive view of self depends on how the self is construed. For those with independent selves, feeling good about oneself means being unique and expressing one's inner attributes. For those with an interdependent self, a positive self-image is derived from belonging, fitting in, occupying one's proper place, engaging in appropriate action, and maintaining harmony.

In summary, cultural differences might be expected in motivation based on an individual's internal representation of self. Although all people might be motivated by self-interest, a fundamental difference is the role that others play in how people define themselves. That is, individuals are differentially motivated depending on whether they view themselves as independent of or interdependent with others. In intercultural interactions, this motivational difference influences behavior throughout the interaction sequence just described.

Summary

This chapter presented a more sophisticated approach to specifying the effects of culture on behavior. The basics of social cognition were applied to the context of cross-cultural interactions that are fundamental to management across cultures. By doing this, it is possible to identify a number of mechanisms or conduits through which culture manifests its influence. In addition to the effect that variations in national culture have on the normative behavior of individuals in that culture, several other influence mechanisms exist. These include the development of normative scripts for particular situations, culturally based selective perception of the behavior of others, and differential attributions for behavior founded in culturally based expectations. These mechanisms can be seen to operate in a basic interaction sequence that underlies the interpersonal interaction between culturally different individuals in a variety of organizational settings. This sequence of behavior-perception-attribution-reaction is central to our understanding of intercultural interactions. However, it is important to recognize that motivational differences based on differing conceptualizations of the self can influence behavior throughout the interaction sequence. In recognizing the possible influence of culture through the types of mechanisms suggested in this chapter, it is possible to develop an understanding of the effect of culture that extends beyond the simple projection of cultural stereotypes.

Section II
Roles of the International Manager

Five

The Manager as Decision Maker:

Cross-Cultural Dimensions of Decision Making

The organizational and social environment in which the decision maker finds himself determines what consequences he will anticipate, what ones he will not; what alternatives he will consider, what ones he will ignore.
March & Simon, 1958: 139

International managers are faced with a variety of decisions every day. Resources must be allocated, employees selected, and the attractiveness of joint venture partners evaluated; all must be done in a highly complex international environment. All decisions involve choices among alternatives. However, many of these choices are made almost automatically because of culturally based scripts that individual managers have for the situation. In addition, when confronted with a new or very important decision, managers can invoke a more thorough consideration of differently weighted alternatives.

This chapter reviews the process of individual decision making and explores the opportunity for cultural variation in the ways that managers simplify this complex decision-making process. In addition, this chapter discusses the ethical dilemmas presented by decision making in an international context.

Rational Decision Making

The study of managerial decision making is typically divided into *prescriptive* approaches, what managers should do, and *descriptive* approaches, what managers actually do. On the prescriptive side, the rational model of decision making is based on a set of assumptions that indicates how a decision should be made. The goal of the *rational* decision maker is to make an *optimal* choice among specific and clearly defined alternatives (Simon, 1955). In order to optimize a particular outcome, individuals must progress either implicitly or explicitly through six steps in the decision-making process. These steps are described in Box 5.1.

As shown in Box 5.1, the rational decision maker has a clear goal, a comprehensive set of alternatives from which to choose, which are themselves weighted according to known criteria and preferences, and can choose the alternative that has the highest score.

Cultural Differences in the Optimization Model

The rational or optimizing model is best thought of as a prescriptive or normative approach that demonstrates how managerial decisions should be made. While recognizing that decisions are actually made within limitations that put boundaries on rationality (discussed in this section), it is useful to consider the opportunity for cultural variation in this normative framework.

Based on the descriptions of cultural variation (Chapter 3) that indicate preferences for certain modes of behavior, it is possible to suggest cultural differences in the rational model, and therefore in the related decision structures within organizations. For example, at the problem-

BOX 5.1

Steps in the Rational Decision Process

1. *Problem definition.* First, managers must recognize that a decision is required and identify the problem to be solved. A problem is typically a difference between the actual situation and what is desired. However, managers often act without understanding the problem to be solved and define the problem in terms of a proposed solution, or in terms of its symptoms (Bazerman, 1998). For example, in response to employee complaints about salaries being too low (a symptom), managers might define the problem as a comparison of salaries to industry averages. However, the true problem could be that the total compensation package, including benefits, does not suit the demographic characteristics of the firm's employees.

2. *Identify decision criteria.* Decisions often require the consideration of more than one objective. For example, in selecting a manager for an overseas operation, you may want to maximize that manager's ability to adapt to the new culture, maximize the level of technical skill brought to the situation, and also minimize the cost of the assignment. To be rational, a decision maker must identify all of the criteria that should be considered in the decision-making process.

3. *Weigh the criteria.* The criteria identified in the previous step may not be of equal importance to the decision maker. In order to prioritize their importance to the decision, they must be assigned weights. A rational decision maker will know individual preference for certain criteria and assign relative weights accordingly (e.g., cost of the assignment versus technical skills in the previous example).

4. *Generate the alternatives.* This step requires the rational decision maker to identify all possible alternatives that will satisfy the decision criteria. No attempt is made at this step to evaluate the alternatives.

5. *Evaluate the alternatives.* Each alternative must now be evaluated against the weighted criteria. This is often the most difficult part of the decision-making process because it requires the decision maker to predict the future outcomes of each choice. However, the rational decision maker is able to assess the consequences of each alternative.

6. *Select the optimal solution.* The optimal solution is computed by simply multiplying the expected effectiveness of each alternative on each criterion times the weighting of each criterion for each solution. The sum of these scores is an evaluation of each alternative against the weighted decision criteria. The optimal alternative should then be selected.

definition step, the activity orientation of the culture can influence when a situation is defined as a problem. Managers from cultures with a "doing" or problem-solving orientation like the United States might identify a situation as a problem to be solved well before managers from "being" or situation-accepting cultures such as Indonesia or Malaysia (Kluckhohn & Strodtbeck, 1961). Likewise, the identification and weighting of criteria can be affected by the culturally different value orientations. For example, when asked to identify and rank criteria regarding a desirable acquisition target, U.S. and Korean managers had different opinions as shown in Box 5.2.

An examination of Box 5.2 reveals the cultural variation in decision criteria consistent with what we might expect, based on the cultural orientations of the two sets of managers. That is, with the exception of the fourth item in the U.S. list, all of the criteria relate to short-term financial measures consistent with U.S. short-term orientation (Doktor, 1983). In contrast, with the exception of the second item in the Korean managers' list, all of the criteria relate to long-term growth-oriented measures.

Cultural variation might also be anticipated in the generation and evaluation of alternatives. Cultures with a strong past orientation tend to place more value on alternative solutions that have been used successfully in the past. Whereas, present- or future-oriented cultures are more likely to favor unique and creative solutions to problems. In addition, the motivational differences mentioned in Chapter 4 can influence the weighting of alternatives, for example, in favor of those alternatives that have the most highly valued outcomes for individuals or for a collective.

Finally, who makes the choice and how long the decision process takes can be culture bound. Vertical individualist cultures, like the United States and France, are likely to have decision-making authority vested in only a few high-ranking individuals (Heller & Wilpert, 1981). In contrast, horizontal collectivist cultures (e.g., Israeli kibbutz) are likely to push decision making well down in the organizational structure and involve large numbers of people. In addition, a culture's orientation toward time might influence the pace of decision making. For example, the longer time orientation of Arab cultures is reflected in a more deliberate pace of decision making than is found in North America, where being decisive means making choices quickly (Morrison, Conaway, & Borden, 1994).

Research on the decision-making structures of organizations in different countries tends to support the kind of cultural variation in normative decision-making processes proposed earlier. For example, in a very comprehensive study of this type (IDE Research Group, 1993), the level at which major decisions were taken and the degree of employee involvement in decision making varied significantly across the 10 European

---

BOX 5.2

Desirable Characteristics of an Acquisition Target

United States Managers	*Korean Managers*
1. Demand for target's products	1. Attractiveness of industry
2. Discounted cash flow	2. Sales revenue
3. Return on investment	3. Market structure
4. Attractiveness of industry	4. Manufacturing capabilities
5. Management talent	5. Research and development capabilities

SOURCE: Chung & Lee, 1989.

---

countries surveyed. The decision structures in organizations are likely to reflect a culturally based view of a rational decision process. For example, the *ringi-sei* decision-making process characteristic of Japanese organizations (Misumi, 1984) is consistent with cultural orientations of both collectivism and high power distance (verticality). In this system, decisions are made using a participative procedure in which a subordinate submits a tentative solution that often reflects guidance from a superior (Nakane, 1970). The idea is then cleared through successive levels of the organization, where it is altered and approved by the people who must implement it. The final decision is the result of a managed form of participation that maintains the existing status hierarchy (Earley, 1999).

Limits to Rationality

Regardless of the type of normative cultural variation previously suggested, the optimization model assumes that decision makers can

1. accurately define the problem,
2. identify all decision criteria,
3. accurately weigh the criteria according to known preferences,

4. be aware of all available alternatives, and

5. accurately assess each alternative.

However, although decision makers might attempt to follow a rational model consistent with their cultural norms, they are limited in their ability to do so. That is, individual judgment is restricted or "bounded" in its ability to be rational (Simon, 1955). These boundaries exist because decision makers must often deal with incomplete information about the problem, the decision criteria, and even their own preferences. The cognitive limitations mentioned in Chapter 4 apply. That is, decision makers can only handle a small portion of the information available to them, and their perceptions are not always accurate.

An alternative to the rational model of decision making that recognizes these limitations is the "satisficing" model (March & Simon, 1958; Simon, 1955). Essentially, it suggests that decision makers forego optimal solutions for ones that are acceptable. That is, they do not evaluate all possible alternatives but search for a solution that meets a minimally satisfactory set of criteria. If a particular alternative meets these criteria, the search ends. If, however, it does not, they continue to the next alternative, and the next until a satisfactory solution is found. That is, because of limits to rationality, in reality, decision makers most often satisfice as opposed to optimize.

Cultural Constraints on Rationality

In addition to the cognitive limits to rationality, the concept of rationality itself may be culture bound. Rationality, or being motivated by self-interest, as discussed in Chapter 4, might be defined differently depending on how individuals from different cultures define themselves. Moreover, even though a manager makes a decision in a less than rational way, it could be more important to appear rational in some cultures than in others. For example, conflict models of decision making (e.g., Janis & Mann, 1977) suggest that decision makers use one of four decision styles to cope with the psychological stress of making a decision. According to the model, the optimal decision style is *vigilance*, which is a pattern consisting of a careful collection of facts and consideration of alternatives. In contrast are three alternative or maladaptive styles. *Complacency* involves either ignoring the decision completely or simply taking the first available course of action. *Defensive avoidance* is passing the decision off to someone else, putting off the decision, or devaluing the importance of making a decision. Finally, *hypervigilance* is making a hasty, ill-conceived decision, also called panicking. Research using this model with Japanese and other non-Western samples has found significantly greater use of the alternatives to vigilance as compared to Western (Australia, New Zealand, and United States) samples (Radford, Mann, Ohta, & Nakane, 1989). This is not to imply that Japanese are less efficient decision makers. On the contrary, what might be presented as less efficient decision processes in the West could be the dominant patterns in other (predominantly collectivist) cultures. Other research in the Japanese culture suggests that they are less likely than are Western cultures to report that they employ systematic rational processes in favor of more intuitive decision making (Torrence, 1980). That is, as opposed to focusing on collecting facts, defining the problem, and considering all alternatives, their primary considerations are the impressions of others, feelings and emotions, and intuition (Radford, Mann, Ohta, & Nakane, 1991).

International management decisions are complex and are required frequently. Bounded rationality and satisficing concepts indicate that these managerial decisions will typically not conform to a rational model. In fact, an observation of what managers do indicates that they might actually avoid analytical processes (Mintzberg, 1973). To determine more specifically in what way international managers' decisions might deviate from rationality, we must consider the ways in which they simplify the complex environment surrounding their decisions (Bazerman, 1998). The next section discusses simplifying strategies called heuristics (Tversky & Kahneman, 1974) that apply to decision making in general. In addition, because managers from different cultures simplify complex realities in different ways, the opportunity for culturally based differences in the application of these heuristics is discussed.

Heuristics

Heuristics are rules of thumb (cognitive tools) that individuals use to simplify decision making (Bazerman, 1998). Heuristics can result in biases in the decision, but often the increased speed of decision making outweighs the loss in decision quality. However, managers do not consciously make this trade-off between decision quality and speed because they are typically unaware that they are employing a heuristic. By becoming aware of the impact of heuristics, they might learn to use them to advantage. The three general heuristics that are employed to simplify decision making are availability, representativeness, and anchoring and adjustment.

Availability

Availability is the extent to which instances or occurrences of an event are readily available in memory. It influences managers' judgments of the frequency, probability, or likely causes of that event (Tversky & Kahneman, 1973). An event easily imagined or that evokes emotions will be more easily recalled than vague or bland events. For example, in a U.S. experiment (Russo & Shoemaker, 1989), participants said that motor vehicle accidents caused more deaths each year than stomach cancer. In fact, stomach cancer causes twice as many deaths. However, vivid and numerous media accounts of motor vehicle deaths had created a bias in the perception of the frequency of the two events.

Because the availability heuristic is based on life experiences, cultural differences in judgments that result from availability are easily suggested. For example, Thai people are likely to have much higher estimates of the worldwide death rate from being trampled by a water buffalo than are people living in the United States. That is, culturally different individuals might differ systematically in the way they apply their available recollections to larger situations outside their experience.

Representativeness

Managers' assessment of the likelihood that an event will occur is influenced by how similar the occurrence is to their mental representation (stereotype) of similar experiences. For example, people do not enter prenuptial agreements because they do not believe that the high base rate for divorce applies to them, and they do not consider that when "four out of five dentists recommend" that the five dentists might not be representative of the total population of dentists.

Another example of the representativeness heuristic in action involves misconceptions of chance. People often inappropriately expect that random and nonrandom events will even out. That is, after a run of bad outcomes, they believe they are "due" for a positive result. For example, a belief that after hiring five poor performers, the chances that the next hire will also perform poorly is lower. In reality, of course, the outcome of a random event is independent of the outcomes of previous events, and the next person hired is just as likely to perform poorly as the previous five.

An extension of this idea, that has cross-cultural implications, is reflected in the confidence that a decision maker has in the correctness of the decision. Evidence suggests that once having made a decision, collectivists display greater confidence in its correctness (Yates, Zhu, et al., 1989). This greater confidence is probably the result of the tendency of collectivists to view the world, and hence categorize decisions, in terms of perfect certainty or perfect uncertainty (Wright & Phillips, 1980). In contrast, individualists might consider more possible negative outcomes of their decision and therefore be less certain. For example, when asked to list possible reasons why their decision might be wrong, Chinese respondents produced far fewer reasons than U.S. respondents (Yates, Lee, & Shinotsuka, 1996).

Anchoring and Adjustment

A manager's judgment is often made by starting from some initial point and then adjusting to yield a final decision. The initial point, or anchor, can come from the way a problem is framed, from historical factors, or from random information. Even when an anchor is absurd, and people recognize it as such, their subsequent judgments are often very close to that starting point (Dawes, 1988). That is, regardless of the initial anchor point, subsequent adjustments tend to be insufficient (Tversky & Kahneman, 1974). There are numerous examples of bias resulting from anchoring and adjustment. For example, some school systems categorize children into certain performance categories at an early age. Although a child anchored in a low-performance group might meet expectations, another child of similar ability but anchored in a higher-performance category could be perceived as being a better performer simply because of being categorized as being a high performer. Similarly, a low starting salary could be an anchor that a high-performing employee has difficulty overcoming even with substantial annual increases in terms of a percentage of base salary. Both the source of an anchor and norms for adjustment might vary with cultural experience. For example, the willingness of new migrants from Hong Kong to Vancouver to pay far above market prices for residential property might be explained by this heuristic. The Hong Kong Chinese might have anchored their initial estimate of the cost of housing in Vancouver in their previous experience. Subsequent estimates might still have been higher than reality because of the general tendency to make an insufficient adjustment mentioned earlier plus a collectivist norm for avoiding extremes in evaluations.

These three general heuristics represent ways in which managers might simplify the decision-making process. As shown, these simplifications can result in specific types of biases. By considering cultural variation and the role it plays in social cognition, systematic differences in how these heuristics are applied and the resulting biases can be anticipated. In reality, more than one of the heuristics might be in use in any single decision. In addition, there are many other types of biases resulting from the use of these three rules of thumb. However, a complete discussion of all of the possible effects of cognitive simplification of the decision-making process is beyond the scope of this book (see Bazerman, 1998). What is important to note is that in making decisions, managers simplify reality in predictable ways. Additionally, because managers from different cultures perceive the world differently, their subjective realities differ; therefore, so will the way in which they simplify complex realities.

Motivational Biases in Decision Making

In addition to the cognitive simplification effects previously discussed, many of the decision choices that managers make can be influenced by motivational biases. Motivational biases in decision making are based on the differences in motivation described in Chapter 4. First, decision makers with interdependent self-concepts should be more highly influenced by those motives that are social or refer to others such as deference, affiliation, nurturance, avoidance of blame, and the need to comply. An example of a culturally guided motivational difference specific to decision making is provided in a study of Brazilians (interdependent self) and people from the United States (independent self). In that study, Brazilians were more likely than U. S. people to perform and enjoy performing a behavior costly to themselves, that is, forgo personal benefit to visit a sick friend (Bontempo, Lobel, & Triandis, 1990).

As suggested in Chapter 4, a culturally based motivational difference might exist about the need for consistency in internal attitudes and external behavior. For example, some authors (Doi, 1986) have argued that U.S. people are much more concerned with consistency between feelings and actions than are the Japanese. The independence of the Japanese expressions *honne* (true feelings privately held) and *tatatmae* (the truth that is presented) reflects this lower need for those people with interdependent self-concepts to reconcile the inner self with external behavior (Hall & Hall, 1987). Therefore, we might not expect decisions made by those with interdependent self-concepts to be motivated by the same sort of cognitive consistency that drives those with independent notions of self.

A common decision bias relates to an unrealistically positive self-evaluation (Taylor, 1989). For example, studies with U.S. people (independent self) indicate that they often expect that they are far more likely to graduate at the top of their class, to get a good job, to obtain a high salary, or to give birth to a gifted child than reality actually suggests.

Research suggests that this optimism bias is stronger in those people with an independent self-concept. For example, Canadians (independent self) seem to demonstrate this self-enhancing bias, whereas Japanese (interdependent self) do not (Heine & Lehman, 1995). This overoptimistic view of outcomes can be related to individual self-esteem, which is higher in those with independent self-concepts (Mann, Burnett, Radford, & Ford, 1997).

The previous section introduces several motivational biases in decision making that can vary across cultures. That is, differences in decision motives can be expected based on the decision maker's internal representation of self. Certainly, other motivational biases exist. However, what is important to recognize is that patterns of decision making that vary from a normative "rational" model can be the result of the culturally based motivation of the decision maker as well as the cognitive simplification of the process.

Selection and Reward Allocation Decisions

Two common managerial decisions that have a considerable relevance in terms of cross-cultural interactions are the selection of employees and the allocation of rewards. All organizations have the need to recruit and select new members. Based on the previous discussion, we would expect considerable variation around the world in the procedures used to conduct this important decision-making activity. The research on selection procedures in different cultures is far from complete, but it does demonstrate systematic variation in the decision process. For example, in a survey of the selection processes of 250 companies in five European nations, a significant pattern of similarities and differences in the selection procedures used was found (Shackleton & Newell, 1994). Table 5.1 reports the percentage of companies that reported they always used a particular technique.

As shown in Table 5.1, both cognitive and personality tests were popular only in Belgium, and references were more commonly used in Germany and the United Kingdom than in the other three countries. In addition, handwriting analysis was popular only in France and in French-speaking Belgium. This variation in selection techniques is consistent with the suggestion that cultural differences influence the institutionalization of the selection process. However, similarities also existed because interviews were commonly used across all of the Western European firms surveyed. In contrast, Chinese firms rarely report using interviews for selection purposes (Huo & Von Glinow, 1995) with more important selec-

TABLE 5.1   Percentage of Companies Reporting They Always Used the
Selection Technique

Country	Interviews	Application form	References	Personality tests	Cognitive tests	Handwriting analysis
Belgium (F)	91	74	15	35	30	2
Belgium (W)	100	92	12	25	32	12
France	94	89	11	17	7	17
Italy	96	45	32	8	8	0
Germany	60	83	76	2	2	0
U.K.	91	70	74	10	12	0

SOURCE: Based on Shackleton & Newell, 1994.

tion criteria being the institution from which the individual graduated or
their "home province" (Redding, Norman, & Schlander, 1994). The importance of graduating from a prestigious institution or having positive
kinship ties is characteristic of vertical collectivists and reflects their
belief that this background knowledge is more important than the small
amount of information that can be gained from a brief interview. Other
vertical collectivist countries, such as Japan, demonstrate similar reliance
on a candidate's associations in their selection procedures. For more
senior appointments in these cultures, the network of an individual's
relationships, called *guanxi* in China, can far outweigh any other factor in
being selected (Child, 1994; Wu, 1999).

    Related to the selection decision is the development of a potentially
qualified pool of applicants from which to choose. Again, cultural variation in the specifications of job requirements used in recruiting candidates
is evident. For example, in an analysis of hundreds of newspaper adver-
tisements in eight European countries, 80% of the ads in Scandinavian
countries (Sweden, Norway, and Denmark) emphasized the interpersonal
skills that would be required, whereas in Germany and the United
Kingdom, the percentage dropped to 65%, and in France, Italy, and
Spain to 50%. Ads in France, Italy, and Spain emphasized a particular age
as a requirement. In the more egalitarian Scandinavian countries, the
interpersonal skills required for collaboration were of most importance,
whereas in higher power-distance countries, age was more important.
These examples provide evidence of cultural differences, both in the

processes used in the selection decision and in the criteria that are most important in the decision.

Another key decision in the management of international organizations is the allocation of rewards. A substantial number of studies have examined reward allocation decisions, and most of these dealt with differences in perceptions of fairness by individualists and collectivists in relation to in-groups and out-groups. Although many of these studies may have ignored important contextual factors (Leung, 1997), they still provide some basis for understanding cultural variation in reward allocation.

Reward allocation criteria include equity, equality, need, and seniority. Cultural differences appear to exist regarding the fairness associated with each of these decision criteria. The emphasis on harmony in collectivist cultures suggests that fairness might be perceived to result from equality as opposed to equity in reward allocation. Also, in general, individualists do prefer reward allocations based on equity, and collectivists prefer more equal distributions (Kim, Park, & Suzuki, 1990; Leung & Bond, 1982). However, for individualists, this preference might be moderated by the expectation of future interaction among work-group members (Elliot & Meeker, 1984). In addition, the preference of collectivists for equality versus equity in reward allocation is affected by whether the reward is to be received by an in-group or out-group member. For example, when allocating rewards to in-group members, Chinese used an equality norm, whereas U.S. people used an equity norm. However, when the allocation was made to out-group members, Chinese adhered more closely to an equity norm than did U.S. people (Leung & Bond, 1984). Collectivists also show a higher propensity to allocate rewards according to need than do individualists (Berman, Murphy-Berman, & Singh, 1985). When present, need seems to override other preferences for reward distribution in all cultures; however, this effect is more pronounced for collectivists.

Cultural differences in reward allocation based on seniority also exist. Collectivist logic suggests that this group might be more prone than individualists to see reward allocation based on seniority as fair. In general, this relationship seems to be true (Chen, 1995) and is more pronounced, as would be expected, for vertical collectivists (Chen, Meindl, & Hunt, 1997). However, it is possible that gender roles specific to a given culture might influence the extent to which a seniority norm for reward allocation is invoked. For example, in one study, it was male subjects in Taiwan who were more prone to use seniority to allocate rewards, whereas in the United States, female subjects used this norm (Rusbult, Insko, & Lin, 1993).

In summary, both selection decisions and reward-allocation decisions vary across cultures in a systematic fashion. Much of what we know about this variability relies on the cultural dimensions of individualism and collectivism or power distance (verticality) for explanation. Although relying on this limited evidence is far from satisfactory, it does point out that we must be very careful in trying to apply decision models based on Western modes of thought to non-Western cultures.

Ethical Dilemmas in Decision Making

Increasingly, managers around the world are recognizing the ethical dimension involved in their decisions. Although they generally agree that sound ethics is good for business, they are very skeptical in their views on what they and their peers actually do and about the existence of unethical practices in their industry (Brenner & Molander, 1977). The decisions that international managers make cross cultural as well as geographic boundaries. In crossing these boundaries, the consensus about what is morally correct erodes in the face of differing values and norms. For example, payments that are considered bribes in the United States can be viewed as a perfectly acceptable business practice in other cultures. Discrimination in employment against women that is reprehensible in one culture is a normal expression of appropriate gender-based roles in another.

The study of ethical decision making, like decision making in general, has resulted in both normative or prescriptive models and in descriptive models. However, because managers are reluctant to have their "ethics" directly observed or measured, empirical tests are rare. This section outlines the common normative frameworks or moral philosophies for ethical decision making. Then it presents a descriptive model based on the cognitive moral development of managers that provides for the effect of culture.

Moral Philosophies

A moral philosophy is a set of principles used to decide what is right or wrong (Ferrell & Fraedrich, 1994). Managers can be guided by one of several moral philosophies when making decisions that present an ethical dilemma. The main categories of moral philosophies that are relevant to international management decisions are (a) teleology or consequential models, (b) deontology or rule-based models, and (c) cultural relativism.

Consequential Models

Consequential models focus on the outcomes or consequences of a decision to determine if the decision is ethical. A key precept of this principle as a guide for decision making is utilitarianism (Mill, 1863). Utilitarianism is the moral doctrine that we should always act to produce the greatest possible balance of good over harm for everyone affected by our decision (Shaw, 1996). Selecting a decision that considers the interests and maximizes the utility for all individuals and groups affected by a decision is, in reality, extremely difficult. It becomes even more difficult when those stakeholders affected by a decision have culturally different values and attitudes.

Some philosophers (called *rule utilitarians* in contrast to *act utilitarians* described previously in the moral doctrine) suggest general rules (religious norms, for example) that, if followed, will maximize the benefits to all and can be used as a shortcut to the complexity of evaluating the utility of each decision (Shaw, 1996). That is, they are guided by the belief that some types of behavior (e.g., refraining from excess profits) will always maximize the utility of everyone involved.

Deontological or Rule-Based Models

Deontological principles hold that human beings have certain fundamental rights and that a sense of duty to uphold these rights is the basis of ethical decision making rather than a concern for consequences (Borchert & Stewart, 1986). One of the best known of these rule-based approaches is the categorical imperative of Immanuel Kant (1724-1804). Essentially, the categorical imperative asserts that individuals have the right to be treated as an entity unto themselves and not simply as a means to an end. Unlike utilitarianism, deontology argues that some behaviors exist that are never moral even though they maximize utility. An obvious difficulty with rule-based normative approaches to decision making is achieving wide consensus on which rules (whose values) to base fundamental rights (Donaldson, 1989). Despite this difficulty, a number of transnational corporate codes have been promulgated that attempt to codify a set of universal guides for international managers. By reducing these transnational codes to their key common elements, guidelines can be suggested for ethical practice that have some degree of cross-national acceptance (Frederick, 1991). Box 5.3 presents an example of these guidelines that refer to business operations as well as to basic human rights and fundamental freedoms.

BOX 5.3

Normative Corporate Guidelines

Employment Practices and Policies

- MNCs should not contravene the manpower policies of host nations (ILO);
- MNCs should respect the right of employees to join trade unions and to bargain collectively (ILO, OECD, UDHR);
- MNCs should develop nondiscriminatory employment policies and promote equal job opportunities (ILO, OECD, UDHR);
- MNCs should provide equal pay for equal work (ILO, UDHR);
- MNCs should give advance notice of changes in operations, especially plant closings, and mitigate the adverse effects of these changes (ILO, OECD);
- MNCs should provide favorable work conditions, limited working hours, holidays with pay, and protection against unemployment (UDHR);
- MNCs should promote job stability and job security, avoiding arbitrary dismissals and providing severance pay for those unemployed (ILO, UDHR);
- MNCs should respect local host-country job standards and upgrade the local labor force through training (ILO, OECD);
- MNCs should adopt adequate health and safety standards for employees and grant them the right to know about job-related health hazards (ILO);
- MNCs should, minimally, pay basic living wages to employees (ILO, UDHR);
- MNCs' operations should benefit lower-income groups of the host nation (ILO); and
- MNCs should balance job opportunities, work conditions, job training, and living conditions among migrant workers and host-country nationals (Helsinki).

Consumer Protection

- MNCs should respect host-country laws and policies regarding the protection of consumers (OECD, TNC Code); and
- MNCs should safeguard the health and safety of consumers by various disclosures, safe packaging, proper labeling, and accurate advertising (TNC Code).

Environmental Protection

- MNCs should respect host-country laws, goals, and priorities concerning protection of the environment (OECD, TNC Code, Helsinki);
- MNCs should preserve ecological balance, protect the environment, adopt preventive measures to avoid environmental harm, and rehabilitate environments damaged by operations (OECD, TNC Code, Helsinki);
- MNCs should disclose likely environmental harms and minimize risks of accidents that could cause environmental damage (OECD, TNC Code);
- MNCs should promote the development of international environmental standards (TNC Code, Helsinki);
- MNCs should control specific operations that contribute to pollution of air, water, and soils (Helsinki); and

(continued)

(continued)

- MNCs should develop and use technology that can monitor, protect, and enhance the environment (OECD, Helsinki).

Political Payments and Involvement

- MNCs should not pay bribes nor make improper payments to public officials (OECD, TNC Code);
- MNCs should avoid improper or illegal involvement or interference in the internal politics of host countries (OECD, TNC Code); and
- MNCs should not interfere in intergovernmental relations (TNC Code).

Basic Human Rights and Fundamental Freedoms

- MNCs should respect the rights of all persons to life, liberty, security of person, and privacy (UDHR, ECHR, Helsinki, ILO, TNC Code);
- MNCs should respect the rights of all persons to equal protection of the law, work, choice of job, just and favorable work conditions, and protection against unemployment and discrimination (UDHR, Helsinki, ILO, TNC Code);
- MNCs should respect all persons' freedom of thought, conscience, religion, opinion and expression, communication, peaceful assembly and association, and movement and residence within each state (YDHR, ECHR, Helsinki, ILO, TNC Code);
- The United Nations Universal Declaration of Human Rights (UDHR) (1948);
- The European Convention on Human Rights (ECHR) (1950);
- The Helsinki Final Act (Helsinki) (1975);
- The OECD Guidelines for Multinational Enterprises (OECD) (1976);
- The International Labor Office Tripartite Declaration of Principles Concerning Multinational Enterprises and Social Policy (ILO) (1977); and
- The United Nations Code of Conduct on Transnational Corporations (TNC Code) (not yet completed nor promulgated but originating in 1972).

NOTE: MNC = multinational corporation.
SOURCE: Frederick, W. C. (1991). The Moral Authority of Transnational Corporate Codes. *Journal of Business Ethics, 10*, pp. 166-167. Reprinted with kind permission from Kluwer Academic Publishers.

It might be possible to gain universal acceptance for a set of fundamental rights if they protect something of great importance in all cultures, if they are under continuous threat, and if all cultures can absorb the cost of protecting them (Donaldson, 1989). However, some research suggests that national culture affects the preference of individuals for consequential versus nonconsequential or rule-based principles in ethical decision making. For example, a comparison of four countries found a preference for consequential principles in China but a preference for nonconsequential approaches in the United States, Mexico, and, to some extent, Korea. More important, perhaps, is that managers in different cultures can subscribe to the same moral philosophy (e.g., utilitarianism or fundamental rights) but still choose to behave in ways that are very different (Phatak & Habib, 1998). This is the problem of cultural relativism.

Cultural Relativism

In cultural relativism, moral concepts are legitimate only to the extent that they reflect the habits and attitudes of a given culture (Donaldson, 1989). That is, ethical standards are specific to a particular culture and any cross-cultural comparison is meaningless. What is considered un-ethical in one culture might be quite acceptable in another even though the same moral principle is being adhered to. An example of cultural relativism in a selection decision is demonstrated in Box 5.4.

Cultural relativism implies that one should not impose one's own ethical or moral standards on others (a practice particularly characteristic of individualists according to Triandis, 1995) and that international decisions should be evaluated in the context of differences in legal, political, and cultural systems. However, it also leaves open the opportunity to attribute a wide range of behavior to cultural norms. The use of child labor in Myanmar and China (Beaver, 1995) and discrimination against women in Japan and Saudi Arabia (Mayer & Cava, 1993) are just two examples of conduct that is attributed to cultural relativism. To adopt the concept of cultural relativism in its entirety declares the international decision arena a moral-free zone where anything goes (Donaldson, 1989). For cultural relativism to hold up as a normative model, we must declare that even the most hideous or reprehensible acts are not objectively wrong but depend on how a culture defines "wrong." However, most of us can imagine acts that we cannot defend in terms of variation in cultural practice.

These prescriptive or normative models suggest how one should behave in making an ethical decision. However, like all prescriptive models, they tell us little about how managers actually behave (Fritzsche & Becker, 1984). The development of descriptive ethical decision-making models has lagged these prescriptive models. However, one approach that shows promise because it allows for both cultural and situational influence is the idea of stages of cognitive moral development.

Cognitive Moral Development

Cognitive moral development is an approach to understanding ethical decision making that focuses on the mental determination of right and wrong based on values and social judgments (Kohlberg, 1984). It is

---

BOX 5.4

Cultural Relativism in a Selection Decision

Moral Principle: Attributes of individuals must not be used for differential treatment of the individuals unless they are clearly connected to the goals and tasks required.

Indian Manager: I must hire persons whom I know or who belong to my network of friends and relatives, because I can trust them to be dependable employees.

American Manager: I must hire the best person for the job regardless of class, race, religion, gender, or national origin.

SOURCE: Adapted from Phatak & Habib, 1998.

---

particularly appropriate in understanding managers' responses to ethical dilemmas across cultures. This model suggests that all individuals pass through stages of moral development and that ethical behavior can be understood by identifying a person's level of moral maturity. As shown in Table 5.2, the six stages of development comprise three distinctive levels.

Stages in the model relate to age-based stages in human development. That is, in general, children under the age of nine are at Level One, adolescents and most adults plateau at Level Two, and only a small percentage of people reach Level Three. Level Three is the stage at which people will only accept society's rules if they agree with the moral foundation upon which the rules are based (Kohlberg, 1984). However, level of moral development is not exclusively age based and is found to be related to intelligence, level of education, work experience (Colby, Kohlberg, Gibbs, & Lieberman, 1983), and degree of ethical training (Penn & Collier, 1985). That is, as individuals' cognitive process of moral decision making becomes more complex, they progress to higher stages of moral development. The existence of cognitive development stages was tested with participants of both sexes, from a range of social classes, and in a number of cultures. Stages One through Four were found to exist in all cultures, and evidence of the principled perspective was found in both Western and Eastern cultures (Snarey, 1985).

TABLE 5.2 Stages of Moral Development

STAGE OF MORAL DEVELOPMENT	SOCIAL PERSPECTIVE
LEVEL ONE—PRECONVENTIONAL	_INDIVIDUAL PERSPECTIVE_
Stage One—Obedience and punishment	Sticking to rules to avoid physical punishment. Obedience for its own sake.
Stage Two—Instrumental purpose and exchange	Following rules only when it is in one's immediate interest. Right is an equal exchange, a fair deal.
LEVEL TWO—CONVENTIONAL	_MEMBER OF SOCIETY PERSPECTIVE_
Stage Three—Interpersonal accord, conformity, mutual expectations	Stereotypical "good" behavior. Living up to what is expected by people close to you.
Stage Four—Social accord and system maintenance	Fulfilling duties and obligations to which you have agreed. Upholding laws except in extreme cases where they conflict with fixed social duties. Contributing to the society, group.
LEVEL THREE—POSTCONVENTIONAL	_PRINCIPLED PERSPECTIVE_
Stage Five—Social contract and individual rights	Being aware that people hold a variety of values; that rules are relative to the group. Upholding rules because they are the social contract. Upholding nonrelative values and rights regardless of majority opinion.
Stage Six—Universal ethical principles	Following self-chosen ethical principles. When laws violate these principles, act in accord with principles.

SOURCE: Adapted from Kohlberg, 1969, 1984.

Managers' stage of cognitive moral development determines their mental process of deciding what is right or wrong; and, as noted previously, these stages of moral development seem to exist in all cultures. However, both individual and situational factors have the potential to affect the relationship between the assessment of what is right or wrong and actual ethical decision making in organizations (Trevino, 1986). In addition, these individual and situational differences may be culture bound. Figure 5.1 is a graphic representation of this process.

As shown in Figure 5.1, the model suggests that individual differences can influence the likelihood of people acting on the choice of what they believe to be ethical. For example, individual factors, such as the extent to which one believes that an outcome is the result of one's own efforts (*locus of control*—Rotter, 1966) and the extent to which people depend on information from external reference points (*field dependence*—Witkin & Goodenough, 1977), might influence their reliance on their own internal beliefs about what is right or wrong. In this example, decisions by managers with high field dependence and external locus of control can be less consistent with their level of moral judgment than managers with internal locus of control and field independence. Both the expectation about the outcomes of one's actions and the reliance on social information to make decisions are strongly shaped by culture (Leung, Bond, & Schwartz, 1995; Smith & Bond, 1999; Smith, Trompenaars, & Dugan, 1995). In this way, culture might influence the relationship between level of moral development and making an ethical or unethical decision.

Managers approach an ethical dilemma with a particular level of cognitive moral development. However, decisions taken in a social context can be strongly influenced by the situation. The susceptibility of an individual to external influence is related to the stage of moral development, with individuals at lower levels more susceptible (Trevino, 1986). Situational factors that might be proposed to influence the relationship between stage of moral development and ethical decision making include such factors as the extent to which the environment specifies normative behavior, whether the social referents in the situation are members of one's in-group or out-group, and the extent to which demands are placed on the decision maker by persons in authority. For example, normative behavior regarding sexual harassment might be very easy for U.S. people to recall from memory, whereas for Indonesians, appropriate behavior in this situation is more ambiguous. In addition, for example, social information provided by a superior has a more dramatic influence on decisions for vertical collectivists compared to horizontal individualists (Liu, 1986). The social context for managers also includes the organization in which they function. Organizations differ in adopted principles of social re-

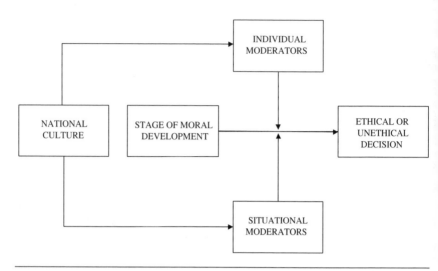

Figure 5.1. Culture's Influence on Ethical Decision Making
SOURCE: Adapted from Trevino, 1986; Robertson & Fadil, 1999.

sponsibility and have processes for social responsiveness (Wood, 1991). In addition, these organizational features can vary across cultures (Donaldson, 1993). These principles and processes can facilitate or impede ethical decision making.

The concepts presented in the model (Figure 5.1) have been subjected to only limited empirical tests. For example, an analysis of the ethical judgments of U.S., Eastern European, and Indonesian participants indicated that the type of ethical issue influenced cultural differences. However, after controlling for situational characteristics and the cultural background of participants, the moral judgments they made were consistent with their ethical ideology (Davis, Johnson, & Ohmer, 1998). Other research points to the effect of social influence on ethical decision making. In a comparison of U.S. people and Israelis across a range of ethical issues, the best predictor of ethical judgments was what participants felt peers would do (Izraeli, 1988).

Thus, the limited amount of research on descriptive models of ethical behavior illuminates the importance of the three factors: (a) level of moral development, (b) individual factors, and (c) situational factors, in describing ethical decision making in an international environment. First, the level of cognitive moral development appears to be a concept that applies across cultures. However, it would be naive to believe that managers' decisions are somehow hardwired to their value judgments about what is right or wrong. Therefore, both individual characteristics of the manager such as culturally based values and the situational (organizational) context in which the decision is being made are logical moderators of the relationship between the level of cognitive moral development and ethical behavior.

Summary

The decisions that international managers make are made more complex by an environment that includes stakeholders with potentially very different perspectives on desirable outcomes. Because of limits to rationality, managers rely on heuristics or rules of thumb to guide decision making. These heuristics simplify the decision-making process; because managers from different cultures perceive the world differently, they differ in the way that they simplify complex realities. In addition to cognitive simplification, the decision choices made are influenced by motivational biases, based in part on cultural values, and different definitions of self-interest.

International management decisions are further complicated by legal, political, and cultural boundaries. In crossing these boundaries, what is moral can be blurred by cultural differences. There is no shortage of prescriptive models on which managers can draw for ethical guidance. However, actual ethical decision making is probably the result of the complex interplay of the level of cognitive moral development of the manager with other individual and situational factors.

Six

The Manager as Negotiator

Communicating and Negotiating Across Cultures

Americans who travel abroad for the first time are often shocked to discover that, despite all the progress made in the past 30 years, many foreign people still speak in foreign languages. Oh sure, they speak some English, but usually just barely well enough to receive a high school diploma here in the United States.

Dave Barry, Humor Columnist (1988)

A significant part of every manager's job involves the role of negotiator. That negotiator role can involve activity across the boundary of the organization, such as buyer-seller negotiations, or within the company such as negotiating performance expectations with an employee. Underlying every negotiation that takes place in an international context is the process of cross-cultural communication. This chapter discusses the behavioral aspects of international negotiation. This discussion is grounded in the more general topic of cross-cultural communication.

Cross-Cultural Communication Process

Communication is the act of transmitting messages, including information about the nature of the relationship, to another person who interprets these messages and gives them meaning (Berlo, 1960). Therefore, both the sender and the receiver of the message play an active role in the communication process. Successful communication requires not only that the message is transmitted but also that it is understood. For this understanding to occur, the sender and receiver must share a vast amount of common information called grounding (Clark & Brennan, 1991). This grounding information is updated moment by moment during the communication process. Probably all of us have noticed how people who have extensive common information can communicate very effectively with a minimum of distortion. For example, hospital emergency room personnel depend on sharing a great deal of information, such as medical jargon and the seriousness of the situation, in order to communicate complex messages efficiently.

Cross-cultural communication is significantly more demanding than communicating in a single culture because culturally different individuals have less common information. They have less "grounding" because of differences in their field of experience (Schramm, 1980). In this chapter, the term *cultural field* is used to refer to those culturally based elements of a person's background (e.g., education, values, attitudes, etc.) that influence communication. The additional complexity that this adds to the basic communication process is presented graphically in Figure 6.1.

Figure 6.1 shows how the communication process involves the sender of the message, some channel through which the message is transmitted, and the receiver of the message. All of these elements are embedded in their respective cultural fields. The message is encoded (converted to symbolic form) and sent by some means (channel) to the receiver, who then interprets (decodes) the message. The effectiveness of the communication depends on a lack of distortion, which can occur at all the stages of the communication process.

First, the encoded message can be affected by the communication skills and knowledge of the sender, as well as the associated cultural field. That is, we cannot communicate what we do not know, and our ability to encode accurately is determined by our skill in the chosen channel (e.g.,

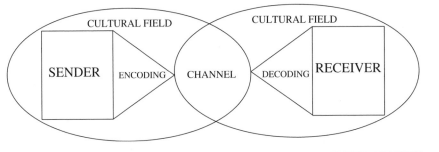

Figure 6.1. Cross-Cultural Communication Process
SOURCE: Based on Schramm, 1980.

speaking or writing). In addition, like all behavior, much communication behavior is scripted and proceeds in a routine manner consistent with the cultural field. For example, in North America, the response to "How are you today?" is often "Fine, thanks!" without any real consideration being given to one's actual physical condition, and the Chinese response to the common greeting "Have you eaten yet?" is similarly automatic.

Second, the symbols that an individual uses to express an idea vary with the cultural field. This includes not only the language used but also aspects of communication that transcend language, such as communication style, conventions, and practices. We might think that people would choose a different communication channel depending on the goal of the communication: written for task-oriented communications and verbal for relationship-oriented communications, for example. However, the reality seems to be that convenience and skill in the use of the medium is more important (Kayany, Wotring, & Forrest, 1996). Today, for example, e-mail substitutes for a variety of communication channels for those who know how to use it.

Finally, all of the factors that affect the sender also influence the receiver. The symbols must be decoded into a form that can be understood by the receiver. Just like the sender, the receiver must be skilled in the channel in use and also have sufficient knowledge to correctly interpret the message. As in any cross-cultural interaction (Chapter 4), the ability of receivers to accurately perceive the communication behavior is influenced by their cultural field. In addition, the extent to which the cultural fields of individuals overlap reduces the opportunity for distortion in the communications process. That is, the more each party understands the other's situation, perspectives, and culture, the easier it is to use symbols that will be encoded and decoded similarly.

Language

One obvious consideration in cross-cultural communication is the language being used. Language is a symbolic code of communication consisting of a set of sounds with understood meanings and a set of rules for constructing messages. The meanings attached to any word by a language are completely arbitrary, but cultural conventions control the features of language use (Triandis, 1972). For example, the Japanese word for cat (*neko*) does not look or sound any more like a cat than does the English word. Somewhere during the development of the two languages, these words were chosen to represent the animal. Similarly, the Cantonese word for the number four (*sei*) has the same sound as the word for death, whereas the word for the number eight sounds like *faat* (prosperity). Therefore, some Chinese avoid things numbered four and are attracted to things numbered eight, although there are no such connotations for English speakers.

Although English may be becoming the major lingua franca of international business (Naisbitt & Aburdene, 1990), culturally based conventions create differences even among English speakers. In Britain, a *rubber* is an eraser, to *knock someone up* means to call at their house, and *tabling* an item means to put in *on* the agenda, not to defer it. Likewise, British people live in flats and might stand in a queue, U.S. people live in apartments and stand in line, and Canadians live in suites and stand in a lineup.

Even when translators know the meaning of words and the grammatical rules for putting them together, effective communication is often not achieved. The following notices written in English and discovered throughout the world illustrate the point.

> In an Austrian ski resort hotel: *Not to perambulate the corridors during the hours of repose in the boots of ascension.*

> Outside a Hong Kong tailor shop: *Ladies may have a fit upstairs.*

> From a Japanese car rental brochure: *When passenger of foot heave in sight, tootle the horn. Trumpet him melodiously at first, but if he still obstacles your passage then tootle him with vigor.*

There could be as many as 10,000 languages in the world. However, 95% of the world's population speaks one of about 100 different languages, and the number of languages spoken by large numbers of people is considerably smaller than that (Katzner, 1975). Still, a significant amount of language diversity exists, and international managers must be concerned with foreign-language competency.

The diversity of languages means an important issue in cross-cultural communication is finding a common language that both parties can use to work effectively. Practically, this means that one of the two parties must use a second language. In part, because the majority of Westerners in international business are monolingual (Ferraro, 1994), English is often the bridge language. This suggests that the second language in use in international business is most often English.

The use of a second language has a number of implications for cross-cultural communication. First, using a second language creates cognitive strain (Smith & Bond, 1999). That is, it requires more effort on the part of the second-language user who could already be contending with other demands of communication or of the task at hand. Over long periods of time, second-language use is exhausting. Second, the greater the fluency of second-language speakers, the more likely they will be seen as competent in other respects (Hui & Cheng, 1987). Third, first-language speakers in a cross-language interaction tend to respond to lower linguistic competency of their partner by modifying aspects of their speech such as slowing the rate of speech and reducing sentence complexity (Gass & Varonis, 1985). This simplification of speech can improve communication by removing redundancy of content (Giles & Smith, 1979). However, this type of speech accommodation, called "foreigner speak," can be perceived as ingratiating and might not be well-received. Box 6.1 is an example of a conversation degenerating into "foreigner speak."

Finally, if the first-language speaker is unable to recognize signals that indicate lack of understanding or does not work to create an environment in which it is acceptable to check for understanding, the second-language speaker may pretend to understand in order to avoid embarrassment or appear competent (Li, 1994). The end result of these factors is that a cross-language communication can be as demanding for the native speaker of the language as for the second-language speaker. Both participants must devote more attention to the communications process in order to achieve an effective transfer of understanding.

BOX 6.1

Foreigner Speak

Manager: Mr. Chan, could you take this report up to Mr. Abercrombie ASAP?

Mr. Chan: Sorry, I don't understand.

Manager: *In a louder voice*—Could you take this report up to Mr. Abercrombie ASAP?

Mr. Chan: You want that I finish report?

Manager: Chan *pause* take report *pause* Mr. Abercrombie *pause* right now!

Mr. Chan: Sorry!

SOURCE: Adapted from Gallois & Callan, 1997.

Communication Styles

The previous section presented some of the difficulties for the communications process posed by language differences. Primarily, these involved issues of translation and second-language use. However, it is also important to consider those aspects of communication that transcend the specific language being spoken. In general, these communication behaviors are logical extensions of the internalized values and norms of their respective cultures. That is, culturally based rules govern the style, conventions, and practices of language usage. In some cases, a relationship to the key value orientations of individualism and collectivism is apparent.

Explicit Versus Implicit Communication

One way in which cultures vary in terms of communication style is the degree to which they use language itself to communicate the message. For example, in the United States, effective verbal communication is expected to be explicit, direct, and unambiguous (Gallois & Callan, 1997). That is, people are expected to say exactly what they mean. In contrast, communication styles in some other cultures, such as Indonesia (Pekerti, 2001), are considerably more inexact, ambiguous, and implicit. These two styles are characterized by a bipolar typology called high-context and low-context communication styles (Hall, 1976).

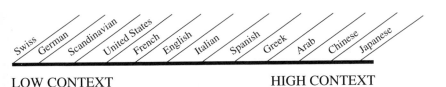

LOW CONTEXT   **HIGH CONTEXT**

Figure 6.2. High- and Low-Context Cultures

> A high-context (HC) communication or message is one in which most of the information is either in the physical context or internalized in the person, while very little is in the coded, explicit, transmitted part of the message. A low-context (LC) communication is just the opposite; i.e., the mass of the message is vested in the explicit code. (Hall, 1976, p. 79)

On the basis of observation, a number of countries have been classified along the continuum according to whether they are primarily high or low context (Hall, 1976). In low-context cultures, the message is largely conveyed by the words spoken. In high-context cultures, a good deal of the meaning is implicit and the words convey only a small part of the message. The receiver must fill in the gaps from past knowledge of the speaker, the setting, or other contextual cues. Figure 6.2 shows the relationship of 12 countries along the high-context and low-context continuum.

Researchers have noted that there is a close agreement between the position of countries on this scale and their location on Hofstede's (1980) individualism-collectivism index (Gudykunst, Ting-Toomey, & Chua, 1988; Pekerti, 2001). Furthermore, they suggest that high- and low-context communication styles can actually help to perpetuate collectivism and individualism, respectively. For example, in individualist cultures, speech will be more focused, briefer with more reference to *I* and to specific goals. However, in collectivist cultures, speech will include more qualifiers such as *maybe, perhaps, somewhat,* and *probably* (Smith & Bond, 1999). Some support for this idea is found in comparisons of pairs of cultures. Systematic differences in communication styles along the lines suggested here have been found for Jews and Arabs in Israel (Katriel, 1986), for U.S. people and Koreans (Kim, 1994), and for Indonesians and New Zealanders (Pekerti, 2001). Box 6.2 gives an example of how high-context communication might operate in practice.

> **BOX 6.2**
>
> **High-Context Communication**
>
> An Indonesian woman had invited the mother of the young man who was courting her daughter to tea. The woman was not pleased with the possibility that her daughter might marry into a family that she viewed as of lower socioeconomic status. During the meeting, she never mentioned the relationship of their children, but she served bananas with the tea. The message that her son didn't belong with the woman's daughter any more than bananas go with tea was subtle and implicit, but was received loud and clear nonetheless.

Direct Versus Indirect Communication

An idea complementary to the high-context versus low-context communication styles just discussed is the degree of directness of communication. Directness is associated with individualist cultures and indirectness with collectivist cultures (Levine, 1985). A pertinent example of this difference is expressed in the indirect style in which a collectivist might say no without really saying it, as shown in Box 6.3.

Direct communication is required at some time in all cultural groups. However, as shown in Box 6.3, directness depends on the social context. The relationship to the social context is evident if we consider the motive for indirectness. In collectivist cultures, politeness and a desire to avoid embarrassment often take precedence over *truth,* as truth is defined in individualist cultures. That is, for collectivists, truth is not absolute but depends on the social situation. Therefore, the social situation is an important indicator for the appropriate degree of directness or "truthfulness." Although making untrue statements to preserve harmony (white lies) is probably universal, the extent of its use is probably higher in collectivist cultures (Smith & Bond, 1999).

Silence and Verbal Overkill

Just as cultural differences exist in language usage, they also exist in how silence is used in communication. To some extent, collectivist cultures value silence as a way of controlling the communication interaction, whereas individualists value talking in the same way (Giles, Coupland,

---

BOX 6.3

Saying "No" in Response to "Has My Proposal Been Accepted?"

Conditional "yes"	If everything proceeds as planned, the proposal will be approved.
Counterquestion	Have you submitted a copy of your proposal to the ministry of . . .
Criticizing the question	Your question is very difficult to answer.
Refusing the question	We cannot answer this question at this time.
Tangential reply	Will you be staying longer than you had originally planned?
Yes, but	Yes, approval looks likely, but . . .
Delayed answer	You should know shortly.

SOURCE: C. Engholm, *When Business East Meets Business West: The Guide to Practice and Protocol in the Pacific Rim.* Copyright ©1991, John Wiley. Reprinted by permission of John Wiley & Sons, Inc.

& Wiemann, 1992). For example, Japanese negotiators allow long periods of silence to develop (or use it strategically) in order to control the negotiation process (Graham, 1985; Morsbach, 1982). These periods of silence are often misunderstood by Westerners who interpret them as a lack of understanding and try to shorten them with further explanation or by moving on to the next point.

Even among individualist cultures, the use of silence versus talking can vary. For example, Australians have a lower tendency to communicate verbally than do people from the United States (Barraclough, Christophel, & McCroskey, 1988), and in Finland, silence is valued as a way of showing encouragement for the speaker to continue (Wiemann, Chen, & Giles, 1986).

Other speech communities have a similar indirectness and ambiguity to that associated with many Asian cultures. However, this indirectness causes them to use speaking versus silence in a different way. For example, Arab-language countries engage in what is called *mubalaqha* or exaggeration to make their point (Almaney & Ahwan, 1982). In the Arab language, some common words used at the end of sentences are put there in order to be emphasized, pronouns will be repeated, also for emphasis, and highly graphic metaphors and similes are commonly used. It is typical for an Arab speaker to modify a single noun with numerous adjectives for added effect. Research indicates that what would be an assertive statement in North America would likely be viewed as weak and equivocating by an Arab (Prothro, 1955). Smith and Bond (1999) suggest, for example, that this might have been at the heart of the Iraqi government's failure to heed the warnings in 1990 of then U.S. Secretary of State James Baker that an invasion of Kuwait would lead to retaliation. Baker might not have delivered his message with sufficient exaggeration to be taken seriously.

Use of Praise

One additional stylistic element that has a systematic relationship to culture is the use of praise and the response to praise (Triandis, 1978). Several comparative studies have demonstrated stylistic differences about giving and receiving praise. Cultural differences exist regarding how frequently praise is used, what is praised, and in how people respond. For example, in comparing Japanese and U.S. people, U.S. people use praise more frequently and are more apt to praise people who are close to them such as friends or family, whereas Japanese are more likely to praise strangers (Barnlund & Araki, 1985). Moreover, U.S. people are more likely to praise physical appearance, whereas Arabs, like Japanese, are more likely to praise skill and work than physical characteristics (Nelson, El Bakary, & Al Batal, 1993). However, consistent with the propensity to exaggerate just noted, Arab praise is typically more elaborate, often containing metaphors.

Response to praise also seems to vary across cultures. For cultures like China, where modesty is a virtue, praise can cause embarrassment. For example, Hong Kong Chinese tend to deflect praise, whereas British people are more likely to politely accept it (Loh, 1993). The cartoon in Figure 6.3 provides an example.

Other Language Considerations

To function effectively in a cross-cultural communication, it is important to understand not only the formal structure of the language but also how it is used in certain social situations. We all have a large repertoire of language styles and registers (formality of language) that we adopt depending on the situation. For example, the language U.S. teenagers use with

Figure 6.3. Response to Praise
SOURCE: Copyright ©1985, Larry Feign. Used with permission.

their peers is often quite different from that they would use with teachers or parents. Similarly, a Japanese adult would use very different language to address a superior at work from that used to speak to a child. In our native language, we have a fairly sophisticated grasp of style. However, cultural rules about style and register vary. For example, Chinese and Japanese have a much more complex range of formal styles than does English (Gallois & Callan, 1997). In addition, most languages have nonstandard forms and usage, such as slang, which make understanding this process more difficult.

Slang and Jargon

Many languages change register by the amount of slang they include. Slang is an informal usage of language typically more playful or metaphorical and associated with a particular subgroup. Jargon, like slang, is associated with a particular subgroup but is often a very specialized or technical language of people engaged in a similar occupation or activity. In both cases, these specialized forms of language can enhance communications for members of the group with which they are associated but can be almost unintelligible for nongroup members. Being able to communicate in the slang or jargon of a particular group helps to define one's membership in that group. For example, the terms *browser, web page, server*, and *wysiwyg* will be familiar to people who share an interest in computers, and the rough dialect heard by young people on the streets of Paris is still French, but serves to identify them as a distinct group.

The use of slang or jargon presents three issues for cross-cultural communications. First, the number of possible variations in expression in any particular language group is increased. Second, these nonstandard terms or usage might only last for a few years before disappearing, unless they are incorporated into the standard form of the language. Finally, however, the knowledge of a shared specialized language by culturally different individuals can to some extent enhance their communication ability. For example, engineers or computer technicians from different cultures might share a significant amount of technical jargon that improves their grounding.

Euphemisms

All cultures seem to have words that by tradition or convention are not often used publicly. These prohibited words are often, but not necessarily, associated with sexual relations or bodily functions (Ferraro, 1994). These prohibited words are often handled by substituting a bland or less direct expression, or euphemism. In the United States, people don't die, they "pass away," they aren't blind but are "visually impaired;" in some Latin American countries, being in an "interesting" condition means a women is pregnant; and in 1997, Hong Kong was not "handed over" to China, it "returned home." Obviously, an in-depth knowledge of another culture is required to understand what topics can be referred to directly and which require a more indirect expression.

Idioms

Every language has unique ways of combining words to express a particular thought. Often, a particular phrase or construction will differ from its literal meaning. This poses a particular problem for translation. Box 6.4 compares idiomatic expressions that convey the same meaning in U.S and French-Canadian usage.

The problem of literal versus idiomatic translation has resulted in a number of humorous (although probably not to those involved) examples of international business blunders. For example, one European firm mistranslated "out of sight, out of mind" to "invisible things are insane" in Thailand (Ricks, 1993).

Proverbs and Maxims

These short sayings express things that are obviously true in a particular culture and often advise people how they should behave. Therefore, they can provide insight into some of a culture's central values. Proverbs are found in all languages, and often the same basic idea can be found in widely different expressions. For example, the maxim "an eye for an eye" is expressed in East Africa as "a goat's hide buys a goat's hide" (Ferraro, 1994). Different cultures rely on proverbs to varying degrees to guide their behavior. That is, proverbs are often widely understood, if not followed, in a particular culture. For example, the "silence is golden" message seems to have been lost on at least some U.S. people.

Language Pragmatics

In addition to the dimensions of language as a communications medium discussed earlier, there are several practical considerations to language usage. These include which language will be used in an intercultural interaction, the effect of linguistic and stylistic accommodation by one speaker, and the effects of second-language ability.

Language Accommodation

Who will accommodate whom in an intercultural communication raises practical questions of language usage in addition to the language fluency of the parties involved. Speech accommodation involves shifting one's speech patterns so that one achieves greater language similarity. Sometimes, because of a previous history of antagonism, one language group will refuse to speak another group's language (Bourhis, Giles, Leyens, & Tajfel, 1979). However, even when historical relationships between two groups are positive, the issue of who will accommodate whom must be resolved. Who will accommodate whom in an intercultural interaction can be complex and depends on the motives of the parties in the interaction, the identities of the parties, and the situation itself (Gallois & Callan, 1997). In business situations, the default language, because of lack of fluency or cultural conflicts, is often English. For example, Japanese people tend to believe that it is not possible for foreigners to be really fluent in their language and will automatically switch to the foreigner's language (Ross & Shortreed, 1990). In reality, however, the kind of situation in which only one person needs to adapt may be fairly uncommon. The effort that one party puts into accommodating the other's language is often appreciated and reciprocated (Giles, Bourhis, & Taylor, 1977). An example of how the role of the participant can influence the choice of language is presented in Figure 6.4.

Stylistic Accommodation

The idea that adapting one's communication style to that of the other culture participant in an intercultural communication will help to bridge cultural distance and improve communication is based on the similarity-attraction paradigm (Byrne, 1971) mentioned in Chapter 4. That is, stylistic accommodation leads to perceptions of similarity, which, in turn, lead to positive attitudes toward the member of the other culture. Research has indicated that some linguistic and behavioral accommodation can have a positive effect but that there might be some optimal level of adaptation of the patterns of the other culture beyond which the effects are less positive (Francis, 1991; Giles & Smith, 1979). The extent to which stylistic accommodation is viewed positively seems to depend on the motive to which it is attributed (Thomas & Ravlin, 1995). For example, if speech or behavioral accommodation is perceived as being patronizing or ingratiating, its positive effects are lost. Research indicates that some stylistic accommodation on the part of both parties in the cross-cultural communication can help to overcome communication difficulties

Figure 6.4. Language Accommodation
SOURCE: Copyright ©1985, Larry Feign. Used with permission.

(Miller, 1995). However, the optimal level of accommodation can be quite difficult to pinpoint.

Language Fluency

The degree of language fluency creates several issues for the second-language user that extend beyond just the user's ability. Higher degrees of language fluency can lead to the second-language user being perceived as having a higher competency in other areas, such as knowledge of cultural norms (Hui & Cheng, 1987). For example, cultural blunders by a foreigner who is not competent in the foreign language might be forgiven as consistent with their lack of language skills and hence cultural knowledge. However, the same behavior by a fluent speaker of the language might be perceived negatively, because they should know better based on their level of language fluency. Fluency in a foreign language can also cause a person to be perceived as having beliefs more closely aligned with the foreign-language group (Bond, 1985). Additionally, foreign-language use can have implications for the attitudes and behavior of the second-language user. For example, individuals have shown differences in attitudes (Guthrie & Azores, 1968) and in linguistic style

(Loh, 1993) when responding in a second language. These shifts in attitudes and behavior are generally in the direction of those of the foreign-language group (Bond & Yang, 1982).

Nonverbal Communication

Just as important to communication as the verbal components previously discussed are the nonverbal aspects of communication. Nonverbal communications convey important messages and are produced more automatically than are words (Argyle, 1988). They include body movements and gestures, facial expressions and facial gazing, tone of voice, and the emphasis of certain words. Some researchers suggest that as much as 70% of communication between people in the same language group is nonverbal (Noller, 1984). In cross-cultural communications, it is possible that people rely even more heavily on the nonverbal component (Gallois & Callan, 1997).

Nonverbal communication helps to regulate intercultural interaction by providing information about our feelings and emotional state, adding meaning to our verbal messages, and governing the timing and sequencing of the interaction (Patterson, 1991). Nonverbal behaviors have the same functions across cultures. However, nonverbal systems of communication, like language, have a significant amount of variation around the world. In general, two types of differences exist. First, the same nonverbal behavior can have very different meanings across cultures. For example, sucking in one's breath across the teeth is a sign of interest or admiration in New Zealand but indicates distress or even anger in Japan, and pulling the lower eyelid with the index finger is a sign of disbelief in France but means "I promise" in Iran. Second, different nonverbal cues can be used to mean the same thing in different cultures. For people from the United States and most Europeans, nodding the head up and down indicates agreement. However, this gesture is not universal. For example, in Calcutta, the rocking of the head from side to side has the same meaning (Jensen, 1982).

The systematic study of nonverbal communication across cultures has been hampered by the lack of an underlying theory or framework. Attempts to systematize have included classifying nonverbal cues as conversational, topical, or interactive (Eisenberg & Smith, 1971). Other approaches have focused on the origin of the cues resulting in many more categories (Condon & Yousef, 1975). There seems to be little agreement on appropriate typologies, and some researchers (Hecht, Andersen, & Ribeau, 1989) have shifted to a functional approach, in which nonverbal behaviors are grouped by the outcomes they achieve as opposed to their origin (e.g., hands, eyes, body, voice). At present, however, the international manager must rely largely on descriptions of the peculiarities of nonverbal communication in various cultures. The following discussion outlines some of the more important categories of nonverbal behaviors (cues) in terms of cross-cultural communication.

Tone of Voice

Along with the words we speak, the way we say them communicates feelings and attitudes (Pittman, 1994). This nonverbal behavior includes pitch, volume, speed, tension, variation, enunciation, and a number of other voice qualities such as breathiness or creakiness (Gallois & Callan, 1997). In addition, these and other features of voice, such as accent, can indicate the cultural identity of the speaker. Cultural norms ascribe different meanings to features and qualities of tone of voice. These meanings can be categorized along the dimensions of dominance, positivity, and arousal (Gallois & Callan, 1997). For example, dominance in the United States is indicated by loud, low-pitched, and fast speech, whereas in Germany, dominance is indicated by soft, low-pitched, breathy speech (Scherer, 1979). As in the interpretation of other behavior across cultures, individuals often fall into the trap of using self-referent criteria in explaining tone of voice. That is, they interpret tone of voice as if it were them speaking.

Proxemics

Another nonverbal component of communication that must be considered in cross-cultural interactions is the way in which people use personal space in their interactions with others. The term coined to describe the study of this dimension of human behavior is *proxemics* (Hall, 1966). People seem to follow predictable patterns when establishing distance between themselves and others that are consistent with cultural norms. For example, based on observation of middle-class North Americans, a typology of distances has been formulated (Hall, 1966) and is shown in Box 6.5.

Because cultural norms influence the appropriateness of a particular spatial relationship, what is an appropriate distance in one culture might seem unusual or even offensive in another. For example, in a study of five different cultures, the appropriate "conversational distance" (between two persons without regard for topic or their relationship) was greatest for Scots, followed by Swedes, U.S. people, Italians, and Greeks, in that

---

BOX 6.5

Typology of Distances

Intimate Distance	Contact–18 inches—a distance reserved for comforting, protecting, and lovemaking
Personal Distance	18 inches–4 feet—a bubble of personal space the size of which depends on the relationship to the other person
Social Distance	4–12 feet—used by acquaintances and strangers in more formal settings
Public Distance	12–25 feet—distance at which the recognition of others is not required

SOURCE: Adapted from Hall, 1966.

---

order (Little, 1968). Although North Americans might prefer a conversational distance of, say, 20 inches, Greeks might be more comfortable at about 9 or 10 inches. The opportunities for misunderstandings in an intercultural interaction are obvious as each party tries to establish a comfortable distance.

Although much of the evidence for cultural-based proximity norms in conversation is anecdotal, the few studies that have been conducted support their existence. For example, in a study of students who were friends, Arabs sat closer, talked more loudly, and touched each other more often than people from the United States (Watson & Graves, 1966). In other research (Watson, 1970), South Americans, Asians, and Indians chose spatial distances midway between that of Arabs and Europeans (including U.S. people and Australians). In yet another study, Japanese chose larger spatial distances than did Venezuelans, with people from the United States choosing a distance in between the two (Shuter, 1977). These findings are for individuals engaged in an interaction. Where there is no requirement for interaction, the findings are somewhat less clear. As is often the case in nonverbal communication, the cultural rules can be different from one situation to the next.

At one extreme of the proximity scale is touching. Individuals touch in a variety of ways depending on purpose. For example, hand to arm to show guidance, kissing the cheek to show affection. Cultures vary widely regarding the meanings associated with the various forms of touching, and who can touch whom and on what part of the body in what circumstances. For example, in North America, it is typical for two men to show friendliness by shaking hands. However, if these same two men held hands while walking down the street in the United States, a behavior common in Thailand (Warren, Black, & Rangsit, 1985), this would be less conventional.

Cultures have been classified as high-touch versus low-touch, with Mediterranean cultures, eastern Europeans, and Arabs and Jews as high-touch; and English, Germans, Northern European, and Asian cultures as low-touch (Montagu, 1972). However, as with any classification scheme this broad, it is important not to overgeneralize. Touching behavior in any culture is likely to depend on a number of factors including age, gender, and social status as well as the situation (Shuter, 1977). For example, a light touch on the back is usually initiated by people of power in the United States as a signal of dominance (Henley, 1977). However, in cultures where touch is common, such as Latin America, such touches might not even be noticed.

Proxemics has some additional implications for the international manager. For example, cultures use office space differently and this can influence cross-cultural communication. Many North Americans close their office doors only for private conferences while Germans are likely to keep their office doors closed at all times. In Japan, offices are often shared among a number of managers. Meetings are held in separate meeting rooms, whereas in the United States, private offices or partitions between workstations are the norm. Hall (1966) reported that one German executive was so protective of his personal space that he had the visitor's chair in his office bolted to the floor in the "proper" place to keep his U.S. visitors from adjusting it to their preferred distance. These patterns of spatial orientations are important in part because they are subtle channels for communicating a significant amount of information, which are often overlooked.

Body Position and Gestures

Unlike languages, which are generally well-documented in structure and meaning, the descriptions of nonverbal elements of communication are usually incomplete and somewhat superficial. The way people position their body conveys information in all cultures. However, people learn which body position is appropriate in a given situation in the same way that they internalize other aspects of culture. The vast array of possible body positions is difficult to categorize in any systematic way. For example, in the United States, people stand up to show respect, whereas in Samoa, they sit down; and showing the sole of your shoe in a Moslem society is a sign of great disrespect (Morrison et al., 1994).

One suggestion is that body positions that make one appear smaller indicate submissiveness and that rounded body postures communicate friendliness, whereas angular postures communicate threat or hostility (Aronoff, Woike, & Hyman, 1992). People from high-power-distance cultures might show more bodily tension as a way of indicating submissiveness or deference (Andersen & Bowman, 1985). For example, bowing is a subtle lowering of the body to show deference to a person of higher status. Bowing is so pervasive in Japan that some department store employees are hired to bow to customers at escalators, and many Japanese bow to their unseen partners in a telephone conversation (Morsbach, 1982). Bowing in Japan is an intricate process, which is determined by the relative social status of the parties and, like many subtle nonverbal elements, is difficult for outsiders to master.

Hand gestures are used both intentionally and unintentionally in communication. Hand gestures used as a substitute for words are called emblems. Because the hand can be configured in numerous ways and with great precision, the number of possible hand gestures is enormous. However, one study has documented the major hand gestures used in western Europe (Morris, Collett, Marsh, & O'Shaugnessy, 1979). Upon examination, the vast array of alternative hand gestures to indicate the same idea is revealed. For example, Box 6.6 illustrates the variety of ways in which men in different parts of the world show their appreciation for an attractive woman.

Further complicating matters, the same hand gesture can have different meanings in different parts of the world. For example, repeatedly crooking the index finger with the palm up beacons another person to come closer in North America. However, the same gesture is obscene in some cultures. Emblems like these are often quite explicit and can be learned by watching what people do and do not do. However, trying to learn all the hand gestures that exist across cultures would be virtually impossible. Therefore, the best advice is probably to avoid gestures until one is very sure what they mean.

Facial Expression

Facial expression is a key source of conveying information, particularly about emotional states. That is, underlying emotional states seem to be closely linked to facial expression. In addition, people tend to be more accurate in making judgments about emotional state based on facial expressions than based on body movement (Ekman, 1982). Early research

BOX 6.6

Showing Appreciation for an Attractive Woman

The cheek stroke (Greece, Italy, and Spain)—the gesturer places his forefinger and thumb on his cheekbone and strokes them gently toward the chin.

The cheek screw (Italy, Sardinia)—the forefinger is pressed into the cheek and rotated.

The breast curve (found in a wide range of cultures)—hands simulate the curve of the female breast.

The waist curve (common in English-speaking countries)—the hands sweep down to make the curvaceous outline of the female trunk.

The eye touch (South America, Italy)—a straight forefinger is placed on the lower eyelid and pulled down slightly.

The two-handed telescope (Brazil)—the hands are curled one in front of the other as the man looks through them in telescope style.

The moustache twist (Italy)—the thumb and forefinger twist an imaginary moustache.

The hand on heart (South America)—the right hand is placed over the heart, signifying a "heart throb."

The fingertip kiss (France)—the fingertips are kissed and then spread out in the direction of the woman.

The air kiss (English-speaking countries)—a man kisses the air in the direction of the woman.

The cheek pinch (Sicily)—a man pinches his own cheek.

The breast cup (Europe in general)—both hands make a cupping movement in the air, simulating the squeezing of the woman's breast.

SOURCE: Adapted from Morris, 1977.

indicated that the same facial expressions were associated with certain emotions in all cultures (Ekman, Friesen, & Ellsworth, 1972). Indeed, it appears that six basic emotions of anger, fear, sadness, disgust, happiness, and surprise are evident in facial expressions around the world from a very early age (Izard, 1991). The three main parts of the face, (a) forehead and eyebrows, (b) eyes, and (c) mouth, express emotions in roughly the following ways (Gallois & Callan, 1997):

Happiness: smiling mouth, puffed lower eyelids, smooth brow and forehead

Surprise: raised eyebrows, wide-open eyes, open mouth

Disgust: brow lowered and drawn inward, upper lip raised, which sometimes causes the nose to wrinkle

Fear: brow raised, furrowed, and drawn inward, wide open eyes, mouth open with lips drawn back

Anger: lowered brow, staring (sometimes narrowed) eyes, jaw clenched, mouth either closed or open with teeth bared

Sadness: brow lowered (sometimes drawn inward), inside corners of eyelid raised, corners of the mouth pulled down (p. 57)

The link between facial expressions and emotions is a direct one that operates without conscious thought (DePaulo, 1992). However, individuals often deliberately seek to override the linkage between their emotions and their facial expression. In this way, culture can influence facial expression. That is, facial expressions are influenced by an individual's culturally learned display rules (Levenson, Ekman, Heider, & Friesen, 1992). An examination of smiling behavior provides an example. In one study, people from the United States and Japan both found a smiling face to be more sociable (Matsumoto & Kudoh, 1993), consistent with the universal association of smiling with happiness. However, in Japan, smiling can also be used to hide displeasure, sorrow, or anger (Morsbach, 1982), and in China, smiling is often associated with a lack of self-control and calmness (Albright, Malloy, Dong, Kenny, & Fang, 1997). Therefore, although all people smile, the meaning of this and other facial expressions can vary across cultures to the extent that people are controlling their facial display.

Some researchers have suggested that cultures can be classified regarding emotional expression rules as either affective or neutral (Trompenaars, 1993). For example, in collectivist cultures, in which people have more interdependent self-concepts, the expression of emotion in public is often suppressed in order to maintain harmony (Ekman, 1982). This is one reason why Japanese and Chinese people often appear inscrutable to Europeans. Research indicates that it is much harder to guess how a Japanese person feels from facial expression than it is for British or Italians (Shimoda, Argyle, & Ricci-Bitti, 1984)

Eye Contact (Gaze)

When two pairs of eyes meet, it is very noticeable. Perhaps this is why writers often refer to the eyes as "windows to the soul." All cultures use gaze (eye contact) in nonverbal communication. Both maintaining eye contact and avoiding eye contact communicate important messages. In North America, a high level of gazing from another is typically interpreted as a sign of friendliness (Kleinke, 1986) unless it persists regardless of the person's response. Then, it can be interpreted as hostile or aggressive (Ellsworth & Carlsmith, 1973). Avoidance of eye contact often suggests shyness, unfriendliness, or insincerity to North Americans (Zimbardo, 1977). However, these patterns are not consistent across cultures.

Cultural differences in gaze patterns seem to be fixed relatively early in life and persist regardless of subsequent cross-cultural experiences (Watson, 1970). For example, Arabs, Latins, Indians, and Pakistanis maintain a significantly higher level of eye contact in normal conversation than do North Americans. Conversely, Africans and East Asians interpret high levels of eye contact as conveying anger or insubordination and hence avoid it. In Japan, for example, rather than looking a person in the eyes, the gaze is focused downward toward the neck region (Morsbach, 1982). The appropriate level of eye contact in conversation can also vary according to the relative status of the individuals involved, and appropriate eye contact in public space also varies across cultures (Davis, 1971).

The previous discussion of nonverbal communication behavior must be treated with some caution. First, it is not possible to rely on uniformity even within a single culture since other factors, such as education, occupation, religion, and the relative status of the individuals involved, can have a significant impact on nonverbal behavior. Second, not all nonverbal behaviors are of equal importance even within a culture. Finally, as noted earlier, there are similarities as well as differences in nonverbal communication across cultures.

Negotiating Across Cultures

An important application of cross-cultural communication for the international manager is face-to-face negotiation. All negotiations share some universal characteristics. They involve two or more parties who have conflicting interests but a common need to reach an agreement, the content of which is not clearly defined at the outset (Hofstede & Usunier, 1996). A substantial body of literature exists about the effects of both contextual and individual factors on the negotiation process and on outcomes (Neale & Northcraft, 1991). However, the extent to which these findings generalize across cultures is largely unknown.

The study of cross-cultural business negotiation has produced several analytical models (e.g., Graham, 1987; Tung, 1988; Weiss, 1993). Consistent among them is that the outcomes of negotiation are thought to be contingent on (a) factors associated with the behavior of individuals involved in the negotiation, (b) factors associated with the process of negotiation, and (c) factors associated with the negotiation situation. In general, culture probably has an indirect effect on the outcome of negotiations by influencing all these contingency variables (Usunier, 1996). However, the state of knowledge of cross-cultural negotiation is largely descriptive. That is, we know that cultural differences in negotiation exist but know less about why these differences occur.

Negotiation Process

A number of efforts have been made to describe the stages of the negotiation process. The number of stages suggested ranges from three (Salacuse, 1991) to twelve (Gulliver, 1979), with the most widely used of these consisting of four (Graham, 1987) or five (McCall & Warrington, 1990) stages. Although the idea of a sequential, phased structure to negotiations might be a peculiarly Western notion (Weiss, 1993), the concept is nevertheless appealing from a comparative standpoint. The Graham four-stage model seems to have the most elements in common with the other popular models. Essentially, the model suggests that all business negotiations proceed through four stages:

1. nontask sounding or relationship building,

2. task-related exchange of information,

3. persuasion, and

4. making concessions and reaching agreement.

Graham (1987) suggests that the content, duration, and importance of each of these stages can be seen to differ across cultures. That is, the internalized cultural values and norms of the negotiator influence which aspect of the process is emphasized. Although no direct tests of the model exist, descriptions of the negotiation process in different cultures (e.g., Pye, 1982; Tung, 1984) support the notion that different aspects of the negotiation process are emphasized in different cultures. For example, Japanese negotiators spend considerable time in nontask sounding or relationship building as compared to U.S. people, and they also emphasize an exchange of information as opposed to the persuasion tactics preferred by people from the United States (Graham, 1987). These differences are reflected in the behavioral styles of negotiators discussed next.

Negotiator Behavior

Several studies have documented the negotiating styles of individuals from different cultures. Differences have been recorded about styles of persuasion, conflict-resolution preferences, and initial bargaining positions and concession patterns (Leung & Wu, 1990). Regarding styles of persuasion, one study (Glenn, Witmeyer, & Stevenson, 1977) analyzed the transcripts of the United Nations Security Council meetings during disarmament negotiations and illustrated cultural differences in the styles of persuasion used by the U.S. and Syrian representatives. The factual-inductive style of the U.S. representatives, which relied on appeals to logic, contrasted dramatically with the more affective-intuitive style of the Syrians, which relied on emotional appeals. The differences in style were consistent with what might be predicted based on the orientations of the two cultures along the individualism-collectivism cultural dimension (Smith & Bond, 1999). The same study documented the persuasion style of Russian negotiators, which relied on references to ideology. These three styles of persuasion were labeled rational, affective, and ideological.

Culture also seems to influence the preference that individuals have for a particular conflict-resolution style. For example, some cultures prefer confrontation in the negotiation process, whereas others prefer a more subtle form of bargaining in which balance and restraint are important. France, Brazil, and the United States are typically competitive, whereas Japanese and Malaysian negotiators are characterized by their politeness, ambiguous objections, and restraint (Leung & Wu, 1990). In addition, Indians can be even more competitive in negotiations than people from the United States (Druckman, Benton, Ali, & Bagur, 1976). Tinsley (1998) found systematic differences among Japanese, German, and U.S. managers regarding preference for a particular conflict-resolution model. Japanese managers preferred a status-power model in which conflicts are resolved by a higher authority. Germans preferred a regulations model in which preexisting procedures or rules resolve problems. People from the United States preferred an interest model that focuses on discovering and resolving the underlying concerns of the other party to make it worthwhile to reach an agreement. Other research indicates that the cultural dimensions of individualism and collectivism can be predictive of a preference for a particular conflict-resolution preference (e.g., Gabrielidis, Stephen, Ybarra, Dos Santos

Pearson, & Villareal, 1997). For example, collectivists prefer bargaining and mediation as conflict-resolution strategies, whereas individualists prefer adversarial adjudicative procedures in which the development of arguments and the presentation of positions are done by the parties to the dispute (Leung, 1987). The rationale for this difference is that collectivists might actually perceive an adversarial procedure to be desirable but that the confrontational and competitiveness inherent in the procedure reduces their preference for it (Bond, Leung, & Schwartz, 1992; Leung & Lind, 1986).

Culture also seems to influence the initial offers and concession patterns of negotiators. Some cultural groups use very extreme initial offers, such as Russians, Arabs (Glenn et al., 1977), and Chinese (Pye, 1982), whereas others, like people from the United States, are more moderate regarding initial positions. Similarly, cultural differences exist in the willingness of negotiators to make concessions. Russians, for example, seem to view concessions as a weakness, whereas other groups, such as North Americans, Arabs, and Norwegians, are more likely to make concessions and to reciprocate an opponent's concessions (Glenn et al., 1977; Maxwell & Schmitt, 1975).

A series of studies by Graham and his colleagues (Graham, 1983, 1985; Graham, Kim, Lin, & Robinson, 1988; Graham, Mintu, & Rodgers, 1994) documented differences in the tactics used by negotiators from a number of different countries. For example, the differences in both verbal and nonverbal behaviors of negotiators from Japan, the United States, and Brazil is presented in Table 6.1.

These descriptions are informative and indicate that negotiator behavior is highly variable across cultures. On examination, they reveal consistency with what is known about communication styles and with underlying cultural-value orientations. We know that both verbal and nonverbal behavior, such as facial gazing, can have a significant effect on negotiation outcomes (Lewis & Fry, 1977). In addition, negotiators are inclined to think in terms of responding to or countering the tactics of their counterparts. As discussed earlier, however, accurate interpretation of the meaning of behavior from outside a particular culture is difficult.

Knowledge of the preferred negotiating style of individuals from another culture might help negotiators prepare a negotiator profile (e.g., Weiss, 1994) of their counterpart. However, an additional complication is that negotiators may change their behavior when negotiating with someone from another culture. Cultural differences have been reported regarding how often negotiators change tactics during a negotiation, with negotiators from Spain the most flexible, followed in order by the United Kingdom, Switzerland, Denmark, and Sweden (Porat, 1970). In addition, research found that Japanese in negotiation with Canadians

TABLE 6.1 Negotiator Behavior in Three Cultures

	Individual Tactics as a Percentage of Total Tactics		
	Japanese $N = 6$	American $N = 6$	Brazilian $N = 6$
Promise	7	8	3
Threat	4	4	2
Recommendation	7	4	5
Warning	2	1	1
Reward	1	2	2
Punishment	1	3	3
Positive normative appeal	1	1	0
Negative normative appeal	3	1	1
Commitment	15	13	8
Self-disclosure	34	36	39
Question	20	20	22
Command	8	6	14
	Occurrences in a 30-Minute Bargaining Session		
Number of times word "No" used	5.7	9.0	83.4
Silent periods of 10 seconds or more	5.5	3.5	0
Conversational overlaps (interruptions)	12.6	10.3	28.6
Gazing (minutes per random 10 min period)	1.3 min	3.3 min	5.2 min
Touching	0	0	4.7

SOURCE: J. L. Graham, 1985. The Influence of Culture on the Process of Business Negotiations: An Exploratory Study, Table 3. *Journal of International Business Studies, 16*, p. 88. Reprinted with persmission.

used different types of influence tactics (more assertiveness, threats, appeals to reason, and appeals to a higher authority) than when interacting with members of their own culture (Rao & Hashimoto, 1996), and Chinese, when trying to resolve a disagreement, used tactics designed to embarrass a Chinese counterpart, but tried to resolve the situation and preserve the relationship with people from the United States (Weldon et al., 1996, cited in Smith & Bond, 1999). However, contrary findings about the extent to which negotiators change their behavior in intercultural interactions exits. For example, in a study of Canadian and Chinese executives, neither group altered its negotiation strategy when negotiating across cultures (Tse, Francis, & Walls, 1994). These contradictory findings suggest that situational differences can influence the extent to which culturally based preferences for negotiation behavior are altered in cross-cultural interactions.

Problem-Solving Approach

Some research on cross-cultural negotiation sought to test the generalizability of what is called the Problem-Solving Approach (PSA) to negotiation. The PSA involves emphasizing cooperative, integrative, and information-oriented strategies over competitive, individualistic, and persuasion-oriented strategies. In general, the PSA positively affects joint negotiation outcomes (Graham, 1986). However, this effect does not seem to be consistent across cultures. Although the PSA was found to improve negotiation outcomes in U.S. negotiator dyads, this effect failed to generalize to British, French, and German dyads (Graham et al., 1988; Campbell, Graham, Jolibert, & Meissner, 1988). In addition, in one study, the PSA had a significant negative effect on outcomes for Chinese negotiators (Graham et al., 1988). These results might also be affected by the roles of the parties engaged in the negotiation. For example, in a negotiation simulation, Japanese buyers achieved a significantly higher profit than did Japanese sellers (Graham, 1983), and a similar result was found for Korean dyads (Graham et al., 1988). It seems, in these high-power-distance, high-context cultures, that the negotiators' behavior was significantly affected by their role. That is, in these cultures, sellers consistently defer to buyers, a norm that does not appear in low-power-distance, low-context cultures (Graham & Sanyo, 1984).

Implications

Taken as a whole, the research to date suggests that significant difficulties exist concerning generalization about the negotiation styles of different cultures. Some valuable prescriptions can be drawn from the experiences of effective negotiators in a particular culture (e.g., Pye, 1982; Tung, 1984). However, more general prescriptions that apply to a wide variety of cultures must be significantly more circumspect. The following points are based on the model of cross-cultural interactions presented in

Chapter 4 and what we have learned about cross-cultural communications and negotiations.

Anticipating Differences

Differences in communication and negotiation behavior across cultures should be anticipated. In addition to language differences, both the communication styles and negotiation styles of individuals, including the preference for conflict-resolution strategies, will likely vary across cultures. Substantial evidence documents these differences, and, in some cases, enough description might be available to construct a profile of the preferred style of the other culture. Also, although evidence is limited, it is reasonable to expect that these behavioral styles are consistent with the dominant cultural values of the country. Even so, this information must be treated with caution, because it is possible that individuals tend to change their behavior when interacting with members of another culture. In addition, the nonverbal component of the message, conveys a substantial amount of information (Gallois & Callan, 1997) and can be very difficult for an out-group member to correctly interpret. Because we selectively perceive based on understandings in our own culture (Markus & Zajonc, 1985), nonverbal cues that communicate an obvious message in one culture might be unnoticed or misinterpreted in another. In addition, cultural differences can influence more than just the behavior that conveys the message. As discussed in Chapter 4, the goals of the interaction, the underlying concept of what a negotiation is supposed to achieve, or both, can vary according to the culturally influenced motives of the individual. For example, studies of negotiators from individualist and collectivist cultures have documented individual-serving and group-serving motives, respectively (Tse, Francis, & Walls, 1994).

Attribution Accuracy

Self-reference in making attributions is unlikely to be accurate. The recommendation to expect differences in culturally different others made earlier assumes a degree of self-understanding. Understanding our own values, attitudes, and culturally based behavioral preferences can help in preventing the misattributions for culturally different behavior that are common in intercultural interactions (Cushner & Brislin, 1996). By recognizing that the communication or negotiation behavior we observe can have very different motives to our own, we can then try to accurately assess its cause. Ideally, managers would view the behavior from the perspective of the other culture. Practically, they might need to use informants with knowledge of the other culture to achieve a satisfactory understanding of the meaning of a particular behavior pattern or what Triandis (1972) calls "isomorphic attributions."

Adaptation

Adapting to the behavioral style of the other culture should be done with some caution. Prescriptions for effective negotiation that suggest adapting one's behavior to that of the other participant's culture are common. For example, Weiss (1994) suggests that negotiators have several options as to what behavioral style to use depending on the cultural knowledge of the parties involved. In general, the model suggests adapting to the party with the least cultural knowledge of the other, or in cases of low knowledge by both, employing a mediator. Although adaptation may have a positive effect based on similarity-attraction (Chapter 4), there is substantial evidence that high levels of both linguistic and stylistic adaptation lead to less positive responses. That is, there might be some optimal level of cultural adaptation, which is difficult to recognize until it has passed.

Context Factors

Focusing on the behavior of the other party may neglect other important consideration. In this chapter, cross-cultural communication formed the basis of the discussion of negotiating in an international context. As a result, the behavior of the participants to the negotiation process was emphasized. One evident issue is the difficulty in predicting the behavioral tactics of a negotiator from another culture. A practical implication is that managers might wish to focus more attention on those factors over which they can have more of an influence. These contextual factors include the relationship between the negotiating parties, the levels of trust among the negotiators, as well as a host of situational elements, such as the location of the negotiation, the physical characteristics of the negotiation venue, and the size and composition of the negotiation team. All of these contextual elements can have an important influence on the outcomes of the negotiation (Fayweather & Kapoor, 1972).

Summary

This chapter presented the behavioral aspects of international negotiation and its foundation in cross-cultural communication. Communication across cultures presents additional opportunities for messages to be misunderstood because of lack of common grounding. In addition, cross-cultural communication is significantly more demanding on both the sender and receiver of the message. Negotiation is a communication in which the parties have a need to reach an agreement, but have potentially conflicting interests. Consistent with variation in communication behavior, negotiators exhibit characteristic differences in terms of their preferred negotiating style, conflict-resolution preferences, and persuasion styles. Some evidence suggests that their behavior changes depending on whether the negotiation is within or across cultures. The lack of definitive research in this area suggests that prescriptions for improving negotiation across cultures might best be drawn from more general models of cross-cultural interactions.

Seven

The Manager as Leader:

The Leadership Role Across Cultures

Japanese and American management is 95% the same and differs in all important respects.

> T. Fujisawa, Cofounder, Honda Motor Company
> (as cited in Smith & Bond, 1999)

One of the most difficult tasks that international managers face is the need to motivate and lead individuals from different cultures. However, leadership is perhaps the most studied but least understood concept in management, and as yet, there is no theory of cross-cultural leadership grounded in research. This chapter examines concepts of leadership as developed in Western countries in terms of their applicability to other cultures. Then, examples of indigenous, non-Western theories of leadership are presented. Finally, this chapter presents a cross-cultural model of leadership that synthesizes some of the newest thinking on the topic. This model is consistent with the influence of social cognition in an intercultural interaction as presented in earlier chapters.

Leadership

Although the word *leadership* is a relatively new addition to the English language, evidence exists that the concept of leadership has existed throughout recorded history (Dorfman, 1996). Descriptions of great leaders are present in such culturally diverse manuscripts as Homer's *Iliad,* the Bible, and the writings of Confucius. Despite the thousands of research articles and books written on this subject, no generally accepted definition of leadership exists (Bass, 1990). Western definitions tend to focus on the ability of individuals to influence organization members toward the accomplishment of goals (Yukl, 1994a), and some international consensus seems to be building toward this definition (House, Wright, & Aditya, 1997). However, based on the discussion of systematic variations in values, attitudes, beliefs, and behavior across cultures presented earlier in this book, it seems likely that the meaning and importance of leadership varies across cultures. To examine the possible nature of this variation, a brief review of the development of leadership theory is helpful.

Western Leadership Theory

Leadership theory is often described as having progressed through four distinct periods, each with a dominant theoretical approach. These approaches are trait, behavioral, contingency, and implicit theories. Examples of each of these theoretical approaches and their applicability across cultures are presented in the following sections.

Trait Theories

Because the world has been greatly influenced by outstanding individuals, it is not surprising that the study of leadership began as a search for those personality characteristics possessed by great leaders. That is, what were the unique qualities that differentiated people from such diverse backgrounds as Winston Churchill, Mohandas Gandhi, Alexander the Great, Sun Tzu, and Miyamoto Musashi from their followers? These so-called great man theories of the early 1900s failed to stand up to scientific tests because of their inability to consistently identify traits that are necessary and sufficient for leadership success. However, we still do not know if there are certain traits that are universally important for leadership. Recent studies reveal that some individual traits are related to leader emergence and leader effectiveness (Dorfman, 1996). For example, although correlations between traits and leadership are moderate (Stogdill, 1974), leaders in Western cultures often exhibit high intelligence, dominance, self-confidence, integrity, energy levels, and task-relevant knowledge (Kirkpatrick & Locke, 1991). In addition, some research suggests that individuals who are flexible in adjusting their behavior to the situation, high self-monitors, are more likely to emerge as leaders (Dobbins, Long, Dedrick, & Clemons, 1990). However, there is also evidence to suggest that some of the traits thought to be important to leadership are culturally determined. For example, authoritarianism and dominance seem to be more acceptable in some developing countries (Tannenbaum, 1980) than in more developed countries like the United States. Also, the notion of self-monitoring is founded in how individuals define themselves and, as such, is influenced by cultural variation (Gudykunst, Gao, & Franklyn-Stokes, 1996). If the trait approach to leadership is to be validated, it is necessary to identify a consistent set of traits characteristic of successful leaders in all cultures. The inherent difficulty with predicting leadership success from such traits, coupled with the fact that these theories ignore both followers and the effects of differing situations, has led researchers in other directions in search of explanations of leadership. A comparison of leading examples of the major leadership theories with some applicability to the cross-cultural context is presented in Table 7.1

Behavioral Theories

Deficiencies in trait theories first led researchers to study the specific behaviors that leaders exhibited. This consisted of a shift in focus from what leaders are to what they actually do on the job. It also indicated a change in the assumption that leaders are born to the notion that leaders could be developed. The most well known of these research programs are the Ohio State University Studies (Fleishman, 1953) and the University of Michigan Studies (Bowers & Seashore, 1966). The Ohio State studies were responsible for defining two dimensions that accounted for most leader behavior described by subordinates. These dimensions, factor analyzed from an original list of over 1,000 behaviors, were called *initiating structure* and *consideration*. Initiating structure included such leader behaviors as assigning tasks to subordinates, coordinating activ-

TABLE 7.1 Major Leadership Theories

MODEL	LEADER BEHAVIORS	SITUATIONAL VARIABLES	OUTCOMES CRITERIA
Ohio State Leadership Studies	Initiating structure Consideration	None	Satisfaction Performance Grievances Turnover
Michigan Leadership Studies	Support Interaction facilitation Goal emphasis Work facilitation	None	Satisfaction Performance
Fiedler's Contingency Model	Task oriented (low LPC) Relationship oriented (high LPC)	Leader-member relations Task structure Position power	Performance
Vertical Dyad Linkage	Differential treatment of subordinates	Subordinate competence Subordinate loyalty	Satisfaction Performance
Transformational Leadership	Leader's personality	Subordinate trust and willingness to follow	Turnover Effectiveness
Substitutes for Leadership	Directive Supportive Participative Charismatic	Characteristics of the subordinate, task, or organization	Satisfaction Performance Commitment

SOURCE: Adapted from Dorfman, 1996.

ities, emphasizing deadlines, and evaluating subordinates' work. Consideration behaviors were those that showed concern for subordinates, such as showing regard for their feelings, respecting their ideas, and being friendly and supportive. Similarly, the University of Michigan studies identified two dimensions of leader behavior labeled *employee oriented* and *production oriented*. In general, the Ohio State studies suggested that, with some notable exceptions, leaders high on both initiating structure and consideration tended to achieve higher subordinate performance. However, the University of Michigan studies found that leaders who were employee oriented were associated with higher group productivity and group-member satisfaction.

Another popular representation of the two-dimensional approach to leadership is Blake and Mouton's (1964) managerial grid, which derived five leadership styles. Figure 7.1 depicts these leadership styles along the two dimensions of *Concern for People* and *Concern for Production*.

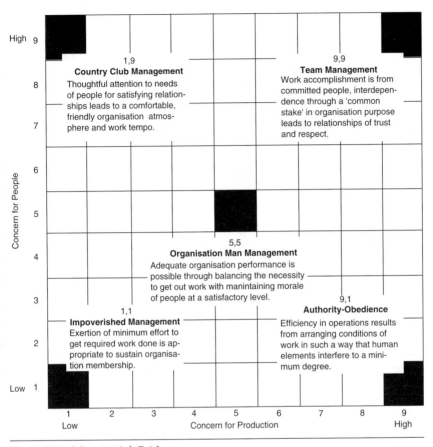

Figure 7.1. Managerial Grid
SOURCE: Reprinted by permission of *Harvard Business Review*. From "Breakthrough in Organization Development," by R. R. Blake, J. S. Mouton, L. B. Barnes, & L. E. Greiner, Vol. 6/1964. Copyright ©1964, Harvard Business School Publishing Corporation. All rights reserved.

Although the grid offers a framework for categorizing leadership styles, there is little evidence to support that the 9,9 (Team Management) leadership style is the most effective across situations (Larson, Hunt, & Osborn, 1974).

A number of cross-cultural studies have found that the two dimensions of leader behavior (task vs. relationship orientation) are important across cultures (e.g., Ah Chong & Thomas, 1997; Ayman & Chemers, 1983; Tscheulin, 1973). Studies using the two-dimensional approach have been conducted in dozens of different countries with the usual, and unsurprising, result that relationship-oriented leaders increase subordinates' satisfaction (Dorfman, 1996). However, the influence of task orientation is more complex across cultures and is not so simply explained. The sometimes-conflicting results found in different cultures for this dimension (e.g., Kakar, 1971; Kenis, 1977) suggest a culture-specific interpretation of task-oriented leadership (e.g., Ah Chong & Thomas, 1997; Howell, Dorfman, Hibino, Lee, & Tate, 1994). That is, although subordinates' response to relationship-oriented leadership might be somewhat consistent across cultures, responses to task-oriented behavior seem likely to be more highly variable depending on what cultures are involved. This finding, coupled with the fact that behavioral theories ignore the influence of subordinates and the situation, probably renders this approach much too simplistic to explain leader behavior in cross-cultural context. The notion that to be effective, leaders must adapt their behavior to the situation and the needs of their followers (Yukl & Van Fleet, 1992) can be even more important in cross-cultural situations.

Contingency Theories

This body of theory was developed in order to reconcile differences among the findings of behavioral approaches to leadership. The first, and most widely researched, contingency model of leadership is Fiedler's (1967) contingency model. The basic idea presented in this model is that the situation moderates the relationship between the leader's style and effectiveness. A leader's style (task- or relationship- oriented) is in effect an assessment of personality characteristics determined by responses on the least preferred coworker (LPC) scale. The situation is assessed for the quality of leader-member relations, degree of task structure, and the leader's position power. According to the theory, leaders cannot change their style, but the better the leader-member relationship, the more highly structured the task, and the stronger the position power, the more control the leader has (Fiedler, 1993). For example, task-oriented leaders perform best in situations in which they have very high or very low position power, and relationship-oriented leaders perform best in situations in which they have moderate position power.

Considerable criticism has been leveled at this theory both for how it is conceptualized (Schriesheim & Kerr, 1977) and for inconsistent findings (Yukl, 1989). However, there is a suggestion that by appropriately including cultural differences as part of the theory, it could prove to be universally applicable (Triandis, 1993).

A number of cross-cultural tests of the theory have been conducted. According to Fiedler (1966), initial tests of the theory in Holland and Belgium were very supportive of the model. The possible moderating role of culture was demonstrated in a study by Bennett (1977) in which high-performing Filipino managers were more task oriented and high-performing Chinese managers were more relationship oriented. Tests of the theory in Japan (Misumi, 1985; Misumi & Peterson, 1987) failed to find the proposed relationships between leadership types and LPC scores, and somewhat mixed support for the theory was found in a study in Mexico (Ayman & Chemers, 1991) by including self-monitoring as an additional leader characteristic. Although Fiedler's (1966) theory has clearly made an important contribution toward understanding leader effectiveness, its use as a cross-cultural theory awaits additional development.

Another significant development in response to conflicting results from behavioral approaches was path-goal theory (House, 1971; House & Mitchell, 1974). Path-goal theory identifies four leader behaviors and specifies a number of situational and follower characteristic moderators of the relationship between leader style and follower satisfaction and performance. Figure 7.2 illustrates the relationships among these elements and Box 7.1 gives some examples of predictions developed from path-goal theory.

Research has generally shown good support for the predictability of the theory, but some predictions have not been supported (Indvik, 1986). In addition, because the theory is complex, it might not have been adequately tested (House & Aditya, 1997; Schriesheim & Kerr, 1977). Regardless, it provides a good basis for considering a number of moderators in the study of leadership (Yukl, 1994b). Because culture might be considered a key situational moderator, it could serve as a platform for considering the moderating effect of culture on the relationship between leader behavior and outcomes (Triandis, 1993).

An idea related to path-goal theory is that the attributes of situations and the characteristics of subordinates could enhance, neutralize, or substitute for some leadership behaviors. So-called leadership substitutes theory (Howell, Dorfman, & Kerr, 1986; Kerr & Jermier, 1978) suggests, for example, that characteristics of subordinates, such as their professionalism, can act as substitutes for such leader behavior as being "directive" while actually enhancing the effect of other types of leader behavior, such as being "supportive" (Dorfman, 1996). Some support exists for the main propositions of the theory (Yukl, 1994a). In addition, it seems that some leader substitutes, such as workers' professionalism and their work experience, are applicable in a number of countries

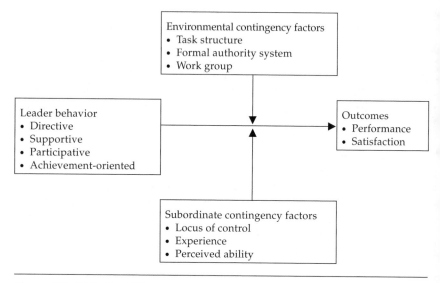

Figure 7.2. Path-Goal Theory
SOURCE: Based on House, 1971.

(Howell et al., 1994). However, contradictory results have also been found, and the cross-cultural applicability of the idea of substitutes for leadership has yet to be fully tested (Misumi & Peterson, 1985).

Implicit Theories

Implicit theories of leadership define leadership as the process of being perceived as a leader (Lord & Maher, 1991). According to the theory, followers develop mental representations or prototypes of leaders through exposure to social situations and interactions with others (Lord, Foti, & DeVader, 1984). After the formation of this leader prototype, individuals are perceived as leaders by the extent to which their behavior matches the behavior expected of a prototypical leader. That is, specific leader behaviors do not make a person a leader unless that person is perceived as a leader by followers. A number of laboratory studies supported the notion that leaders who meet the expectations of followers for leader behavior were more likely to be described as leaders (Lord et al., 1984; Lord & Maher, 1991). This idea has been extended across cultures to show that individuals from different cultures can have different leader prototypes (Ah Chong & Thomas, 1997; O'Connell, Lord, & O'Connell,

BOX 7.1

Examples of Hypotheses That Have Evolved out of Path-Goal Theory

- Directive leadership leads to greater satisfaction when tasks are ambiguous or stressful than when they are highly structured and well laid out.

- Supportive leadership results in high employee performance and satisfaction when subordinates are performing structured tasks.

- Directive leadership is likely to be perceived as redundant among subordinates with high-perceived ability or with considerable experience.

- The more clear and bureaucratic the formal authority relationships, the more leaders should exhibit supportive behavior and de-emphasize directive behavior.

- Directive leadership will lead to higher employee satisfaction when there is substantive conflict within a work group.

- Subordinates with an internal locus of control (those who believe they control their own destiny) will be more satisfied with a participative style. Subordinates with an external locus of control will be more satisfied with a directive style.

- Achievement-oriented leadership will increase subordinates' expectancies that effort will lead to high performance when tasks are ambiguously structured.

SOURCE: From *Essentials of Organizational Behavior, Third Edition*, by Robbins, S. P. Copyright ©1992. Reprinted by permission of Prentice-Hall, Inc., Upper Saddle River, NJ.

1990) and that meeting followers' expectations of leader behavior can result in higher perceptions of trust and leader effectiveness (Thomas & Ravlin, 1995). Although these results suggest culturally specific expectations of leadership, it is also possible that there are some universally endorsed attributes and behaviors that comprise implicit leadership. An example of this possibility is charismatic or transformational theories of leadership (Bass, 1985; Burns, 1978; Conger & Kanungo, 1988; House, 1977).

Charismatic or transformational leaders are those leaders who are able to inspire their followers to transcend their own self-interests for the good of the organization. As noted in the beginning of this chapter, examples of these leaders are to be found in all cultures. They have an extraordinary effect on followers, which garners the followers' admiration, respect, trust, commitment, dedication, and loyalty. In order to have this effect, followers must attribute extraordinary leadership abilities to those people who exhibit certain behaviors. Several studies have tried to identify those traits or behaviors that are characteristic of charismatic leaders (Bennis, 1984; Conger & Kanungo, 1987; House, 1977). They concluded that charismatic leaders are self-confident, have an idealized goal or vision, are very committed to that goal, and are perceived as unconventional and agents of radical change. Box 7.2 presents a summary of the characteristics of charismatic leaders.

Proponents of these theories (e.g., Bass, 1991; House, 1991) argue that charismatic leaders are more effective than noncharismatic leaders regardless of culture. Indeed, a number of studies show a nearly universal relationship for charismatic leadership across cultures (Dorfman, 1996). However, a few recent studies suggest that culture does influence the charismatic leadership process. For example, results from the Dominican Republic (Echavarria & Davis, 1994), the Netherlands (Hartog, Van Muijen, & Koopman, 1994), and Singapore (Koh, 1990) suggest that although the concept of a charismatic leader might be universal, the way such a leader is described by followers can differ markedly. Other evidence suggests that this model of leadership might not hold for some unique cultures such as Japan (Bass, 1991; Howell et al., 1994). In addition, the effect of charismatic leadership has been found to be stronger for people from the United States than for Mexicans (Howell & Dorfman, 1988), indicating that cultural differences might influence the effectiveness of the transformational or charismatic approach. Although encouraging as a potential pan-cultural theory, these results indicate the need for more research before the precise influence of culture on the mechanisms through which charismatic leaders influence followers can be specified.

Non-Western Theories of Leadership

This review of the cross-cultural applicability of leadership theory as developed in the West suggests that although some applicability to other cultures has been found, they are largely inadequate to explain or predict leadership across cultures. An alternative to trying to determine the boundaries or contingencies associated with these theories is to examine leadership theories that are indigenous to non-Western cultures. The following section describes two theories of leadership, one developed in Japan and the other in Arab societies.

BOX 7.2

Characteristics of Charismatic Leaders

1. *Self-confidence.* They have complete confidence in their judgment and ability.

2. *A vision.* This is an idealized goal that proposes a future better than the status quo. The greater the disparity between *this* idealized goal and the status quo, the more likely that followers will attribute extraordinary vision to the leader.

3. *Ability to articulate the vision.* They are able to clarify and state the vision in terms that are understandable to others. This articulation demonstrates an understanding of the followers' needs and, hence, acts as a motivating force.

4. *Strong convictions about the vision.* Charismatic leaders are perceived as being strongly committed, and willing to take on high personal risk, incur high costs, and engage in self-sacrifice to achieve their vision.

5. *Behavior that is out of the ordinary.* Those with charisma engage in behavior that is perceived as being novel, unconventional, and counter to norms. When successful, these behaviors evoke surprise and admiration in followers.

6. *Perceived as being a change agent.* Charismatic leaders are perceived as agents of radical change rather than as caretakers of the status quo.

7. *Environment sensitivity.* These leaders are able to make realistic assessments of the environmental constraints and resources needed to bring about change.

SOURCE: Adapted from *Charismatic Leadership: The Elusive Factor in Organizational Effectiveness*, by Conger, J. A., & Kanungo, R. Copyright ©1988. Reprinted by permission of John Wiley and Sons, Inc.

Leadership in Japan

Descriptions of Japanese management practices abound. However, the systematic evaluation of leadership behavior in this culture, which is governed more by group norms than individual direction, is rare. An exception is a theory influenced by Western conceptions of leadership but developed over 40 years of extensive research in Japan. Misumi's

(1985) Performance-Maintenance (PM) theory identifies four types of leaders based on two basic dimensions of leadership—performance or maintenance. The Performance dimension (P) describes behavior directed toward achieving group goals and includes pressure-type and planning-type behavior. Pressure-type behavior is described by Misumi (1985, pp. 34-35) as "supervisory behavior regarding strict observance of regulations and pressure for production," whereas planning-type behaviors "concern the planning and processing of work." The Maintenance dimension (M) relates to behavior directed at group maintenance and preservation. These dimensions are conceptually similar to the task-oriented and relationship-oriented dimensions found in Western theories of leadership. However, the theory differs in some significant ways from traditional leadership theory (Peterson, 1988). The P and M dimensions are concerned with behavior as experienced by followers and can therefore differ according to the context in which the behavior takes place. That is, certain factors that represent M in Japan would seem inappropriate to followers in a Western culture, such as the United States. For example, discussing an employee's personal problems with other organization members in that employee's absence is consistent with a Japanese manager who would be highly rated on the Maintenance factor (Smith, Misumi, Tayeb, Peterson, & Bond, 1989). Also, some P-type behaviors, such as "your supervisor is strict about the work you do," "your supervisor is strict about observing regulations," and "your supervisor makes you work to your maximum capacity," might carry less positive connotations outside Japanese culture (Dorfman, 1996). Misumi's (1985) theory also treats the two leadership dimensions as complementary. That is, to be effective, Japanese managers must emphasize both P and M such that a manager rated by followers as high on both (PM) would be more effective than a manager rated high on one behavior and low on the other (Pm or pM) or low on both (pm). For example, a P-type behavior exhibited by a manager rated high on M would be perceived by followers as reflecting "planning." The same behavior performed by a manager who was low on M would be perceived as "pressure." It is possible that leaders who emphasize both P- and M-type behaviors are effective in some Asian cultures because the M gives followers the feeling that they are members of the leader's in-group and the P behaviors lead to high performance beneficial to all group members (Hui, 1990).

   Tests of PM theory outside Japan lend support to the idea that both culture-free and culture-specific leadership behaviors can exist (e.g., Peterson, Smith & Tayeb, 1993). That is, although the broad dimensions of Performance and Maintenance seem to be applicable across cultures (Smith, Peterson, Bond, & Misumi, 1992), the specific leader behaviors perceived by followers to indicate these dimensions seem, at least to some extent, to vary across cultures. Additional research indicates that the Performance (P) or task-oriented dimension is the most susceptible to the influence of a specific cultural interpretation (Ah Chong & Thomas, 1997; Peterson et al., 1993).

Leadership in the Arab World

Leadership behavior in Arab societies is strongly influenced by the Islamic religion and tribal traditions, as well as by contact with Western culture (Ali, 1990). The tribal influence is evident because managers are expected to behave like fathers. That is, their roles include protecting and caring for employees, as well as having overall responsibility for the business. Overlaying this tribal influence is the legacy of a rigid bureaucracy introduced during rule by the Ottoman Empire (late 13th century until the end of WWI) and Europeans. The combination of these tribal norms with bureaucratic structures resulted in an authoritarian and patriarchal approach to leadership called "sheikocracy" (Al-Kubaisy, 1985). This style is characterized by hierarchical authority, subordination of efficacy to human relations and personal connections, and conformity to rules and regulations based on the personality and power of those who made them. The combination of this leadership style with influences from Western management practices has produced a "duality" in Arab managers who want to be modern by adopting Western practices but simultaneously wish to maintain tradition. According to Ali (1990), this duality results in leadership behaviors such as creating numerous rules and regulations without making any attempt to implement them; creating selection and promotion systems based on performance, but selecting and promoting based on personal relationships and family and social ties; and paying people from powerful families who are not required to report for work.

The "prophetic-caliphal" model of leadership developed by Khadra (1990) typifies this duality of relationships prevalent in Arab culture. The model specifies two distinctly different leadership types that can emerge to fill the leadership vacuum created by the lack of institutionalism prevalent in Arab society. According to the theory, the very existence of the rational bureaucratic procedures of institutions is undermined by the prevalence of two societal characteristics called individualism and personalism. Individualism, in this case, refers to the tendency to make decisions without considering the opinions of others. Personalism involves viewing one's relationship to others from an egocentric perspective in which one's own set of needs dominates. There is a strong predisposition in Arab society for a great man or "prophetic" leader to emerge to fill the leadership vacuum. If such a prophetic leader emerges, indicated by the ability to accomplish some great feat, he will garner feelings of love, unity of purpose, and voluntary submission to authority by followers. If, however, an ordinary or "caliphal" leader emerges, conflict and strife will result, and he must use coercion and fear in order to maintain his status as a leader. Although the prophetic-caliphal model has yet to be broadly tested, Khadra (1990) presents substantial evidence that the basic premise of the model makes sense to Arab managers. In addition, this model appears to have many consistencies with the notions of charismatic leadership developed in the West.

The preceding sections indicate that there is certainly no lack of theories of leadership from which to choose. Both traditional and indigenous theories provide useful insights into the process of leadership in a cross-cultural context. Yet, no single theoretical perspective is adequate to explain and predict the complexities of leadership in the international context. The following section presents a model that synthesizes much of what we know about cross-cultural leadership to derive implications for today's manager.

Integrated Cross-Cultural Model of Leadership

The model of leadership presented in Figure 7.3 is grounded in work by Dorfman (1996), Erez and Earley (1993), and Yukl (1989) and is consistent with the emphasis on social cognition taken in this book. That is, it has as its basis a cognitive information processing approach to leadership.

This approach is similar to the implicit theories presented previously, in that the ability of the leader to influence others is largely dependent on presenting an image consistent with followers' expectations of a leader. The three key elements of the theory—leader image, follower and group characteristics, and substitutes for leadership—are all affected by cultural variation. That is, culture is considered an all-encompassing or enveloping influence on leadership processes (Dorfman, 1996). For example, cultural differences influence the conceptions that people have of an ideal leader. This culturally determined image defines the behavior required to be perceived as a leader by followers. For example, Pacific Islanders expect leaders to give specific instructions and orders and to insist on adherence to rules and regulations, whereas these same behaviors would not portray an ideal image in Anglo-European culture (Ah Chong & Thomas, 1997). In addition, consistent with the model presented in Chapter 4, the interpersonal interactions between the leader and follow-

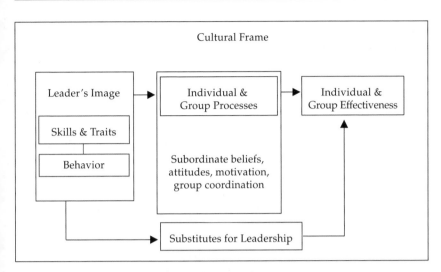

Figure 7.3. Cross-Cultural Model of Leadership
SOURCE: Adapted from Dorfman, 1996; Erez & Earley, 1993; Yukl, 1989.

ers are subject to cultural influence. For example, authoritarian leadership approaches are likely to be more acceptable in high-power-distance cultures, and the relationship of the leader to the group will likely vary along the cultural dimensions of individualism and collectivism. Situational moderators of various types act as substitutes for particular leadership behavior in a number of cultures (Howell et al., 1994). As discussed earlier, culture can be viewed as an underlying factor that determines the nature of the situational characteristics that will act as effective substitutes for leadership. For example, the technical expertise of followers is, in part, a result of the orientation of a particular society toward education. Finally, the outcomes of leadership are also embedded in a cultural context, in that the evaluation of leader effectiveness can be primarily based on either the performance of individuals or groups. For example, in collectivist cultures, individual performance that does not contribute to group harmony and cohesiveness might not be evaluated positively (Dorfman, 1996).

Implications for the Practice of Leadership

The early stage of development of cross-cultural theories of leadership raises the question of what practical value these theories hold for management. The following ideas are based on the cross-cultural model presented previously as well as the empirical evidence presented earlier in this chapter.

Universal Leadership Functions

The general functions of leadership are probably universal across cultures. Substantial evidence in a variety of cultures supports the idea of two dimensions of leadership. Leadership in a number of cultures is categorized as concerned with the task, with the relationship with members, or both (e.g., Ah Chong & Thomas, 1997; Smith et al., 1989). In a study of 12 different countries, Bass, Burger, Doktor, and Barrett (1979) found that managers, regardless of culture, indicated a desire to get things done while using less authority. In addition, Smith and Peterson (1994) found that managers in 25 countries reported more satisfaction for activities in which they had higher discretion. Bass (1997) makes a powerful argument for the universality of the main components of transformational leadership. That is, these leaders, regardless of culture, have a vision, are able to inspire followers to work toward that vision, and are able to organize the activities of followers to keep them focused. Transformational leadership has been found to exist and be effective in a number of different countries (House et al., 1997). It seems, therefore, that leaders in all cultures have certain characteristics or exhibit certain behaviors that allow them to be regarded as leaders by their followers. However, as discussed subsequently, it is likely that the specific behaviors that are appropriate for different cultures will be highly variable.

Culture-Specific Leader Behaviors

Culture seems to affect the type of leader behavior accepted and effective in a given society. In general, research has indicated that the leadership styles across cultures are consistent with the dominant cultural values of the country (Jackofsky, Slocum, & McQuaid, 1988). In addition, earlier in this chapter, examples of indigenous approaches to leadership were presented. The integrated model shown previously (Figure 7.3) suggests that leader behavior consistent with what followers expect will be more likely to result in an individual being perceived as a leader and, therefore, make that individual more effective. Considerable evidence suggests that being perceived as a leader and meeting followers' expectations result in greater leader effectiveness (e.g., Lord et al., 1984; Thomas & Ravlin, 1995). For example, the direct assertive behavior of John F. Kennedy and Martin Luther King, Jr. was very different from the quiet, nonaggressive styles of Mahatma Gandhi and Nelson Mandela. However, all could properly be categorized as effective transformational leaders in their respective cultures. In addition, recent research indicates that the specific behaviors that indicate a particular leadership dimension are contingent on culture. For example, specific behaviors considered either task or relationship oriented by followers differ in ways consistent with the cultural setting. For example, being perceived as treating people fairly is an important leadership characteristic in both Polynesian and Anglo-European culture. However, the specific behavior that indicates fair treatment can be very different for each cultural group (Ah Chong & Thomas, 1997). Therefore, regardless of whether a more traditional behavioral or newer transformational approaches to understanding leadership are taken, it seems that differences in the cultural setting must be taken into account in determining who is likely to be perceived as a leader and what leader behavior is most likely to be effective.

Situational Moderators

The characteristics of the situation influence, to varying degrees, the extent to which leadership can make a difference. A number of the theoretical approaches reviewed in this chapter recognize that leadership is situation specific. Under certain circumstances, the characteristics of the situation might constrain the leader's ability to have very much of an effect on followers. That is, leaders are always under pressure to conform to the social situation in which they must operate. As noted in Chapter 1, the behavior that managers exhibit is determined in part by the expectations for behavior that are sent by their superiors, their peers, and their followers. In addition, many of the factors that influence the performance of followers, such as organizational policies and procedures, are outside of a manager's control. For example, research on charismatic leaders (Conger & Kanungo, 1988) indicates this type of leader is most likely to emerge during periods of rapid growth, change, or crisis.

In addition, different cultures tend to place different degrees of importance on the role of leadership. In the United States, leaders in corporations are often paid many times the salary of those in nonleadership roles, indicating a belief that leaders do indeed make a difference. Typical of an individualist culture, in mainstream New Zealand, the search for the cause of an event more often than not leads to the individual who was in charge. In contrast, Maori (indigenous New Zealanders) leaders often regard themselves as representatives of work groups as opposed to authority figures and face a dual obligation to both the *iwi* or tribal group and the work situation (Reichers, 1986).

Summary: Leadership in an Intercultural Interaction

This chapter illuminates the concept of leadership from a cross-cultural perspective by presenting traditional theories of leadership and their application across cultures. In addition, examples of indigenous non-Western theories of leadership were explored. Finally, the chapter introduces an integrative model of cross-cultural leadership and implications for managers of what we know. This model highlights one of the most important, but rarely addressed aspects of leadership: the question of how to best manage the interaction between leaders and managers who are culturally different. Very little research exists to address this question, which is a very salient issue for managers faced with a culturally diverse workforce. The few studies conducted (Ah Chong & Thomas, 1997; Peterson, Brannen, & Smith, 1994; Thomas & Ravlin, 1995) suggest two important considerations. First, followers are likely to have an expectation of leadership behavior based on the leader's culture. For example, some research indicates that U.S. subordinates of Japanese managers expect them to be strongly task oriented (Smith et al., 1992). Second, like communication and negotiation behavior, adapting leader behavior to be more like that typical of the followers' culture is risky. For example, Thomas and Ravlin (1995) found that such adaptation of behaviors characteristic of the followers' culture was effective only to the extent that this behavior was perceived as genuine by followers. Therefore, one might adapt too much to the followers' culture. The logical conclusion from this limited evidence is that managers seeking to be favorably perceived need to exercise care in choosing which leader behaviors of a culture to emulate. The best model for leader behavior is probably not a manager from the indigenous culture but another manager of one's own culture who is particularly effective.

Section III
International Management Challenges

Eight

The Challenge of Multicultural Work Groups and Teams

When we sit together as Germans, Swiss, Americans, and Swedes, with many of us living, working, traveling in different places, the insights can be remarkable. But, you have to force people into these situations. Mixing nationalities just doesn't happen.

Percy Barnevik (as cited in Taylor, 1991)
Former CEO of Asea Brown Boveri

Groups are a part of almost every organization, and as jobs become more complex, groups will accomplish more of the world's work. Group behavior is more than the sum total of each individual acting in their own way. When people must work together in groups to perform a task, the cultural differences among group members often become more apparent. Because of the reality of a multicultural workforce in most industrialized countries, managers are now more than ever faced with the task of managing work groups composed of culturally different members. In addition, as geographic boundaries become less important in business, managers are finding themselves involved in work groups composed of culturally different members. This chapter explores the influence of cultural diversity on the functioning of work groups and the role that managers can play in getting the most from, and as members of, these groups.

Work Groups

Although people join various groups, both formal and informal, for reasons as varied as their security, their need for affiliation, to enhance their status, and to maintain their self-esteem, the types of work groups that are of most concern to managers have some specific characteristics. Three distinctive characteristics of work groups in organizations have been identified (Hackman, 1991). First, work groups are social systems that have boundaries with members who have different roles and are dependent on each other (Aldefer, 1977). That is, both people within the group and those on the outside will recognize the group's existence and which individuals are members and which are not. Second, these groups have a task to perform. Finally, work groups function within an organizational context. That is, the group exists only within and as part of a larger organization.

Because of the popularity of team-based management techniques (Hoerr, 1989), there is a tendency by some authors to treat all work groups as teams. Although all work groups have the characteristics just noted, not all work groups are teams. A useful categorization of work-group types by Arrow and McGrath (1995) makes a distinction among three primary types of work groups. That is, work groups in organizations are classified as task forces, crews, or teams. Task forces focus on the completion of a specific project typically within a limited time frame. The group comes together for the length of time required, and members are selected based on the task-related skills required by the group. A group of bankers designing a new money market instrument is an example. Crews, in contrast, focus on the tools required in the performance of the task, and the appropriate interaction with, or use of, a tool specifies the interaction among group members. Tools are defined broadly to include a wide variety of task-related implements or devices. For example, airline flight deck crews interact with each other in a very regimented way as dictated by the requirements of effectively operating the aircraft. That is, the flight deck crew of one 747 will behave in very much the same way as any other flight deck crew during routine operations. By contrast, organizational teams focus on the interrelationships among the group members. These teams are sets of people with specific skills and abilities who are provided with tools and procedures to address certain sets of tasks over a long period of time.

These differences in work-group types highlight the need to recognize the structure of the work group in trying to explain and predict the behavior of different organizational groups. However, as discussed in the following section, to understand work-group effectiveness, the group structure must be considered in concert with other group characteristics. This is especially true when the group is composed of members from different cultures.

Work-Group Effectiveness

Narrowly defined, effectiveness of a work group depends on how well the group uses its resources to accomplish its task. However, not all organizational tasks have clearly defined correct or even best answers. The long-term effectiveness of a work group might not be assessed accurately by considering only how it is performing at a single point in time. Therefore, a broader definition of work-group effectiveness that more accurately portrays whether a work group is functioning well in an organization is suggested (Hackman, 1991). First, the output of the group must meet the quantity, quality, and timeliness standards of the organization. Second, the processes employed by the group should enhance the ability of the group members to work together. Finally, the group experience should contribute to the growth and personal well-being of the group members. This broader definition encourages a longer-term view of work-group effectiveness consistent with the requirement that work groups function within the confines of the larger organization.

To specify the relationship of culture to group effectiveness, it is first necessary to identify the underlying dynamics of work groups. Group dynamics are complex, and research has produced a number of group process models. Here, a model (shown in Figure 8.1) based on the work of Goodman et al. (1987) and Helmreich and Schaefer (1994) identifies six sets of variables that influence the process and performance of work groups. These variables are the following:

1. the external or contextual conditions imposed on the group,

2. the resources of group members,

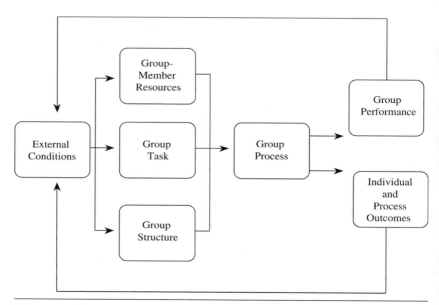

Figure 8.1. Group Process Model
SOURCE: Based on Goodman, Ravlin, & Schminke, 1987; Helmreich & Schaefer, 1994.

3. the structure of the group,

4. the group task,

5. the group process, and

6. the composition of the group.

Although international managers might be most concerned with the cultural composition of the group, this factor cannot be understood in isolation and must be considered in the context of the dynamics of the group. Each of the six sets of variables that affect group processes and performance are discussed briefly in the following sections.

External Conditions

Part of group behavior is determined by the larger organization to which the group belongs (Friedlander, 1989). The strategy of the organization, the authority structures, and regulations employed to implement that strategy determine which groups in organizations get resources and dictate the type of behavior that receives rewards. Research indicates that contextual factors influence both the productivity of work groups and employee satisfaction with the group (Campion, Medsker, & Higgs, 1993). Obviously, large profitable organizations can provide more resources for any type of group that is consistent with the organizational strategy and culture. In addition, the composition of the group is dependent on the selection process of the organization, as group members must first be organization members. This selection process is critical in determining the skills, attitudes, values, and beliefs that organization members bring to work groups.

Group-Member Resources

Group members bring two types of resources to groups: personal attributes, including personality, values, and attitudes, and their skills and abilities, both technical and social. In general, and as one might expect, member skills and abilities are positively related to group performance (Szilagyi & Wallace, 1987).

No single personal attribute has been found to facilitate group performance, and little research has examined the relationship between personality and group dynamics (Hoyle & Crawford, 1994). However, some evidence exists to suggest that the characteristics of individuals in groups influence the overall affective tone, or climate, of the group. This, in turn, relates to the extent to which the group engages in prosocial behavior (George, 1990). Moreover, some research argues that personality variables can be powerful predictors of some group outcomes, such as innovation (Bunce & West, 1995). A group member's culture can be considered a personal attribute but can also be task related, as discussed later in this chapter.

Group Structure

As noted earlier, work groups can be categorized as task forces, crews, or teams. Each of these structures shapes the behavior of group members by prescribing the norms, role expectations, and status relationships shared by group members. Of particular importance to the effectiveness of work groups are the norms associated with processes related to task performance (Goodman et al., 1987). These norms specify such things as what methods and channels of communication are important, the level of individual effort expected, and also provide group members with explicit guidance as to how to accomplish the task.

Although all groups share the same types of norms, the norms for a particular group are unique. Group norms can come from explicit statements made by group members, critical incidents in the group's history, an early behavior that emerges and persists, and from other previous group situations (Feldman, 1984). As discussed later in this chapter, group members from different cultures can differ in the source of their normative beliefs of how groups should function because of differences in their prior group experience.

Group-member roles are affected by the conflict created in the process of role assignment (Moreland & Levine, 1982). This is the conflict created by differing opinions about who should assume a role or how it should be played. Some anecdotal evidence suggests that cultural difference in preferences for different roles in multicultural groups exists (Schneider & Barsoux, 1997). Generally, examinations of the effect of role conflict have indicated a negative relationship to group effectiveness (Jackson & Schuler, 1985). However, as noted later in this chapter, not all conflict within a group has negative results.

The effect of status systems in groups can be summarized in three categories. First is the effect of a person's status on his or her relationship with other group members. Second is the effect of a group member's status on his or her evaluation by others. Third is the effect of status on a group member's self-esteem. In general, group members with higher status are more influential in the group, are evaluated more positively, and have higher self-esteem than group members with lower status (Ravlin, Thomas, & Ilsev, 2000).

Group Process

Because groups form their own social systems, the outcomes of work groups are not the same as the sum of their individual members' efforts. When group processes such as communication patterns, decision processes, and conflict reactions cause a group to fail to meet its potential, it has suffered a process loss. When the efforts of the group exceed that of individual members, a process gain or synergy is experienced. This simple formula for group effectiveness is shown graphically in Figure 8.2.

Examples of process losses include "groupthink," in which the norm for group consensus overrides the motivation to realistically appraise alternative courses of action (Janis, 1982), and "social loafing," in which individuals reduce their effort on group tasks (Thomas & Fink, 1963). As discussed in more detail later in this chapter, some process losses are dramatically influenced by cultural differences (Earley, 1989).

Figure 8.2. Group Effectiveness Model

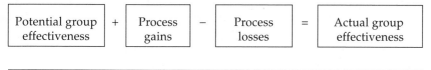

| Potential group effectiveness | + | Process gains | – | Process losses | = | Actual group effectiveness |

Group Processes Over Time

An additional element of group processes is the changes that groups go through over time. Early in the study of group process, Tuckman (1965) proposed that all groups go through five stages called *forming, storming, norming, performing,* and *adjourning.* In the first, or *forming* stage, group members just begin to think of themselves as part of a group and might be uncertain about the group and how they fit into it. In the second, or so-called *storming* stage, the characteristics, attitudes, and expectations of individuals come into conflict with the structure of the group. In the third, or *norming* stage, the group agrees on the expectations that specify the acceptable behavior (norms) of the group. In the fourth, or *performing* stage, the efforts of the group shift to accomplishing the task at hand. As noted previously, some work groups, such as teams, would remain in this stage. Task forces and crews would proceed to the fifth, or *adjourning* stage, once the task was completed. Although this model of group development is informative, research suggests that groups do not necessarily proceed sequentially from one stage to the next and that several stages can occur at the same time (Gersick, 1988). In addition, groups can revert to prior stages.

For groups that have a deadline for the accomplishment of their task, another development model called the punctuated equilibrium model (Gersick, 1989) might be more helpful. In this group development model, the group sets its direction at the first meeting, and this pattern of behavior and approach to the task become firmly adhered to for the first one-half of the group's existence. Although group members might have alternative ideas about the group process, the group is often unable to act on these ideas. Despite the length of time the group has to complete the task, a transition seems to occur at about the midway point between the first meeting and the official deadline. At this point, the group seems to get a wake-up call and drops the previous patterns of behavior and perspectives in favor of a new direction and enhanced activity. Following the transition, another period of equilibrium ensues and the group focuses on implementing the direction set during the transition. At the final meeting of the group, a flurry of activity occurs as the group members press each other to make their contribution to accomplish the task. When combined with the five-stage model, these ideas are valuable to understanding how groups progress over time. An obvious limitation in multicultural groups, however, is the well-established cultural variation in orientations toward time (Boyacigiller & Adler, 1991).

Group Task

The nature of the tasks in which the work group is engaged influences both the processes and outcomes of the group (Goodman, 1986). Jackson (1992) provides a useful classification of group tasks into three primary types: clearly defined production tasks, cognitive or intellective tasks, and creative idea generation and decision-making tasks. Production tasks require motor skills, and some objective standard of performance is assumed to exist. Intellective tasks are problem-solving tasks with a correct answer, whereas decision-making tasks are involved with reaching consensus on the best solution to a problem. In simple routine production tasks, group processes, such as communication, are less important. Therefore, in this type of task, a work group with *potentially* high process losses might still be effective. However, the same group involved in a problem-solving task might suffer the negative effects of those more important process activities. Because intellective tasks (that is, tasks with objectively correct answers) rarely exist in organizations, this type of task has few implications for managers and is not discussed further.

Group Composition

Members of work groups might be similar or different on a number of different dimensions (e.g., gender, age, experience, nationality) important to the performance of the group. Although the focus in this chapter is the cultural composition of groups, research on other dimensions of similarity and difference can shed light on how group composition influences group processes and outcomes. For the purpose of this discussion, group composition can be classified as homogeneous on a particular dimension, heterogeneous on that dimension, or minority-majority. Minority-majority groups consist of groups in which one or a few members are different on the dimension of interest. A single U.S. person in a group of Japanese would be a minority-majority group on the dimension of nationality, whereas a group of all Japanese would be classified as homogeneous on that dimension, and a group with a variety of nationalities would be heterogeneous. Research on the effect of group composition on work-group outcomes has, in many instances, focused on a comparison of homogeneous and heterogeneous groups. Results of this comparison have been mixed. Heterogeneity in observable attributes is generally found to have a negative effect on affective outcomes, such as identification with the group and satisfaction (Milliken & Martins, 1996). In addition, group heterogeneity on underlying attributes, such as skills and tenure in the organization, have a direct relationship to the level of process losses suffered by the group (Milliken & Martins, 1996; Steiner, 1972). However, group heterogeneity on task-related abilities and skills is typically shown to be positively related to group performance on both types of tasks typically found in organizations (Jackson, 1992). In summary, heterogeneous work groups probably have a higher performance potential but also a higher tendency to suffer process losses. Also, however, recent research (e.g., Jehn, Northcraft, & Neale, 1999) emphasizes the need to consider that different types of diversity have different effects on group processes and performance.

Research on the special case of minority-majority groups has tended to focus on the influence of minority members on the majority. For example, research by a number of researchers found that minority members can influence the majority if they are consistent and persistent in their arguments (Nemeth, 1992). However, other research suggests that by expressing alternative views, minority members can improve the decision making and performance of the group by increasing the group's attention to the process of decision making (Nemeth, 1992).

Culture's Influence on Work Groups

Based on the general model of work-group functioning described earlier, it is possible to examine the way in which culture influences work-group processes and function. As suggested earlier, this influence is perhaps most apparent in the cultural composition of the work group. However, the organizational context in which the group functions, the work-group structure, and the task in which the group is involved also influence the extent to which cultural differences affect work-group outcomes.

The cultural composition of work groups affects the way they function through three mechanisms:

(a) cultural norms—the orientations of the specific cultures represented in the group toward the functioning of groups,

(b) cultural diversity—the number of different cultures represented in the group, and

(c) relative cultural distance—the extent to which group members are culturally different from each other.

These mechanisms are interrelated, but each affects the way groups operate in a different way.

Cultural Norms

One of the most important influences on group effectiveness is the mix of cultural norms represented in the work group. Different cultures have very different orientations toward what is appropriate in terms of work-group function and structure (Thomas et al., 1996). These beliefs are not checked at the workplace door but spill over into the workplace. For example, many collectivist cultures believe that maintaining a sense of harmony is extremely important in interpersonal interactions. This contrasts dramatically with notions of constructive conflict and devil's advocacy popular in some individualist cultures like the United States. A number of studies support the idea that individuals bring a mental representation (script) to the work group with which they interpret events, behaviors, expectations, and other group members. For example, studies show that group members initially base their actions on their previous experiences in other groups. In one such study, members of new groups who previously developed norms for cooperation acted co-operatively in a subsequent similar situation (Bettenhausen & Murnighan, 1991). Evidence also exists that people with different cultural orientations have different views of what are appropriate group processes. For example, the task-related norms of a group might be set based on the individual cultural backgrounds of group members (Hackman & Morris, 1978). In addition, one study (Earley, 1989) found that individuals from a collectivist culture were less likely to engage in social loafing than were members from a more individualist culture. The reason that social loafing does not occur among collectivists is that they bring their norms for placing group goals ahead of their own interest to the work-group situation. By contrast, the motivation for personal gain of individualists also carries over into the work-group setting.

In summary, like other behavioral norms, the norms for interacting in a group can vary according to culture. Although the norms for any work group are unique, one of the bases for these norms in all groups is the individuals' previous group experience (Feldman, 1984). Therefore, in multicultural work groups, individuals from different cultures are likely to have very different ideas, at least initially, about how the work group should go about its task, how they should behave, and how they should interact with other group members.

Cultural Diversity

A second influence on work-group effectiveness is the number of different cultures represented in the group—its cultural diversity. Cultural diversity has been shown to have both positive and negative effects on work-group effectiveness. Culturally diverse groups, particularly those acting face to face, are likely to suffer from increased process losses and have lower group performance than homogeneous groups (see Hill, 1982, for a discussion). These increased process losses potentially result from the culturally different perceptions and communication patterns noted in previous chapters. Alternatively, because of the different perspectives of group members, cultural diversity should result in more creative and higher-quality group decisions (Earley & Mosakowski, 2000; Elron, 1997; McLeod, Lobel, & Cox, 1996; Thomas et al., 1996). Moreover, having specific knowledge of another culture can be thought of as a task-relevant ability for some group tasks. Consistent with recent research into minority influence, the expression of alternate views by culturally different group members can raise the quality of group decision making and problem solving by increasing the attention of the group to the decision-making process (Nemeth, 1992).

The effect of process losses and gains is not consistent over the life of the group. Over time, culturally diverse groups achieve a reduction in process losses (Pelz, 1956; Watson, Kumar, & Michaelson, 1993). That is, as groups age, members find ways of dealing with the problems of intercultural interaction thus increasing the possibility that given an appropriate task, they will demonstrate superior performance (Katz, 1982). This can include the development of a "hybrid" team culture (Earley & Mosakowski, 2000) that emerges in similar fashion to the change of direction in Gersick's (1988) model of team development and that facilitates the performance of culturally diverse work groups. In addition, over time, work groups have the opportunity to receive feedback to both individual and group processes (Watson, Johnson, & Merritt, 1998). This feedback can come from both inside and outside the work group and might be particularly useful to culturally diverse work groups that are trying to overcome the problems of cross-cultural interaction (Thomas, 1999).

Therefore, the effect of cultural diversity in the work group has both positive and negative elements. On the one hand, it has the potential to increase group performance through a greater variety of ideas and perspectives and an increased focus on group processes by members. On the other, the probability of increased process losses exists, but this negative effect is likely to diminish over time, particularly if process-related feedback is received.

Relative Cultural Distance

A third way in which the cultural composition of the group influences group effectiveness is the extent to which each individual in the group is culturally different from the other group members. Culturally different work-group members are aware that they are different, and this awareness causes them to compare themselves to the other members of the group (Bochner & Ohsako, 1977; Bochner & Perks, 1971). Based on this comparison, they evaluate the appropriateness of their behavior and their status in the work group. If group members perceive their status in the group favorably, they are likely to participate more fully and to perceive the group more positively (Mullen, 1987; Mullen & Baumeister, 1987; Tajfel & Turner, 1986). For example, a study of multicultural work groups in Japan (Thomas et al., 1996) found that the extent to which individuals were culturally different from other group members affected their assessments of group cohesiveness and satisfaction with the group process. Other research (Thomas, 1999) found that the extent to which group members differed from others on the cultural dimension of collectivism affected their assessment of the level of conflict in the group and their willingness to express their ideas. Greater cultural difference between an individual and the rest of the group makes it more likely that the individual's cultural norms for group behavior vary from those of the group. This difference can result in a lower expectation of a successful interaction with the other group members and a higher estimate of the effort required to achieve success. Individuals might be reluctant to invest high amounts of effort in interacting with other group members who are very different because these interactions might be viewed as costing more in time and effort than the potential benefit (Thibaut & Kelley, 1959).

In summary, the influence of culture is evident through three related mechanisms. These are the culturally based norms that the group members bring to the work-group situation, the cultural diversity or number of cultures in the group, and the degree of cultural difference of group members relative to the group. Each of these mechanisms has different effects on work-group processes and outcomes.

Culture's Effect in Different Group Structures and Tasks

The nature of the task and the structure of the work group influence the extent to which the cultural composition of the work group affects its outcomes. Earlier, group structures were classified as crews, task forces, or teams, and group tasks as production, or creative idea generation and decision making. Both the structure of the work group and the task with which it is involved specify the nature of the relationships among work-group members. Group tasks that allow little employee discretion, are not sensitive to variations among group members, and are not controlled by the group offer very limited opportunities for the characteristics of group members to influence outcomes (Goodman, 1986). Therefore, production tasks would generally offer less opportunity for the effects of cultural composition (either positive or negative) than would creative idea generation and decision-making tasks. Crews, task forces, and teams differ in terms of the importance of member composition to their functioning (Arrow & McGrath, 1995). Because the nature of the interaction of crews is through the tools that they use, who the members are as people is of little importance to the function of the group. For example, a copilot from one culture could replace another from a different culture on short notice with little effect on the routine operation of a flight deck crew. In contrast, the structure of a team makes it very sensitive to member differences. These groups require highly developed intermember relationships and are therefore very sensitive to cultural differences among group members. For task forces, group composition is more important than for crews but less important than for teams. Because task forces are temporary and project focused, member interactions are limited in both intensity and time. The influence of cultural composition in different group structures and tasks is depicted graphically in Figure 8.3.

In summary, both the types of group task and the group structure can affect the extent of influence that the cultural composition of the work group has on group outcomes. For example, a product development task force engaged in planning a product introduction to a foreign market might benefit substantially from having foreign nationals represented in the group. In this case, the national culture of group members might be viewed as a task-relevant skill that members bring to the group and that can be used to the advantage of the group. In contrast, the potential influence of cultural diversity among production workers in a vehicle assembly team is limited by the nature of the task. When this same group is involved in solving problems associated with designing the production

Task Type

Group Type		Decision Making	Production
	Task Force	High	Low
	Crew	Low	Very Low
	Team	Very High	Moderate

Figure 8.3. Effect of Cultural Composition on Different Tasks and Group Types

process, as in quality-improvement teams, the opportunity for cultural differences to influence the group process (either positively or negatively) is enhanced.

Geographically Distributed Work Groups

Up to this point in our discussion, a key underlying assumption about work groups is that they interact face to face. This could be true for the majority of work groups in organizations. However, one way in which many organizations are dealing with the challenges of globalization is by forming work groups with geographically dispersed structures (Greiner & Metes, 1995). Called, variously, virtual teams, ad hoc networks, and electronically mediated groups (Cohen & Gibson, 2000), a key characteristic is that they interact primarily by electronic networks. Therefore, work-group members can be separated by time, space, and culture but also by discipline, organization, or industry. All of these elements can contribute to the degree of distance between work-group members.

These "virtual" work groups are possible because of recent advances in computer and telecommunications technology. Three broad categories of technology can form the infrastructure across which the virtual work group interacts (Townsend, DeMarie, & Hendrickson, 1998). These are desktop videoconferencing, collaborative software systems, such as Lotus Notes, and Internet-Intranet systems. These tools provide a foundation for group work but do not truly replicate face-to-face interaction. For example, differences in information technology and lack of technical support can be major additional barriers to work-group effectiveness (Cohen & Gibson, 2000), and because of electronic mediation, some of the social mechanisms that facilitate communication and decision making are lost.

The study of these rapidly emerging types of work groups is lagging behind their implementation. However, some research indicates that communications and group dynamics develop differently across electronic media than they do face to face. For example, individuals seem to prefer face-to-face communication to electronic media for complex, innovative, subtle, or ambiguous messages (Allen & Hauptman, 1990; DeMeyer, 1993; Trevino, Lengel, & Daft, 1987). In addition, electronically mediated groups tend to form more slowly (Kraut, Egido, & Galegher, 1990) because of asynchronous communication, and the electronic media reduces the ability to sense the social presence of other group members. This lack of "evidence" of cultural differences including the masking of language differences might make culture a somewhat less salient dimension in these groups (Jarvenpaa & Leidner, 1999). However, opportunities for the influence of culturally based characteristics, such as differences in tolerance of ambiguity and explicitness (high- versus low-context) of communication styles, are apparent.

In summary, the use of electronic media allows firms to build work groups with optimum membership without regard for the restrictions of time and space. However, the ability of these work groups to provide effective solutions depends on overcoming the additional barriers presented by the distance among group members and by electronic mediation. Recent theoretical development, based on the existing literature on work groups and technological mediation, suggests that the effectiveness of these types of work groups could depend on three general factors (Cohen & Gibson, 2000). These are the development of shared understandings among group members about goals and processes; the use of information technology to integrate the skills, abilities, and knowledge of work-group members; and the development of trust among group members.

Organizational Conditions and Culturally Diverse Work Groups

Work groups are influenced by the larger organization of which they are a part. The dominant characteristics of the organization influence the types of goals and methods that are acceptable for work groups

(Campion et al., 1993). In addition, management controls the resources required for work groups to be effective. Very little research exists regarding the effect of organizational conditions on culturally diverse work groups (Milliken & Martins, 1996), and the majority of that has involved task forces (ad hoc groups set up to complete an experiment) involved in creative decision making or problem-solving tasks. Therefore, to make inferences about the influence of organizational conditions on culturally diverse work groups, it is necessary to draw on research about work groups in general as well as a small number of experimental studies. Apart from the technological issues mentioned previously, key organizational factors that influence the effectiveness of work groups are the level of management support, the extent to which individual rewards come from the group, the status afforded the group, the amount of training provided to the group, and the extent to which the organization allows groups to be self-managed.

Management Support

It might seem obvious that the most effective work groups exist in organizations that provide high levels of organizational support, such as making sure the work groups have the materials and information necessary to achieve their goals. However, numerous examples exist of organizations setting challenging goals for work groups and then failing to provide adequate support (Hackman, 1991). In addition, recent research suggests that management must either design work around groups or around individuals but that mixing the two designs in so-called hybrid groups is not effective (Wageman, 1995). An additional element of support required for work groups composed of culturally diverse members is an organizational culture that supports diversity as indicated by an organizational culture that treats people of all cultures with respect (Cox, 1993). Research with culturally diverse manufacturing teams indicates that the level of management support is positively related to the task performance of the work group and work-group-member attitudes such as satisfaction with the group, group cohesiveness, commitment, and trust, and negatively related to the amount of conflict felt by group members (Thomas et al., 2000).

Group-Level Rewards

The effect of rewards on individual performance is much better understood than the relationship between rewards and work-group performance. Some research has suggested that a mix of individuals and group rewards will be most effective with work groups, particularly the self-regulating variety (Pearce & Ravlin, 1987). More recently, however, others suggest that these hybrid reward systems can lead to lower individual effort and hence poor group performance (Wageman, 1995). A recent study of culturally diverse teams found that the extent to which individuals derived their rewards from the team was positively related to both team performance and team-member attitudes (Thomas et al., 2000). However, these results must be treated with some caution based on what we know about preferences for reward allocation across cultures. For example, we know that individualists and collectivists are guided by different reward-allocation norms (Leung & Bond, 1984). Individualists are typically more comfortable with rewards based on equity, in which rewards are based on the level of individual contribution. The norm for collectivists is more likely to involve equality of reward allocation in which all group members share equally in group rewards. The effectiveness of a particular reward-allocation system is likely influenced by the cultural composition of the work group and the preferences of group members. For example, in individualist cultures, making the ability to work well in a group a key component in an individual's performance review might be more acceptable than tying rewards more directly to work-group performance.

Work-Group Status

The argument that the status of a work group in the organization will influence its performance is based on the idea that being a member of a high-status group will increase members' feelings of self-worth and effectiveness. As in other groups, individuals are motivated to maintain and enhance their work groups and hence their own standing (Tajfel & Turner, 1986). The positive effect that high group status has on the individual improves both individual and work-group performance (Ravlin, Thomas & Ilsev, 2000). Successful work groups get the recognition that signals to the rest of the organization that they are an important element of organizational success. However, the extent to which individuals from different cultures derive their self-esteem from work groups can vary considerably (Erez & Earley, 1993). For example, people from collectivist cultures are more likely to identify more strongly with their cultural or family group than they are with a work group composed of relative strangers (Triandis, 1995). Therefore, the status of work groups might have a greater influence on the feelings of self-worth, confidence, group potency, and desire to work in the group for some cultures, such as individualists, as opposed to others, such as collectivists. However, affording work groups high status in the organization would seem to make sense in terms of making group membership desirable, regardless of culture.

Training

The concept that work-group success requires training in interaction skills as well as technical skills is well established (Wagner, Hibbits, Rosenblatt, & Schulz, 1977). Often, however, managers seem to assume that employees automatically have the skills to be effective work-group members (Hackman, 1991). In situations in which all work-group activities and tasks cannot be specified in advance, and in which individuals can have different assumptions about how the work group should operate, training in interaction skills is especially important.

Cross-cultural training has the objective of bringing the expectations of individuals from different cultural backgrounds in line with the reality of working in a multicultural context. The effectiveness of cross-cultural training programs on improving interpersonal interactions is documented in a number of studies (e.g., Black & Mendenhall, 1990).

Self-Management

The argument for self-managing work groups (teams) stems from the idea that the benefits of group work are related to the delegation of a substantial amount of authority to the work group or team (Barry, 1991; Pearce & Ravlin, 1987). However, if too much authority is delegated, work groups can charge off in inappropriate directions. Research on multicultural work groups has failed to show clear support for self-management as a determining factor in work-group effectiveness (Thomas et al., 2000). Setting the direction for a work group might empower it, but dictating work processes and procedures can actually inhibit group performance. Alternatively, insufficient direction can result in work groups with an unclear sense of appropriate task-related processes. Recent research in a single culture has suggested that it is the extent to which work-group members feel empowered rather than the degree of self-management that might be most important to group effectiveness (Kirkman & Rosen, 1999) and that empowerment stems from more than just the degree of self-management. In addition, other research (Thomas, 1999) argues that process-related feedback could be the key factor in determining if culturally diverse work groups overcome the process losses associated with diversity. Therefore, achieving an appropriate level and type of delegation for multicultural work groups can be a particularly difficult management task (see Kirkman & Shapiro, 1997).

Managing Multicultural Work Groups

Even if it were possible to determine the optimal cultural mix in a particular work-group situation, it is unrealistic for managers to control the cultural composition of work groups. Instead, they must try to find ways to maximize the positive consequences of both homogeneity and diversity while minimizing the negative consequences of both (Jackson, 1992). The complexity of this endeavor suggests that there is not a universal prescription that can be applied to every multicultural work group. The following ideas are derived from our current knowledge about this management challenge.

Work-Group Task and Structure

The research to date suggests that both the positive and negative effects of cultural diversity depend on how the work group is structured and the nature of the task. Work groups with high degrees of interpersonal interaction, such as teams, will be more susceptible to both the process losses and process gains produced by cultural differences among group members. In addition, less structured tasks, such as creative problem solving and decision making, are more open to the influence of cultural differences than are highly structured and regulated production tasks. For example, cultural differences might be masked on the production line only to become apparent in a weekly team meeting at which improvements in the production process are being discussed. In another example, airline flight deck crews might operate very similarly across cultures under routine conditions, but the influence of cultural differences becomes apparent when handling emergency situations (Merritt & Helmreich, 1996).

Broad Evaluation Criteria

Multicultural work groups should probably be evaluated in terms of group processes and individual outcomes as well as task accomplishment. The long-term effectiveness of a work group depends on the ability of the group to help individuals meet their personal goals and the ability of group processes to facilitate performance. Multicultural work groups often take longer to reach their potential than do homogeneous work groups (Watson, Kumar, & Michaelson, 1993). Assessing how a work group is doing according to broader criteria than just accomplishment of the immediate task can give managers insight into the longer-term potential of the group, regardless of its present level of task accomplishment.

Composition and Task Requirements

Multicultural work groups are very sensitive to the need for resources, including member resources required to accomplish the task. The guiding principle for work-group organization should be to ensure that the work group has the task-related knowledge, skills, and abilities required to complete the group tasks (Hackman, 1987). These task-related requirements can also include culture in that characteristics of specific culturally based knowledge and skills might be appropriate to certain tasks. For example, some recent research with Japanese teams found that when culturally based tacit knowledge "in the bones expertise" was made explicit, greater gains were made in productivity and knowledge (Nonaka, 1994).

Common Purpose

Creating a shared sense of purpose among the work-group members can be even more important in multicultural work groups. The idea that groups with goals that transcend the individual differences of group members (superordinate goals) have better group processes is well established (Sherif, Harvey, White, Hood, & Sherif, 1961). However, establishing this shared sense of purpose among individuals with different values, attitudes, and beliefs is challenging. It requires managers to have an in-depth understanding of the values, attitudes, and beliefs of culturally different work-group members.

Summary

This chapter explored the management challenge of effectively managing culturally diverse work groups and teams. The effective performance of work groups, in general, is affected by six sets of factors:

1. the external or contextual conditions imposed on the group,

2. the resources of group members,

3. the structure of the group,

4. the group task,

5. the group process, and

6. the composition of the group.

Cultural diversity in work groups influences the group through three distinct but interrelated mechanisms of the cultural norms of group members, cultural diversity or the number of different cultures represented in the group, and the extent to which group members are culturally different from each other. In addition, the nature of the task and the structure of the group influence the extent to which the cultural composition of a group affects its processes and outcomes. Key organization factors that influence work-group effectiveness are the level of management support, the extent to which individual rewards come from the group, the status afforded the group, the amount of training provided to the group, and the extent to which the organizations empower the work group. In short, managing multicultural work groups involves trying to find ways to maximize the positive consequences of both homogeneity and diversity, while at the same time minimizing their negative consequences.

Nine

The Challenge of Designing International Organizations

Globalization does not mean imposing homogeneous solutions in a pluralistic world. It means having a global vision and strategy, but it also means cultivating roots and individual identities.

Gucharan Das, former chairman and managing director,
Procter & Gamble, India

All organizations create structure to coordinate activities and control the actions of their members. However, the forms that organizations take both domestically and around the world vary considerably. This chapter reviews the management challenges presented by international organizations. International organizations are discussed both in terms of a universal logic to organizing and the influence of culture on organizational structure. First, the basic dimensions of organizational structure and design are described, and different schools of thought about explaining organizational structure are discussed. Then, the influence of culture and examples of cross-national variation in organizational forms are presented. A discussion of the MNC as a unique organizational form leads to consideration of its influence on managerial roles and the relationship of culturally different individuals to the firm. Finally, the design of work within the context of the multinational and multicultural organization structure is discussed.

Organizations

Organizations are social systems intentionally structured to achieve goals. They are not independent of their surroundings but are open systems that continuously take inputs from the environment, such as raw materials, human resources, and ideas, transform them, and then return output to the environment in the form of products, services, or knowledge (Katz & Kahn, 1978). As systems of people, organizations must be coordinated through a differentiation of roles and a hierarchy of authority to achieve goals. This "structure" of the organization can be described by its degree of complexity, formalization, and centralization (Pugh, Hickson, Hinings, MacDonald, & Turner, 1963).

The complexity of an organization is the extent to which it is differentiated along three dimensions: horizontal, vertical, and spatial. *Horizontal differentiation* refers to the number of different types of jobs that exist in an organization. The greater the number of different occupations in an organization, the greater is its horizontal differentiation. *Vertical differentiation* refers to the number of levels in the hierarchy of the organization. The more levels that exist between the highest and the lowest positions, the more complex the organization is. *Spatial differentiation* refers to the extent to which the organization's physical facilities and personnel are geographically dispersed. Geographic dispersion of activities, as in international organizations, increases complexity.

Formalization is the extent to which rules and procedures govern the activities of organization members. For example, the level of documentation for employee behavior is a good indicator of the formality of an organization. Formal organizations allow little discretion in the way people do their jobs.

The degree of centralization in an organization is indicated by the extent to which decision making is concentrated at a single point. In centralized organizations, virtually all decisions are made in one location typically by top management. In decentralized organizations, decisions are pushed down and out through the organization.

There are a variety of ways in which the three elements of organizational structure—complexity, formalization, and centralization—can be combined. Often, however, an organization's structure is characteristic of one of two fundamental types, *mechanistic* or *organic* (Burns & Stalker, 1961). Mechanistic or bureaucratic organizations are characterized by centralization, high formality, and high complexity (especially in horizontal differentiation). In contrast, organic organizational structures have low formalization and complexity with decision making distributed throughout the organization based on knowledge. Figure 9.1 presents a graphic representation of these two fundamental organizational designs.

Organizational Designs

The general forms of mechanistic versus organic organizational designs are helpful in demonstrating how the various elements of structure might combine. A more refined perspective on the fundamentals of organizational forms is offered by Mintzberg (1983). He proposed that all organizations are composed of five essential parts. As shown in Figure 9.2, these are the operating core, the middle line, the support staff, the technostructure, and the strategic apex.

According to Mintzberg, each of these parts is dominant in one of five basic types of organizational design. The *operating core* consists of the employees who perform the basic tasks related to the production of products and services. This part of the organization is dominant in a *professional bureaucracy,* which is populated by highly trained specialists. Examples include universities, museums, and hospitals. The *strategic apex* is composed of the top-level managers who have overall responsibility for the organization. In *simple* organizational structures, the strategic apex dominates. Simple structures are characteristic of entrepreneurial ventures or small firms in which virtually everyone reports to one person. The direct supervision by this individual is the key coordinating mechanism. The *middle line* consists of those managers that connect the operating core to the strategic apex. Middle-line managers predominate in *divisional structures,* which are characterized by groups of semi-autonomous units coordinated by a central headquarters. Many large multinationals are characteristic of this structure, which depends on standardization of outputs for coordination. The *technostructure* is composed of technical analysts who have responsibility for various forms of standardization in the organization. The influence of the technostructure is strongest in the type of design that Mintzberg calls the *machine bureaucracy.* Organizations that rely on standardized procedures and policies for coordination and control such as banks and government departments are characteristic of this design. *Support staffs* provide indirect support

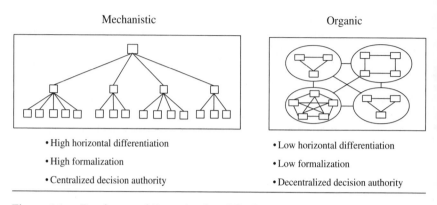

Figure 9.1.   Fundamental Organizational Designs

services to the rest of the organization. The support staff is most influential in an organizational form called an *adhocracy*. The adhocracy, like the professional bureaucracy, is composed of highly skilled professionals. However, it differs because the high degree of standardization and formalization associated with bureaucratic or mechanistic structure is absent. This organizational design depends on mutual adjustment for coordination and is most similar to the organic structure presented previously.

These five types of organizational designs represent a conceptual framework that can be used to understand the variety of organizational forms that exist. Management scholars have drawn on a number of logical approaches and some empirical research to suggest a particular cause or set of causes for organizational structure. These schools of thought tend to focus on a single aspect of the issue and use different logics and terminology. However, some reconciliation of the different points of view is possible (e.g., Astley & Van de Ven, 1983), and each perspective provides some insight into our contemporary understanding of international organizational forms.

Explaining Organizational Structure

Explanations that have evolved for the existence of different organizational structures can be classified into four groups. Roughly in the order of their development, they are deterministic theories, contingency theories, ecological theories, and institutional theories. Both deterministic and contingency theories operate at the level of individual organizations,

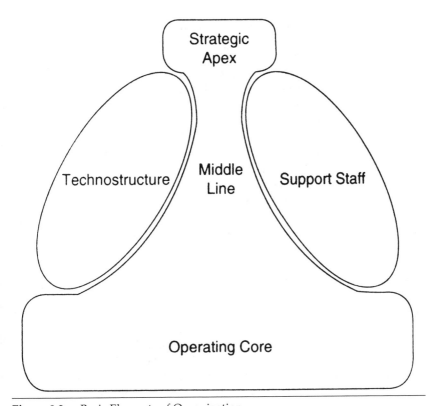

Figure 9.2. Basic Elements of Organization
SOURCE: Mintzberg, Henry. *Structure in Fives: Designing Effective Organizations* (2nd ed.). © 1993 by Prentice Hall, Inc. Reprinted with permission.

whereas ecological and institutional theories deal with populations or communities of organizations.

Deterministic Theory

Much of the initial study of organizational structure focused on the one best way to organize. These approaches proposed that one factor or another was dominant in explaining the structural aspects of organizations. Significant are those that proposed technology, strategy, and size as determinants of structure.

Based on studies of English manufacturing firms, Woodward (1965) found that the three technological classifications of *unit production, mass production,* and *process production* explained the differences in structure she observed. The technology argument was later refined to include knowledge technology as well as production technology (Perrow, 1967). By classifying tasks by the number of exceptions encountered and how well-defined were the methods available to find solutions to these exceptions, organizations could be classified as routine, craft, engineering, or nonroutine. Although the relationship between technology, in terms of routineness, and structure is not particularly strong, organizations composed of routine tasks tend to be more differentiated both horizontally and vertically (Hage & Aiken, 1969).

The origin of the strategy structure relationship lies in Alfred Chandler's study of the development of numerous large U.S. firms (Chandler, 1962). In essence, the argument is that as the strategy of the firm moves from a single product through vertical integration to product diversification, the firm must develop more complex and formal structures to coordinate activities. Over the years, the idea of what constitutes a strategy has matured (e.g., Miles & Snow, 1978; Porter, 1980). However, the basic premise of the relationship to structure remains. This view suggests that some optimal structure exists that reflects a particular strategy.

The argument for organization size as a determinant of organization structure has a long history beginning with studies by Blau (1970) and also the Aston researchers (e.g., Pugh & Hickson, 1976). Although not without its critics (e.g., Argyris, 1972; Hall, Haas, & Johnson, 1967), size seems to be strongly related to at least some elements of structure. The greatest effect of size is on vertical differentiation (Mileti, Gillespie, & Haas, 1977). As organizations increase the number of people employed, the organizations add more levels. The rate of increase in differentiation is initially rapid but decreases as the organization grows. In addition, increases in organizational size are related to increases in formalization but to decreases in centralization (Blau & Schoenherr, 1971). The logic is that as organizations grow, they substitute formal rules for direct supervision, and the ability to centralize decision making effectively declines.

Contingency Theory

Deterministic theories are concerned only with factors internal to the organization. Contingency theories of organization developed because of the recognition that organizations, as open systems, interact with their environment. A popular definition of environment describes it as those institutions and forces that affect the organization but are outside of its control (Churchman, 1968). Therefore, it can include economic, political, legal, and social conditions although management might not be concerned with all of these at any one time. Organizational environments are described in a variety of ways (e.g., Emery & Trist, 1965). However, perhaps the most useful categorization is in terms of environmental uncertainty, because managers will try to reduce uncertainty in order to improve effectiveness (Dill, 1958). Simple static environments create less uncertainty for managers than do complex dynamic environments.

The classic studies of Burns and Stalker (1961) and Lawrence and Lorsch (1967) supported the fundamental idea that managers adjust the organization structure to reduce environmental uncertainty. In general, simple static environments (low environmental uncertainty) give rise to organizations with high complexity, high formalization, and high centralization, whereas complex dynamic environments result in high uncertainty and give rise to organizations with low complexity, low formalization, and decentralization (Duncan, 1972). Although contingency theories allow for multiple causes (e.g., strategy, technology, size, environment) for an organization's structure, there is some question as to whether or not this approach reflects reality (Child, 1974). That is, if environments are increasingly complex and dynamic, most organizations should adopt a more organic structure. However, observation suggests a significant amount of complexity, formalization, and centralization in modern organizations. Even if one's view is restricted to Western cultures, the evidence for the relationship between contingency variables and organizational structure is mixed (Tayeb, 1987). Additionally, the assumption of a Western notion of rational choice (see Chapter 5) of structural forms creates some questions about the applicability of this approach in international contexts. Two alternatives to contingency theory that provide some insight into explaining organizational structure in international environments are ecological and institutional theories.

Ecological Theories

Ecological theories focus not on single organizations but on the structures of whole populations of organizations. These populations are in many cases described in terms that make them equivalent to industries (Westney, 1997). In this view, the environment determines organizational structure not through choice by managers but by selecting out those organizations that do not fit (Hannan & Freeman, 1977). That is, organizations are relatively inert and either die or are absorbed by other organizations as environmental conditions change (Hannan & Freeman, 1984). Managers are viewed as very limited in their ability to adapt their internal structures. Rather, whole populations of organizations survive or fail with little regard for the actions taken by individual firms. This natural selection view of organizations suggests that environmental forces drive the evolution of corporate structures and that actions by managers have little effect (Astley & Van de Ven, 1983). Although an inactive role for managers might be an unpalatable option for some, ecological theories serve to point out possible constraints on the ability of organizations to adapt and suggest reasons for inertia in organizational structures (Westney, 1997).

Institutional Theory

Institutional theory focuses on the ways that organizations in shared environments come to adopt structures viewed as appropriate and that are reinforced in interactions with other organizations (Westney, 1997). That is, it explains the structural similarity (isomorphism) that exists across organizations. For example, commercial banks have a number of structural similarities, as do hospitals, as do universities. Fundamentally, institutional theory suggests that two factors influence organizational structure. The first consists of the effect of the environmental agents (e.g., regulatory agencies, professional societies, consulting firms) in shaping the organization. The second are those processes internal to the firm that interpret certain externally validated structures as appropriate. DiMaggio and Powell (1983) defined three categories of environmental pressures toward institutional isomorphism:

- *coercive* isomorphism—patterns of organization are imposed on the firm by an outside authority such as government,

- *normative* isomorphism—professional bodies promote "proper" organizational structure, and

- *mimetic* isomorphism—organizations copy the structure of firms that have been successful in dealing with a particular environment.

Although institutional theory was not formulated with organizations that operate in multiple environments in mind, it has been recently applied to the study of these international organizations (Rosenzweig & Singh, 1991). Large MNCs often span both countries and industries. Therefore, they can be subjected to competing isomorphic pressures in the different environments in which they operate (Westney, 1993). As discussed later, the structures of these organizations that straddle organizational environments reflect the necessity of accommodating these sometimes conflicting pressures.

The approaches to understanding the structures of organizations described here differ both in terms of the role of managers and in the effect of environmental factors in determining structure. At one end of the continuum, managers make strategic choices regarding adapting the internal structure of the organization to the environment. At the other, managers have little influence, and forces in the external environment largely determine effective structures. The debate among organization theorists concerning the most appropriate approach to studying international organizations continues (Ghoshal, 1997). The view presented here is that although none of the perspectives is entirely satisfactory, they all identify important facets of the pressures and contingencies that face international organizations. As such, they provide a backdrop for the examination of the influence of culture on organizational forms.

Culture and Organizational Structure

A fundamental question concerning international organizational design is why organizations in different societies are alike in some respects and different in others. Reflecting on the organization theories presented previously, we can see why all organizations might share similar characteristics but also why cultural differences in organizational structures exist.

Culture-Free Perspective

One view is that the contingencies that affect organizations operate in a similar fashion across cultures. That is, for organizations to be effective, the design of the organization must fit with their size, technology, and strategy, regardless of culture (Child, 1974, 1981; Hickson, Hinings, McMillan, & Schwitter, 1991). This so-called culture-free approach does not deny the existence of cultural differences; it just considers culture irrelevant. Research from the Aston studies, which over the course of two decades studied over 1,000 organizations in 14 (primarily western European) countries (Hickson & Pugh, 1995), showed a very strong effect of size on organization structure in all countries studied (Hickson & McMillan, 1981). That is, regardless of country, larger organizations tended to be more formalized, specialized, and less centralized. Additional support for the culture-free contingency approach has been found in samples from the Middle and Far East (Donaldson, 1986). It is important to note that this research does not make comparisons across cultures but suggests that organizations in many countries seem to respond similarly to size. The Aston model relies on Western conceptions of organizational structure, which effectively prevented any testing of the cultural assumptions underlying them. Moreover, it implies that the specification of organization structure will have a direct effect on organization members and that the duties and roles implied by structure are not open to cultural interpretation (Smith & Bond, 1999). For example, centralization can be assessed by who makes decisions in the organization, but it does not address the degree of consultation that occurred before the decision. When the contingency perspective has been tested in cross-cultural comparison, organizations demonstrated similar configurations in response to contingency demands; however, the means by which they had done so was found to be different and consistent with the cultural characteristics of the countries studied (Tayeb, 1987). Therefore, the "culture-free" perspective provides insight in terms of very general structural configurations. However, it is not entirely adequate to explain many of the differences observed in organizations across cultures. In addition, even if the structure of organizations appears objectively similar, the meaning that culturally different organization members give to the structure can be different and affect their behavior (Inzerilli & Laurent, 1983).

Structural Variation Across Cultures

Several approaches to describing the how and why of cultural influence have been proposed (e.g., Gibson, 1994; Hofstede, 1991; Lachmann, Nedd, & Hinings, 1994), and some empirical evidence exists that supports a relationship between culture and organizational structure (e.g., Dunphy, 1987). Based on the definition of culture adopted in this book and the perspectives on general causes of organizational structure discussed previously, two mechanisms by which national culture influences organizational structure emerge. In the first case, organizational structure is seen as a manifestation or "symptom" of the manager's cultural values. That is, organizational structures are logical extensions of specific value orientations. For example, in a high-power-distance culture, organizations would be more hierarchical and centralized (Hofstede, 1980). In the second case, national culture influences the extent to which different ways of organizing are accepted by the members of a society. That is, pressures from the organizational environment, which includes the cultural context, dictate the type of structure seen as correct or legitimate. For example, normative pressures influence the tendency of Chinese firms to stay small and family owned (Chen, 1995).

Research directed at determining which of these perspectives is most powerful in explaining the relationship between culture and organizational structure has failed to find overwhelming support for any one perspective (Gibson, 1994). As with the more general approaches to understanding differences in organizational structures, each mechanism can help capture the complexity of the relationship between national culture and organizational structure. Figure 9.3 presents a synthesis of the previous discussion of how culture might influence the design of organizations in different countries.

As shown in Figure 9.3, the contextual variables central to contingency approaches (e.g., size, technology, strategy) can account for the similarity in organizational structures found around the world.

Through one path, differences in the organizational choices that managers make are guided by their culturally based value orientations. Managers are not necessarily aware of these subconscious influences and simply make choices about structure that feel correct. The more hierarchical organizational structures found in German organizations provides an example (Child & Kieser, 1979; Ruedi & Lawrence, 1970). This rigidity in organizational structures is consistent with dominant German value orientations. Likewise, the flat structure of firms in the Swedish automobile industry can be explained as a manifestation of egalitarian cultural values (Ellegard et al., 1992). Examinations of Japanese business organizations operating in the United States are also indicative of this mechanism for culture's influence. In one study, the structural characteristics of the U.S. organization (specialization specifically) varied with the number of Japanese nationals employed (Lincoln et al., 1978). In this case, the characteristic values of the Japanese manifested themselves in lower specialization.

The other avenue for cultural influence relies on environmental pressure to shape organizational structure. That is, organizational structure is less the product of conscious design than it is a reflection of the structures that society will accept as legitimate. Many of the pressures that society brings to bear on organizations emanate from the institutions (e.g., legal, political) of a society. However, the culture and the institutions of society are inevitably linked as they have evolved together over time.

Several examples of this approach exist to support this idea. First, the Chinese family structure of business is an example of a structure that results in part because of isomorphic pressures. The Chinese family business centers on paternalism that results in simple structures that restrict the focus to a single aspect of business (Chen, 1995). The societal characteristics of mutual obligation, familialism, and personal connections (*guanxi*) support the effectiveness of this organizational form (Wu, 1999).

Two organizational forms that have similar orientations to the family business but that reflect different societal pressures are the *keiretsu* in Japan and the *chaebol* in Korea. The Japanese *keiretsu* originated with the pre-WWII family-owned *zaibatsu*. Often the original *zaibatsu* family

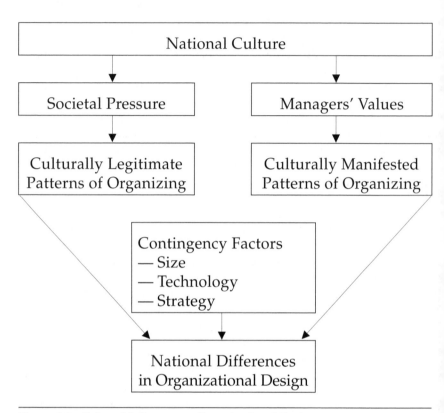

Figure 9.3. Cultural Influence on Organizational Design
SOURCE: Adapted from Cullen, 1999; Gibson, 1994.

name survived as in Mitsui, Mitsubishi, and Sumitomo. The modern *keiretsu*, although no longer family owned, is a complex network of inter-firm networks consisting of a large number of industries, including a trading company (*sogoshosha*), and is usually anchored by a bank. Functioning like an extended family, the coordination and control is facilitated by reciprocal ownership and the focus is typically on long-term gains (Ghauri & Prasad, 1995). This organizational form, although sharing some characteristics with both Korean and Mexican firms, is a unique product of its national environment. The Korean *chaebol* are family dominated, multi-industry conglomerates such as Hyundai, Samsung, Lucky-Goldstar, and Daewoo. They differ from *zaibatsu* in that they are heavily populated with family members, particularly in key positions, and are financed by the government (Steers, Shin, & Ungson, 1989). Although paternalistic and highly centralized like other family business, the *chaebol* is also a unique product of its environment. Korean society, through government policy such as low-interest loans, tax rebates, and access to foreign currency, has favored the development of large-scale business. Therefore, the structure of the huge, but still family-run, Korean *chaebol* is the result of societal pressure for large firms or, in intuitionalism terms, coercive isomorphism.

A final example of environmental influence on organizational structure is the knitwear industry of the Modena region of Italy. In this region of Italy, a system of production called "putting out" that economists consider archaic and inefficient survives. In the putting-out system of organization, the manufacturer "puts out" raw materials to independent artisanal firms, who assemble the goods, often in their homes. In Modena, the putting-out system relies on small (less than nine workers on average), family-owned firms to cut, assemble, dye, press, and package knitwear, and results in high living standards and high organizational efficiency (Lazerson, 1995). The success of the system in modern Modena rests on the presence of cohesive family units, cooperative relationships, and an environment supportive of small, family-run firms. That is, centuries of societal engagement in cooperative endeavors, dating back to straw hat weaving in the 1600s, created a unique set of normative conditions that allow this type of enterprise to flourish (Putnam, 1993). The fit of these small firms with the traditions of family work in the region produced a unique and competitive organizational form.

The model presented in Figure 9.3 is a synthesis of several approaches to understanding organizational structure and seeks to account for both the similarities and differences in organizational structure that are observed in different national cultures. It recognizes the influence of contextual variables such as size, technology, and strategy on organizational design, which accounts for the many similarities. However, it also makes explicit two avenues for the influence of national culture. First, as managers make choices in organizational structure, they are influenced by deeply held values and beliefs that influence what seems normal in terms of organization. In addition, however, organizations are open systems influenced by pressures from the environment. The cultural context of the firm determines, at least in part, what types of organizational structures are viewed as appropriate by society.

Organizing in Multinational Corporations

Thus far in this chapter, our concern has been directed at understanding the forms that organizations might take in different national cultures. However, MNCs operate across cultural boundaries and present a number of additional issues for international managers. The MNC is a single organization with a need to coordinate its operations across multiple environments.

Typical International Structures

The need for MNCs to coordinate and control operations across multiple environments led to several approaches to placing foreign activity within the broader organizational structure. The approach taken can depend on the location and type of foreign subsidiaries, the impact of international operations on corporate performance, and the path through which the firm's international operations have developed over time (e.g., Stopford & Wells, 1972). In addition, the preference for a particular method to integrate international operations can vary according to the firm's country of origin (Leksell, 1981; Marschan, 1996). Five ways of integrating international activity are common. The *international division* groups all international activities together in a single organizational unit and is more popular with U.S. than European MNCs (Daniels & Radebaugh, 1998). This structure has also been the initial choice of a significant number of firms as they expand internationally (Davis, 1992). The *product division* structure groups all units involved with like products together around the world. In this case, it is possible for foreign subsidiaries in the same country to have a different relationship to the firm depending on the product line. The *functional division* expands its domestic functional units into its foreign counterparts (e.g., Marketing Europe, Marketing North America, etc.) based on geography, whereas the *geographic division* structure groups all functional areas into geographic units (e.g., North American Division, European Division, etc.). In the *matrix* structure, each subsidiary reports to more than one group (product, geographic, or functional) for the purpose of integrating international operations with functional areas, product areas, or both. The popularity of this type of structure has waxed and waned as the advantages of integration versus the disadvantages of dual reporting were weighed against each other.

International Collaborative Alliances

A recently emerged international organizational form is that of collaborative alliances with foreign firms. These alliances typically take one of three forms: informal cooperative alliances, formal cooperative alliances, and international joint ventures (Lorange & Roos, 1992). The informal type of arrangement is usually limited in scope and has no contractual requirement. Formal arrangements typically require a contractual agreement and are often indicated by broader involvement. In addition, joint ventures are separate legal entities with joint ownership. A considerable literature has developed concerning these organizational forms, a complete discussion of which is outside the scope of this book (e.g., Beamish & Killing, 1997). However, consistent with the focus on organizational structure in this chapter, it is important to note that collaborative arrangements result in new structures, the form of which must be determined from the organizational preferences of the partners.

Despite the trend toward this organizational form, most international alliances have a short duration with as many as 70% of alliances failing to meet performance expectations (Geringer & Hebert, 1991). The most-often-cited reason for failure is incompatibility of the partners (Dacin, Hitt, & Levitas, 1997). However, when selecting a potential partner to a collaborative agreement, the focus of firms is typically on complementarity of task-related capabilities. That is, a firm searches for partners with capabilities that it lacks itself. However, research indicates that such compatibility factors as the national culture of the partner, its organizational structure, and past experience are as important to success as task-related criteria such as technical know-how, financial assets, and access to markets (Geringer, 1988). This suggests that the selection of partners and the formation of structure in the alliance is facilitated by an understanding of the culturally based organizational design preferences of potential partners.

MNC Subsidiary Structure

Regardless of the overall organizational form, the subunits of the MNC operate in distinct local environments, each with the type of isomorphic pressures noted earlier. This additional complexity has caused some researchers to suggest that the MNC is a unique organizational form and is best understood as a complex network of differentiated subsidiaries (Ghoshal & Bartlett, 1990). This idea shifts the fundamental emphasis from understanding the overall organizational structure to understanding the effects of firm and environmental characteristics on the foreign subsidiary (Roth, Schweiger, & Morrison, 1991).

An idea helpful in understanding these effects is that the organizational structure and management practices of subsidiaries of the MNC are influenced by the opposing forces toward adaptation to the local environment (local responsiveness) and consistency within the organization (global integration) (e.g., Bartlett, 1986; Porter, 1986). According to Rosenzweig and Singh (1991), the pressures for consistency among subsidiaries in the international firm (global integration) stem from two factors: *organizational replication* and the *imperative for control*. Organizational replication is the tendency of the firm to duplicate, in new environments, existing structures and procedures that are effective. For example, Procter & Gamble initially designed each new foreign subsidiary to be an exact replica of the U.S. organization because of a belief that the same policies and procedures that were successful in the United States would work equally well overseas (Bartlett & Ghoshal, 1989). The imperative for control suggests that standardization of policies is used to reduce the complexity and uncertainty inherent in the control of international operations. MNCs are confronted with additional complexity because of geographic and cultural differences among subsidiaries and between the subsidiary and headquarters. As noted previously, in new environments, the pressures for local adaptation derive from the social nature of organizations, and hence their tendency to reflect the values, norms, and accepted practices of the societies in which they operate (Westney, 1993).

The elements of organizational structure in the foreign subsidiaries of MNCs can be represented in terms of these dual pressures as shown in Figure 9.4.

As shown in Figure 9.4, the pressures for conformity to local norms and for internal consistency with the rest of the organization can vary from subsidiary to subsidiary. This results in a variety of structures across the organization. That is, a complex pattern emerges with elements of foreign subsidiaries having various degrees of conformity to local demands and with the subsidiaries in different countries resembling each other to varying degrees. An important distinction of this approach to understanding organizational forms is that it recognizes that the influence of the environment on the MNC is not uniform across the subunits of the firm (Rosenzweig & Singh, 1991). Therefore, it explicitly recognizes the influence of national culture in defining the environment of the organization.

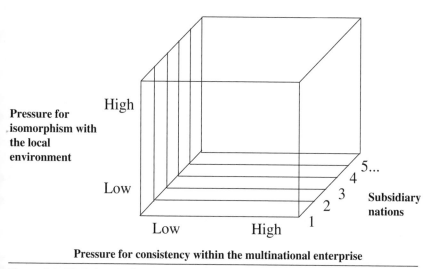

Figure 9.4. Variations in Structure Across Subsidiaries of a Multinational Enterprise
SOURCE: Adapted from Rosenzweig & Singh, 1991.

Subsidiary Manager's Role

Considering the structure of the MNC as a network of subunits that exists in a variety of environments and thus in terms of competing forces on the subsidiary raises issues about the role of the managers of these subunits. Because of the "loose coupling" of subunits of the organization that results from this organizational form, much of the coordination and control shifts to individuals in positions that link the subunits (Bartlett & Ghoshal, 1989).

The managers of subsidiaries of MNCs, because they function across internal and external organizational boundaries, perform this linking function and occupy these unique boundary-spanning roles (Thomas, 1994). The subsidiary manager, because of membership in the two separate but related entities (the larger organization and the local operation), is the recipient of role expectations from both. In the international environment, the opposing pressures for local adaptation and global integration felt by the firm intensify these different role expectations. To the extent that role pressures of the senders differ, are contradictory, or are mutually exclusive, the manager will experience conflict about the appropriate role; and to the extent that these role pressures are incomplete, the manager will experience role ambiguity (Kahn, Wolfe, Quinn, Snoek, & Rosenthal, 1964). Conflicting expectations raise the possibility that subsidiary managers might have difficulty in accommodating both sets of role expectations. In extreme cases, these managers can "go native" and fail to consider the parent company's perspectives in the performance of their duties, or alternatively, can fail to consider local interests. However, managers can respond to these conflicting demands by attempting to alter the way in which they interact with their environment and thereby change their roles. The fact that managers attempt to alter the content of their jobs to make them less reactive and dependent on the demands of others is well-documented (Sayles, 1964; Stewart, 1982).

Mintzberg's (1973) categorization of managerial roles, introduced in Chapter 1, can be used to inform our understanding of the response of subsidiary managers to conflicting role demands. The extent to which any of these roles dominates a particular manager's work is contingent on environmental, job, personal, and situational variables. Conflicting forces toward local responsiveness and global integration are reflected in the emphasis that managers place on their various roles. For example, strong forces toward local adaptation result in an emphasis in liaising with elements of the local environment as opposed to a focus on allocating resources within the organization.

Consistent with the fundamentals of cross-cultural interaction introduced in Chapter 4, in cases in which the expectations of the environment are conflicting or unclear, the emphasis that managers place on different roles can be more susceptible to cultural influence. That is, managers might rely on culturally based scripts to carry out their jobs when the environment does not clearly indicate appropriate behavior. Longstanding empirical support exists for the idea that managers from different cultures view their roles differently (Haire, Ghiselli, & Porter, 1966). More recently, however, researchers have addressed the nature of the relationship between culture and managerial-role characteristics. For example, in a 21-nation study, role conflict, role ambiguity, and role overload were found to be related to Hofstede's national scores on power distance, individualism, uncertainty avoidance, and masculinity (Peterson, Smith, Akande, et al., 1995). In the same study, perceived role stress was found to be more heavily influenced by national culture than by personal or organizational factors (Peterson, Smith, Akande, et al., 1995). Responses to role stress were found to be influenced by national culture in a small number of studies. For example, research found that responses to role ambiguity differed for Chinese and Western managers (Smith, Peterson, & Wang, 1996). Chinese managers responded to this role stress by relying on rules and procedures, whereas Western managers were more likely to rely on their own training and experience. In addition, the relationship between role conflict and commitment was found to be different for Chinese and U.S. managers (Perrewe, Ralston, & Fernandez, 1995). Although research on this issue is limited, what is clear from these results is that in cases in which role expectations are conflicting or ambiguous, such as in the boundary-spanning roles of subsidiary managers, the national culture of the manager can be influential in how the role is perceived and how the manager responds. That is, we might expect that culture would exert an even more pronounced influence under these conditions.

Designing Jobs in International Organizations

The design of jobs in international organizations is a reflection of the structure of the enterprise but also involves the relationship that individuals have with their work environment. As organizations become more global and adopt less tightly coupled structures, the nature of employees' relationship to the organization is affected. In addition, increased globalization typically means increased cultural diversity within the firm. Cultural differences influence how individuals view the nature of work and the characteristics of their relationship to their employer. Moreover, cultural differences can influence the way in which work is organized in these organizations.

Cultural Differences in the Psychological Contract

Because employers can never specify all the terms and conditions of the employment relationship, individuals supplement this information in the formation of what is called their psychological contract. The psychological contract consists of individual beliefs or perceptions concerning the terms of the exchange relationship between the individual and the organization (Rousseau, 1989). It can include beliefs about such things as performance requirements, job security, training, compensation, and career development. Organizations signal their commitments and obligations to the employee through such things as overt statements, expressions of organizational policy, and references to history or reputation. In addition, as noted in Chapter 6, the social context in which these messages are conveyed influences how they are perceived and recorded in memory. A key element of establishing employee expectations is the differentiation of roles and hierarchy of authority embodied in the organizational structure.

Psychological contracts involving the employment relationship have both transactional and relational elements, but they can differ in the extent to which they are transactional versus relational (Morrison & Robinson, 1997). Transactional aspects of contracts emphasize specific, short-term, monetary obligations such as payment for services provided by employees. Contracts of this type require only limited involvement of the parties. Relational contracts, by contrast, emphasize broad, long-term, socioemotional obligations such as commitment and loyalty.

The psychological contract is fundamentally tied to how people view themselves. Because people in different cultures have very different conceptions of the self and the interdependence of themselves and others (Markus & Kitayama, 1991), cultural differences can influence how individuals perceive and manage the social exchange with their employer. In terms of the formulation of the psychological contract, we can predict that cultural differences will exist in terms of the extent to which social cues are important in defining their contract, the extent to which characteristics of the contract are shared among organization members, and the extent to which the contract with the employer is perceived as transactional or relational (Thomas & Au, 2000). For example, we might expect that individualists would have a more transactional perception of the relationship with their employer, whereas a collectivist's perception would be more relational.

In addition to influencing contract formation, cultural variability can influence what is perceived as a violation of the contract and how such violation develops. Culture might also affect employee responses to violations in the psychological contract both directly and indirectly. That is, cultural norms can indicate appropriate responses to changes in the relationship with their employer. For example, the norm for the maintenance of harmony prevalent in some cultures would argue against voicing one's displeasure to a superior as a typical response.

A more indirect means of cultural influence might also exist in the way that individuals evaluate the nature of their relationship with their organization. That is, the context of the situation, such as the availability of good job alternatives or their previous satisfaction with their job can be evaluated differently. For example, Turnley and Feldman (1999) found that high-quality job alternatives promoted exit (leaving the organization) in response to psychological contract violations, but Thomas and Au (1999) found that national culture moderated the effect of quality of job alternatives on loyalty as a response to the more general situation of a decline in job satisfaction.

In summary, the multicultural nature of global organizations, coupled with the requirements of coping with a dynamic and complex environment, make it difficult for organizations to consistently and objectively specify the relationship with their employees. This increases the importance on the perception of the relationship that culturally different employees might hold.

Meaning of Work

The expectation that individuals have about their relationship with their employer is influenced by why they engage in work (their work motivation) and what they value in their work. A major research project conducted in seven industrialized countries addressed these questions (Meaning of Work International Research Team, 1987). This research indicates there is some consistency across countries in what people perceive as the functions of work. For example, when asked to divide 100 points across 11 purposes that work serves, approximately 70% was accounted for by three purposes in all cultures. These were that work provides (a) needed income, (b) an interesting and satisfying experience, and (c) contact with people. However, respondents from different countries placed different levels of importance on these purposes. For example, Japanese gave nearly twice as many points to "needed income" than did respondents from the Netherlands, and Israelis assigned the most points to "an interesting and satisfying experience" (Meaning of Work International Research Team, 1987). Another aspect of the meaning of work is the extent to which work is central in individuals' lives. An index of work centrality for the seven countries measured is shown in Figure 9.5.

As an example of work centrality, the Meaning of Work International Research Team (1987) asked respondents whether or not they would continue work after winning a significant amount of money. The percentage who replied that they would ranged from 93% in Japan to 69% in the United Kingdom indicating significant variation in the centrality of work. However, even a 69% response indicates the high level of importance that people attach to work. Studies in other parts of the world have found similarly high levels of work centrality indicating the importance of nonfinancial aspects of work motivation (Smith & Bond, 1999).

In analyzing the goals that people hope to achieve from work (as opposed to "why people have to work" just discussed), the Meaning of Work International Research Team (1987) discovered an interesting pattern as shown in Table 9.1.

Although a significant amount of variation in the importance of work goals was found, the most important work goal across cultures was that of interesting work (work that you really like). Respondents in four countries (Belgium, Britain, Israel, and the United States) ranked this

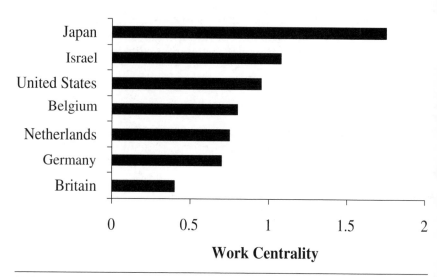

Figure 9.5. Work Centrality Across Seven Countries
SOURCE: Adapted from Meaning of Work International Research Team, 1987.

goal as most important, and the remaining three countries ranked it second or third. This finding suggests that there is some consistency across cultures (at least as represented by these four countries) about what people are looking for in their job. The importance of "interesting work" across cultures has a number of implications, not the least of which is the design of jobs.

Work Design Across Cultures

Work design is often a direct reflection of organizational design because the characteristics of structure affect the nature of jobs. For example, horizontally differentiated firms have more specialist jobs. However, although the initial focus of work design was to improve worker efficiency (Taylor, 1911), more contemporary perspectives have focused on how the characteristics of the job affect worker motivation. Although job design is presented here along with a discussion of organizational structure, it is this newer perspective on motivational aspects that largely informs the following discussion of cultural variation in job design. Three approaches to job design emanating from three different cultures are presented. These are the job characteristics model, sociotechnical systems, and quality-control circles.

TABLE 9.1 Rank Order of Work Goals Across Seven Countries

Work Goals	Belgium	Britain	Germany	Israel	Japan	Netherlands	U.S.A.
Opportunity	7	8	9	5	7	9	5
Interpersonal Relations	5	4	4	2	6	3	7
Opportunity for Promotion	10	11	10	8	11	11	10
Convenient Work Hours	9	5	6	7	8	8	9
Variety	6	7	6	11	9	4	6
Interesting Work	1	1	3	1	2	2	1
Job Security	3	3	2	10	4	7	3
Match Between Person & Job	8	6	5	6	1	6	4
Pay	2	2	1	3	5	5	2
Working Conditions	11	9	11	9	10	10	11
Autonomy	4	10	8	4	3	1	8

SOURCE: Adapted from Harpaz, 1990.

One of the most influential models of work design is the job characteristics model (Hackman & Oldham, 1980) developed in the United States.
Essentially, the model suggest that any job can be defined in terms of the
following five job characteristics:

- *skill variety*—consists of different activities requiring different abilities

- *task identity*—requires the completion of a whole and identifiable piece of
  work

- *task significance*—has a substantial effect on other people

- *autonomy*—has substantial freedom, independence, and discretion

- *feedback*—the activities of the job provide direct and clear information on
  performance

These characteristics combine to influence the psychological states that
are critical to worker motivation. To be motivating, a job must be perceived as *meaningful,* the worker must feel *responsible for outcomes,* and
the worker must *know the actual results of work activities.* The motivating
potential of the job depends on the extent to which individuals have a
strong need for personal growth. That is, individuals with high growth
needs are more likely to experience the psychological states, and they
will respond more positively to these psychological states. Considerable
research has been conducted on the job characteristics model, which generally supports the idea that there are a set of identifiable job characteristics that influence employees' behavior (Loher, Noe, Moeller, & Fitzgerald, 1980). However, alternative approaches to work characteristics
suggest that people respond to socially induced perceptions of their job
as opposed to objective characteristics of the job (Salancik & Pfeffer,
1978). Based on the previous discussion of cultural differences in the
meaning of work, the opportunity for culturally based differences in
these socially induced perceptions of job characteristics is obvious. For
example, it seems that increased job autonomy would be more likely to
increase the motivating potential of a job in the Netherlands than it
would in Britain. In addition, however, job characteristic approaches
were developed in an individualistic culture and designed primarily for
individual employees. Therefore, the application of this approach in
more collectivistic cultures might require modification.

An approach to job design that, although still considering increasing
the motivational potential of the job, was developed and applied in more
collectivist cultures is sociotechnical systems (Trist, 1981). This approach
focuses on integrating the social and technical aspects of the work system.

That is, individual workers are seen as part of a social system that must mesh with the technology of the workplace (Cummings, 1978). Sociotechnical job designs almost always involve autonomous work groups. An autonomous work group has almost complete responsibility for a significant task. The most famous sociotechnical systems application was in the Volvo automobile factories at Kalmar and Uddevalla, Sweden. At the Kalmar plant, the work was organized for teams, and each team had responsibility for a particular portion of the automobile, such as doors, interior, or electrical system. In this approach, the team becomes the focus of job design as opposed to the individual. That is, the team develops task identity by having responsibility for an identifiable portion of the car, team members develop multiple skills that allow them to perform a variety of tasks, and self-inspection of product quality provides feedback (Erez, 1997). Based on measures such as employee morale, employee turnover, and product quality, the experiment at Kalmar was a success. However, the number of hours spent on each car was considerably higher than at U.S. and Japanese manufacturers, suggesting that the teams could have been operating at less than their full capacity (Erez, 1997).

A final example of job design is the quality circles based on the belief that workers understand their own work better than anyone else and can therefore contribute to its improvement. Quality circles are small groups that voluntarily and continuously conduct quality-control activities (Onglatco, 1988). In Japan, quality circles have significantly improved quality, reduced costs, and contributed to innovation. However, they have had very limited success when transplanted to the United States (Cole, 1980). Erez and Earley (1993) suggest that this failure results from an expectation of employee participation that cannot be fulfilled by the more individualistic U.S. management philosophy. That is, quality circles are consistent with the expectation that Japanese employees have for their relationship with their employer but raise unrealistic expectations in U.S. workers.

In summary, the development of individualist job-design approaches in the United States, autonomous work groups in Northern Europe, and quality circles in Japan are congruent with the value orientations of the three regions. That is, the development of work characteristics that are consistent with the motivational requirements of different cultures is not coincidental (Erez & Earley, 1993). Therefore, the choice of job design might be best informed by cultural dimensions that relate to the way in which the characteristics of the job fulfill culturally based expectations of what work is about.

Summary

In this chapter, three challenges presented by international organizations were discussed. First, international managers must confront organizational structures that are both similar and different to their own when interacting with suppliers, competitors, and collaborators. Although all organizations can be defined in terms of their complexity, formalization, and centralization, a variety of organizational forms exist across industries and countries. Theoretical approaches, such as contingency, ecological, and institutional theories, have been formulated in order to explain organizational structure. Although none of these is adequate on its own to explain international organizations, they all provide insight into important contingencies and pressures faced by international firms. Some determinants of organizational structure can have a consistent relationship across cultures. For example, large organizations are consistently more formalized, specialized, and less centralized in all countries. However, culture influences organizational structure through its influence on the choices that managers make about organizational design and through the types of structures that societies view as legitimate.

The second challenge for managers is understanding the MNC as a unique organizational form. MNCs span both industries and countries and are therefore subject to environmental forces not felt by purely domestic organizations. These forces are categorized as pressure for internal consistency within the organization and pressures for adaptation to the local environment. These environmental influences result in a complex but loosely coupled structure with subunits having various degrees of conformity to local demands and resembling each other to varying degrees. These organizations place additional, and often conflicting or ambiguous, demands on the role of the subsidiary manager because they rely on these managers to span the organizational and cultural boundaries and provide coordination and control. Because managers from different national cultures perceive their roles differently, they can respond to these role pressures in different ways.

The third challenge for international managers associated with the structure of the organization is the relationship of employees to the organization and the design of work. Globalization of structures leads to multiculturalism of the workforce. Culturally different employees are likely to have different interpretations of their relationship to the organization and respond to changes in that relationship in different ways. The meaning they give to worklife influences the expectation that individuals have about their relationship with their employer. Both what people perceive as work and how central work is in their lives have similarities and distinct differences across cultures. How people who are culturally different view work has implications for the way work is structured in organizations. Although work can be designed to increase its potential in motivating employees, the way this is done reflects culturally based preferences.

Ten

The Challenge of International Assignments

The best place to get your international experience is beside the globe in the president's office.

Anonymous

Because of increasing diversity in the workforces of industrialized countries, understanding cross-cultural interactions is important for all managers. However, one of the most difficult situations in which to confront cultural differences is as a manager on temporary assignment in a foreign country. Understanding the special circumstances of employees sent overseas for temporary assignments (expatriates) has been a management concern since the rapid expansion of cross-border business activity that occurred following the Second World War. The trends toward staffing with local nationals versus expatriates have certainly varied over time. However, managers on temporary assignments overseas continue to play a very important role in managing today's global organizations (Kobrin, 1988; Thomas, 1994; Torbiorn, 1982). The additional difficulties presented by overseas assignments combined with the often critically important nature of the expatriate role have

perience of these employees of special interest and gener-
icant amount of research.

pter, the term *expatriate experience* is used to encompass both
ce of firms with staffing with expatriates and the experience
loyees with an overseas assignment. First, the firm's perspec-
ng with expatriates and its influence on employee selection
l with the employee's decision to accept an overseas assign-
popular ways of determining whether an overseas experience
are explored. A significant volume of research has attempted
le success of overseas employees by examining individual,
ial, and environmental factors. Reviewing this literature
ntradictions and paradoxes that suggest that an overseas
can be a double-edged sword.

The Role of Expatriates

The role that expatriates must take on is affected by the staffing strategy
that the MNC has for its foreign operations. The fundamental preferences of MNCs for a particular staffing strategy have been described as
"polycentric" (local foreign managers only), "ethnocentric" (home-country
managers predominate), or "geocentric" (a mix of nationalities at home
and abroad) (Perlmutter, 1969). Very little research actually addresses
the reasons that a firm might choose a particular staffing strategy. However, there is some evidence that the use of expatriates (home-country
nationals) follows a cycle consistent with the stage of internationalization of the firm (Franko, 1973). That is, expatriates predominate in top
managerial jobs in early stages of internationalization with the use of
third-country national managers growing as the technology of the firm is
diffused among nations. This staffing pattern was found in both U.S. and
European MNCs (Franko, 1973), but some research suggests that these
patterns might have changed over time. For example, a more recent longitudinal study of the staffing patterns of 50 U.S. affiliates of a Japanese
firm found, contradictory to the stage model suggested earlier, a positive
relationship between the company's international experience, size, and
the use of expatriates (Beechler & Iaquinto, 1994). In addition, other factors, not related to the stage of internationalization, such as the task
complexity found in the affiliate and the cultural distance of the affiliate
from headquarters, have also been found to be related to the use of expatriates (Boyacigiller, 1990). Different staffing patterns can also exist in the
foreign affiliates of firms with different countries of origin. Generally,
research has indicated that Japanese-owned firms have more expatriates

in their foreign affiliates than their U.S. or European counterparts (e.g., Beechler, 1992; Kopp, 1994; Peterson et al., 1995; Tung, 1981).

In summary, the staffing strategy of an MNC is affected by its stage of internationalization, country of origin, the size and the task complexity of its foreign affiliates, and the cultural distance of the affiliate from headquarters. This strategy is important, in part, because it can influence the role expectations that the firm has for its overseas employees (Thomas, 1998). For example, the greater numbers of expatriates in Japanese-owned firms might be an indicator that these firms rely more heavily on expatriates as means of managerial control (Baliga & Jaeger, 1984; Rosenzweig & Nohria, 1994).

Individual Staffing Decisions

Individual staffing decisions reflect the overall firm-level staffing strategy mentioned earlier whether or not this strategy is made explicit. However, some consistency across firms exists. An early study of why firms might fill an overseas position with an expatriate suggested that firms transferred personnel internationally for one of three reasons: to fill a technical requirement, to develop the manager, or to develop the organization (Edstrom & Galbraith, 1977). Recent research indicates some generality on the use of expatriates with British, German, Japanese, and U.S. firms all reporting that filling a technical requirement was the main reason for selecting expatriates (Peterson et al., 1995; Scullion, 1991). However, some variation might exist based on both the home- or host-country culture and conditions. For example, New Zealand firms have been more likely to cite the development of the organization and the expatriate manager as the major reasons for using expatriates (Enderwick & Hodgson, 1993), and a survey of managers of U.S. firms in Korea found that the most important reason stated for staffing with a local national instead of an expatriate was the manager's lack of local knowledge (Park, Sun, & David, 1993).

In summary, the staffing strategy of MNCs affects the role that the employee is expected to fill while on the overseas assignment. This role is very likely to involve the use of his or her technical expertise or the exercise of managerial control over the foreign operation, but can have a developmental component. Although these roles seem fairly consistent across cultures, the nationality of the firm might influence both the strategy of the firm and the role expectation that it has for employees on a foreign assignment.

Selection of Managers for Overseas Assignments

Based on the reasons given by firms for sending a manager on an overseas assignment, it is not surprising that early research indicated that technical competence was the primary decision criteria used by firms in selecting employees for these assignments (e.g., Borrmann, 1968; Hays, 1971; Howard, 1974; Ivancevich, 1969; Miller, 1975; Tung, 1981). A more recent survey of 24 MNCs (Haselberger & Stroh, 1992) indicated that little has changed in expatriate selection in recent years; managerial competence and technical competence continue to lead the list of selection criteria. Other criteria that can have a substantial bearing on an employee's performance seem to be generally neglected. This overemphasis on technical competence as a selection criterion may result because high technical qualifications present a lower perceived risk of adverse consequences to the selecting manager (Miller, 1975). In addition, firms may place the most emphasis on selection criteria that are most easily measured, such as technical skills.

Interestingly, host-country organizations also view technical expertise as an important selection criteria for the expatriates assigned to them (Zeira & Banai, 1985). In addition, consistent with the discussion on decision making in Chapter 5, there seem to be some differences in selection criteria based on the nationality of the firm. For example, one recent study found that the ability to adapt was ranked as the most important selection criteria by Australian managers and by expatriates on assignment and was ranked second to technical competence by Asian managers (Stone, 1991). As is noted later in this chapter, the reliance on technical expertise as the most important selection criteria for success in an overseas assignment is probably not well-founded.

Decision to Accept an Overseas Assignment

The pool of potential applicants available to the manager making a staffing decision is limited by a number of factors, including restrictions imposed by other organizational requirements and those imposed by the individuals themselves. One of these is the willingness and motivation of applicants to accept the overseas posting. Reasons for accepting an overseas posting cover the gamut from personal development to financial gain. Early studies found that the motives of people from the United States for accepting an assignment were (a) a sense of vocation, (b) financial rewards, and (c) the desire to escape undesirable circumstances at home (Cleveland, Mangone, & Adams, 1960). In addition, studies show that U.S. people accepting their first overseas assignment were more likely to be motivated by the opportunity to advance their career than were employees with previous international experience, and that the willingness to relocate overseas was significantly related to the expatriate's focus on career advancement (Brett, Stroh, & Reilly, 1993; Miller & Cheng, 1978).

Taken together, these studies point out the differing perspectives on an overseas assignment from the point of view of the firm versus that of the employee. That is, although firms tend to select expatriates based on technical requirements, the expatriates themselves are primarily motivated, at least on their first posting, by the opportunity for career advancement. It seems, therefore, that conflict between the expectations that firms have for an expatriate and the perceptions that expatriates have of their role is often built-in at the outset of the experience.

Definitions of Success

Firms and expatriate employees are concerned with the success of an overseas assignment. However, whether an overseas assignment is viewed as a success or failure depends, in part, on the definition of success. These definitions often vary widely; however, research in this area has focused primarily on three outcomes of the expatriate experience: turnover, adjustment, and task performance.

Turnover

The most frequently used measure of expatriate success (failure) has been turnover, or more specifically, the premature return of expatriates to their home country (Black & Gregersen, 1990). Most often, this has been measured as the intent to remain on assignment for the time originally agreed upon. Reports that as many as 30% of expatriates failed to complete their initial overseas assignment were responsible for much of the research into the determinants of expatriates' success (Thomas, 1998). Turnover of expatriates is of special concern to firms because of the extra costs of maintaining these employees.

Adjustment

The second major focus of research on expatriate success has been the ability of the expatriate to overcome culture shock (Oberg, 1960) and adjust to the new environment. A psychological definition of adjustment is a condition consisting of a relationship with the environment in which needs are satisfied and the ability to meet physical and social demands exists (English, 1958). This overall adjustment was refined in later research to include three dimensions of adjustment (Black, Gregersen, & Mendenhall, 1992; Black, Mendenhall, & Oddou, 1991; Parker & McEvoy, 1993; Takeuchi & Hannon, 1996). These dimensions are general living adjustment, work adjustment, and interaction adjustment, and they seem to be influenced by somewhat different factors (Black & Gregersen, 1991a; Parker & McEvoy, 1993). Figure 10.1 summarizes the relationships among the three facets of adjustment and their individual, job, cultural, and nonwork antecedents. Noteworthy in this summary of relationships is that job characteristics are primarily related to work adjustment and that individual characteristics are related to all three facets of adjustment.

Much of the research on the expatriate adjustment was based on an assumption of a cycle of adjustment to the foreign environment that follows a U-shaped pattern (Lysgaard, 1955). The model is extended to a W when repatriation is considered (Gullahorn & Gullahorn, 1963). This adjustment cycle is presented graphically in Figure 10.2.

According to the model shown in Figure 10.2, expatriates progress at regular intervals through four phases of honeymoon, culture shock, adjustment, and, finally, mastery. In the honeymoon stage, everything is new, exciting, and interesting, and the new environment intrigues the expatriate in much the same way as if the expatriate were a tourist. At the culture shock stage, the expatriate becomes frustrated and confused because the environment is not providing familiar cues. At the adjustment stage, the expatriate begins to understand cultural differences, learns the ways to get things done, and begins to settle in to the rhythm of daily living in the foreign country. Eventually, the expatriate can achieve the mastery stage and become able to function in the new culture almost as well as at home. Not all expatriates achieve mastery in their new environment. Some return home early, whereas others can complete their assignment but without really adjusting.

Research support for the U-shaped curve of adjustment has not been conclusive (Church, 1982). Although some support has been found (Black & Mendenhall, 1991), in general, research fails to show support for the generality of both the phases and the time parameters of the U-curve, making the description of the curve extremely variable. In addition, different patterns of adjustment in the work and nonwork environments, as well as different adjustment patterns for expatriates and for their spouses, have been found (Briody & Chrisman, 1991; Nicholson &

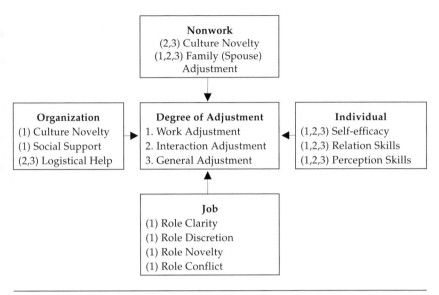

Figure 10.1. Framework of International Adjustment
SOURCE: Republished with permission of Academy of Management Review, from "Toward a Comprehensive Model of International Adjustment: An Integration of Multiple Theoretical Perspectives," by Black, J. S., Mendenhall, M. E., & Oddou, G., Vol. 16, Iss. 2. Copyright ©1991. Permission conveyed through Copyright Clearance Center, Inc.

Imaizumi, 1993). Despite the lack of strong empirical support, the idea that expatriates might go through some systematic and discernible pattern of adjustment remains an attractive notion from both an academic and a practical perspective.

Task Performance

Task performance is the third major indicator of expatriate performance. A distinctive feature of the expatriate role is the requirement that expatriates meet the often-conflicting performance expectations of home-office superiors and host nationals (Mendenhall & Oddou, 1985). Only very recently have researchers begun to examine the processes used to evaluate expatriate performance. In general, this research indicates that accurate appraisals of expatriate performance is difficult to obtain but might be facilitated by balancing the appraisals of home- and host-country raters and by increasing the frequency of appraisal (Gregersen, Hite, & Black, 1996).

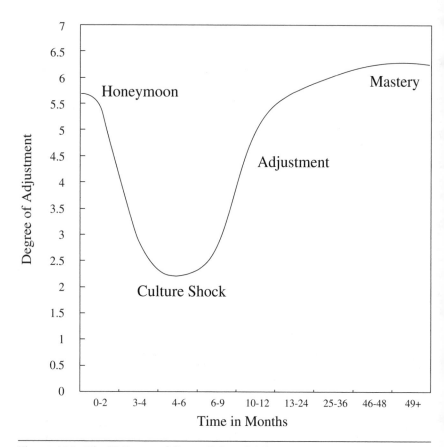

Figure 10.2. The U-Curve of Cross-Cultural Adjustment

Adjustment-Performance Relationship

Much of the research on the expatriate experience has assumed a direct positive relationship between the adjustment and the performance of expatriates (e.g., Mendenhall & Oddou, 1985). However, this relationship might be more complicated than has often been assumed. Research support for a positive relationship between adjustment and performance is somewhat equivocal. Some studies have found performance negatively related to expatriates' perceptions of the intensity of their adjustment to the new culture (Earley, 1987). However, other studies have found different effects depending on the facet of adjustment and the measure of performance used. The following are examples of these findings:

- Work adjustment, but not general adjustment or interaction adjustment, positively related to performance (Nicholson & Imaizumi, 1993).

- Interaction and general adjustment positively related to intent to stay on assignment, whereas no relationship was found for adjustment to work (Gregersen & Black, 1990).

- Work adjustment positively related to performance, but general living adjustment negatively related to performance, after controlling for work adjustment and interaction adjustment (Parker & McEvoy, 1993).

- Performance and adjustment were predicted by different factors in a study of Japanese and U.S. managers (Clarke & Hammer, 1995).

In summary, this evidence suggests that different facets of adjustment can affect the performance of employees on overseas assignment in different ways. The relationship also depends on how performance is assessed. In addition, some research suggests that the highest-performing individuals, at least in terms of their effectiveness in transferring skills and knowledge to host nationals, are also the most likely to experience severe culture shock (Kealey, 1989; Ruben & Kealey, 1979). Overall, the assumption that good adjustment leads to good performance is probably an oversimplification.

The different parties involved in the expatriate experience—the home country, the host country, and the expatriate—can have somewhat different expectations. In addition, the outcomes of an expatriate experience can vary widely. Therefore, the following multidimensional definition of success in an expatriate assignment was devised (Feldman & Thomas, 1992). An overseas assignment is successful if the individual:

- meets the performance expectations of quality and quantity of both home-country and host-country superiors,

- develops and maintains satisfactory relationships with local nationals,

- acquires skills related to managing people of different cultures, and

- remains on assignment the agreed upon length of time.

Factors Affecting Expatriate Success

A number of factors related to one measure or another of expatriate success have been examined. These include individual, organizational, and environmental variables. The following section describes the key research findings regarding the effects of these three categories of variables on outcomes of an overseas assignment.

Individual Factors

Similar to early leadership research, much of the early research of individual differences focused on the personality characteristics of those people who were effective in overseas assignments (e.g., Cleveland et al., 1960; Guthrie & Zektrick, 1967; Mottram, 1963; Sewell & Davidson, 1956; Stein, 1966). However, the failure of empirical tests to establish consistent relationships between personality characteristics and measures of success such as task performance, adjustment, and satisfaction resulted in a shift in emphasis to the behavior of successful individuals or their social skills (Brein & David, 1971; Furnham & Bochner, 1986; Stening, 1979). Individuals who described themselves as being satisfied with and functioning well in a foreign culture identified the following behaviors or personal abilities considered important to their success:

- the ability to manage psychological stress,

- the ability to effectively communicate, and

- the ability to establish interpersonal relationships (Abe & Wiseman 1983; Hammer, 1987; Hammer, Gudykunst, & Wiseman, 1978).

In addition, some research sought the opinions of employees (U.S. people) overseas regarding critical success factors. Consistent among the studies was that family situation (lack of spouse adjustment) was mentioned as the factor most likely linked to expatriate failure (Hays, 1971, 1974; Tung, 1981). A recent study of expatriates from 26 different nationalities (Arthur & Bennett, 1995) identified five characteristics of individuals related to success. In order of importance to respondents, these were the following:

- family situation,

- adaptability,

- job knowledge,

- relational ability, and

- openness to other cultures.

Clearly, a wide range of individual characteristics can influence the success or failure of an expatriate experience. In addition, some evidence suggests that the importance of these factors might be somewhat cross-culturally consistent. However, because of the difficulty involved in defining the prototypical expatriate, the classification of these characteristics into broad skill or behavior dimensions, as suggested earlier, is probably a more useful way to include individual characteristics in the evaluation of antecedents to success in an overseas assignment.

Demographics

In addition to individual differences noted previously, demographic characteristics of expatriates, such as age, tenure, educational level, and marital status, have all been found to influence the expatriate experience. The following is a summary of these research findings:

- The age of the expatriate has been found to be positively related to organizational commitment, work adjustment, and job satisfaction, but negatively correlated with willingness to relocate, intent to leave, and general satisfaction.

- Tenure of expatriates has been found to be positively related to job satisfaction and negatively related to intent to leave.

- The education level of expatriates has been found to be negatively related to job satisfaction and commitment to the organization, and positively related to general adjustment and interaction adjustment, but not work adjustment.

- Married expatriates have been found to be more job satisfied and higher performers.

- The adjustment of the spouse or family is positively related to expatriate adjustment and negatively related to intent to leave (Thomas, 1998).

The rationale for these effects has rarely been specified. Instead, it is assumed that demographic characteristics indicate underlying values, attitudes, and beliefs, which, in turn, relate to outcomes. Like personality characteristics, the contribution of the effect of demographics alone to our understanding of the expatriate experience is somewhat limited. However, as shown later in this chapter, as indicators of life stage, career stage, and family situation in combination with organizational and environmental variables, they prove somewhat more useful in explaining the expatriate experience.

Foreign Language Ability and Previous International Experience

Two individual factors with established theoretical linkages to expatriate success are the ability of the overseas employee to communicate in the host-country language and previous international experience. Both foreign-language fluency and prior overseas experience can be important to expatriate success. However, the particular elements of success to which these factors apply and the mechanisms through which they operate have not been clearly defined. For example, substantial support has been found for a positive relationship between foreign-language fluency and the degree of interaction with host nationals and to a lesser extent with satisfaction, commitment and adjustment (Church, 1982; Thomas, 1998). This effect might be based on the ability of expatriates to develop a so-called conversational currency (being able to make conversation about everyday things such as local sporting events, etc.) that can facilitate interactions with host nationals (Brein & David, 1971). However, several empirical studies suggest that foreign-language skill is not necessarily an effective predictor of expatriate success (Benson, 1978). That is, it might not be language skill that is the critical factor but the willingness to communicate, which is facilitated by skill in the foreign language.

In considering previous overseas experience, it might be that the quality of international experience is as important as the amount in facilitating adjustment to another culture. Recent studies found that the amount of prior overseas experience was positively related to adjustment and to job satisfaction (Naumann, 1993; Parker & McEvoy, 1993; Takeuchi & Hannon, 1996). In addition, one study found that U.S. managers with prior experience abroad were more likely to use appropriate intercultural behaviors (Dunbar, 1992). However, other research suggests that previous overseas experience can be negatively related to some attitudes of expatriates, such as the amount of discretion they feel they have in performing their jobs (Black & Gregersen, 1990).

The intuitively appealing notion that foreign-language fluency and previous overseas experience are positively related to expatriate success seems, at best, to be an oversimplification of the relationship. The likelihood is that the relationship between language fluency and expatriate effectiveness is not a linear one. For example, anecdotal evidence suggests that the returns for a small amount of foreign-language knowledge (knowing a few words) are great but that to achieve substantial additional benefit, a significant degree of language fluency (the ability to develop conversational currency) is required. A similar relationship might be suggested for overseas experience with the additional recognition that all overseas experiences are not identical, and the ability of individuals to learn from prior overseas experiences might be highly variable. In addition, the effects of these two factors are likely to be influenced by the amount of intercultural interaction required by the assignment and the degree of cultural novelty in the situation.

Nationality of Expatriates

Early studies of foreign students (see Church, 1982, for a review) indicated that nationality of the individual was important to adjustment to the foreign environment. However, the vast majority of research on overseas business experiences has been conducted with U.S. expatriates. Some research suggests that U.S. expatriates might have higher rates of premature return from their assignment than, for example, Europeans and Japanese (Tung, 1981) or New Zealanders (Enderwick & Hodgson, 1993). In addition, differences have been found in the cultural skill and knowledge, and in job satisfaction reported by U.S. versus German expatriates living in Japan (Dunbar, 1994), and in the self-perceived effectiveness of Japanese versus U.S. expatriates in Thailand (Stening & Hammer, 1992). These results suggest that the cultural background of the expatriates themselves, as well as the characteristics of the foreign culture, can influence some aspects of their overseas experience.

Gender of Expatriates

Recently, the possible effect of the gender of the expatriate manager has become a more important and recognizable issue. However, as Adler (1987) notes, "... about the single most uncontroversial, incontrovertible statement to make about women in international management is that there are very few of them" (p. 169). Indeed, recent estimates suggest that only about 14% of expatriates are female (Solomon, 1998), and only about 4% of top executives in international subsidiaries are women (Elron, 1997). However, the profile of the typical female expatriate suggests that the small number of female expatriates might be the beginning of a trend. A survey of 52 women expatriates in Asia (Adler, 1987) reported the following characteristics:

- average age of 28.8 years

- 62% were single

- almost all had a graduate degree

- they were in very junior positions

- they spoke 2.5 languages on average

- 90% were the first women in the overseas position

- 22% were the first female manager expatriated anywhere by their firm

A very similar profile was reported in a study of 45 female expatriates in Hong Kong (Westwood & Leung, 1994). A survey of international personnel managers from 60 U.S. and Canadian companies concerning their perceptions of barriers to women expatriates sheds light on the reasons for the profile just mentioned (Adler, 1984). Fifty-four percent indicated that their firm would hesitate in sending women on an expatriate assignment. In order, the personnel managers listed the following reasons:

- foreigner's prejudice against women (72.7%)

- dual careers (69.1%)

- selection bias (53.8%)

- women not interested (24.5%)

- women unqualified (18.2%)

- women not effective (5.6%)

These results are consistent with previous findings that top managers feel that women face significant resistance when seeking overseas assignments (Thal & Cateora, 1979). However, a survey of 1,129 graduating MBAs from the United States, Canada, and Europe indicated that male and female MBA graduates were equally interested in international careers (Adler, 1986). In addition, women are more likely to find an expatriate experience in large firms and with financial institutions (Adler, 1984).

A central issue to women expatriates is the extent to which women face greater difficulty overseas than men. Surveys have generally indicated negative attitudes by local businesspeople toward women expatriates (Stone, 1991), discrimination against them (Westwood & Leung, 1994), and a preference of overseas businesspeople for dealing with male executives (e.g., Izraeli, Banai, & Zeira, 1980). However, some research has suggested that being female can be an advantage overseas. Adler's (1987) survey of 52 women expatriates in Asia indicated the following:

- 42% felt that being female was an advantage,

- 22% found it irrelevant,

- 16% said that being female had both positive and negative effects, and

- 20% found it primarily negative.

Anecdotal reports suggest that advantages can accrue to women expatriates because of their small number that increases visibility, they are afforded higher status because of their uniqueness, or because they have better interpersonal skills than men (Adler, 1987; Taylor & Napier, 1996; Westwood & Leung, 1994).

Some researchers suggest that a greater presence of women in the expatriate community in the future may result from recent developments, such as a shortage of qualified men, legal and social pressure for equal opportunity, the increasing familiarity with women in management positions, and the increasing ability of women to self-select for an overseas assignment because of changing company attitudes (Antal & Izraeli, 1993). This prediction underscores the need to understand the special issues surrounding the placement of women in overseas positions.

Job and Organizational Factors

In addition to characteristics of individuals, aspects of the job and the organization are important to the expatriate experience. Consistent with the managerial-role focus of this book, job-related factors can perhaps best be described in terms of role characteristics, such as novelty, ambiguity, discretion, conflict, and overload. In addition, the job level of the expatriate has an influence on the experience. Important organizational factors are the degree of training provided to the expatriate and, relatedly, the extent to which the expatriate has realistic prior knowledge about the assignment.

Expatriate Job Characteristics

The reason for examining the characteristics of the expatriate experience, in terms of role characteristics, stems from the idea that an expatriate assignment involves the adjustment to a new work role as well as to a new environment (Black, 1988). In general, these results suggest that, as might be expected, work-role characteristics have an influence on the work adjustment of expatriates. Specifically, the amounts of ambiguity, novelty, and conflict in the expatriate's role all have a negative effect on adjustment to a new work role and on job satisfaction (Thomas, 1998). Not surprisingly, work adjustment is, in turn, positively related to the intent to remain on assignment (Black, 1990). A consistent finding is that the amount of discretion that expatriates have in conducting their role has a positive effect on their adjustment to their new work role and their intention to remain on assignment (Thomas, 1998).

Although the main influence of characteristics of the job is on the expatriate's adjustment to the work of the new assignment, in some cases, work-role characteristics have shown some spillover effect on other facets of adjustment. Specifically, discretion in one's work role seems to facilitate general adjustment, and ambiguity and conflict in the role negatively affects both general adjustment and the ability to interact with host nationals (Thomas, 1998).

Job Level

The organizational level of job changers influences the types of strategies available to them to deal with the effects of moving to a new role, and hence on the probability of favorable outcomes (Feldman & Brett, 1983). For example, the organizational level of expatriates was found to be positively related to job satisfaction, intent to remain on assignment, and to self-reports of performance (Thomas, 1998). However higher-level expatriates have also been reported as having more trouble adjusting to new jobs, and some higher-level Japanese expatriates have more difficulty with interaction and general adjustment (Gregersen & Black, 1990; Takeuchi & Hannon, 1996). These results suggest that the organizational level of expatriates might also carry with it other factors, such as more challenging assignments, which may need to be considered in predicting the effect of organizational level on the expatriate experience.

In addition to characteristics of a specific overseas job, more general organizational characteristics have an influence on the expatriate experience. Key organizational factors that influence success include the amount of organizational support provided expatriates and their families, the extent to which the expatriate was provided with realistic information about the country and the assignment, and the amount of cross-cultural training provided. Of these factors, the amount of training has received the most attention.

Expatriate Training

The conventional wisdom regarding cross-cultural training of expatriates is that although the positive effect of such training is well-documented (e.g., Landis & Brislin, 1983), firms often fail to provide training because they believe it is not effective (Mendenhall & Oddou, 1985). The failure of firms to provide extensive cross-cultural training is widespread and documented in studies in a number of different countries (e.g., Enderwick & Hodgson, 1993; Tung, 1981). However, broad support for a positive relationship between cross-cultural training and outcomes related to managerial effectiveness has been documented (Black & Mendenhall, 1990; Deshpande & Viswesvaran, 1992). Specifically, these reviews suggest that cross-cultural training is positively related to the following:

- self development (self-oriented skills, perceptual skills, and relational skills),

- adjustment,

- relationships with host nationals, and

- performance (Black & Mendenhall, 1990; Deshpande & Viswesvaran, 1992).

Despite this general endorsement for the effectiveness of training, less is known about the effects of different training types, such as informational training, area studies, cultural awareness training, and intercultural skills training. In addition, a question remains regarding the appropriateness of predeparture versus in-country training. That is, At what point in the expatriate experience is training most beneficial? Figure 10.3 is derived from recent work by Black and Mendenhall (1989) and draws on social-learning theory for guidance (Bandura, 1977). It suggests that the selection of training methods for a particular situation can be determined by referring to the degree of cultural novelty in the situation, the requirements for intercultural interaction with host nationals, and the degree of novelty in the job.

The rationale presented in the model is that as the requirements of the situation become more demanding, the cross-cultural training required should move from more passive to more participative modes. That is, whereas fact-oriented training might suffice in situations with low cultural novelty, low interaction requirements, and low job novelty—more rigorous training, involving more analytical and experiential elements, is required for situations at the other end of the spectrum.

Related to the issue of cross-cultural training is the expatriate's accurate or realistic conception of the situation to which the expatriate is moving. According to research regarding the realistic expectations of new jobs (e.g., Meglino & DeNisi, 1987), one might anticipate that realistic expectations by the expatriate would be related to positive outcomes. That is, accurate information about the environment provides the opportunity for expatriates to make adjustments in anticipation of environmental differences (Gullahorn & Gullahorn, 1963). For example, realistic expectations have been found to be positively related to expatriate adjustment and job satisfaction (Feldman & Tompson, 1993; Stroh, Dennis, & Cramer, 1994). Similarly, a positive relationship between expatriates' predeparture knowledge about the host country and all the facets of expatriate adjustment has been documented (Black, 1990). These results emphasize

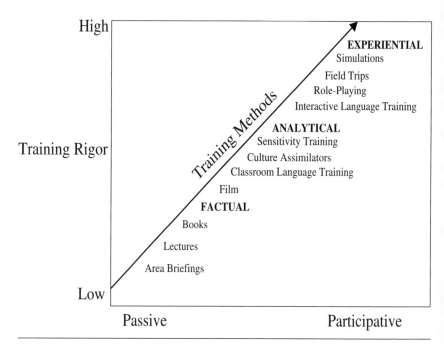

Figure 10.3. Framework for Selecting Cross-Cultural Training
SOURCE: From "A Practical but Theory-Based Framework for Selecting Cross-Cultural Training Methods,"
by J. S. Black & M. Mendenhall, *Human Resource Management,* Copyright ©1989, John Wiley & Sons.
Reprinted by permission of John Wiley & Sons, Inc.

that the reduction of uncertainty is an important consideration in the overseas experience and therefore in cross-cultural training.

A third organizational factor, which is found to be related to elements of expatriate success, is the extent of the organizational support received by expatriates. For example, one measure of organizational support, the amount of contact (through visits to headquarters, letters, telexes) that expatriates have with the parent company, has been positively related to some facets of adjustment (Black, 1990). In addition, the level of company assistance was found to be positively related to expatriate job satisfaction (Stroh et al., 1994) and, in a study of Australian expatriate spouses, also a significant predictor of psychological adjustment (DeCieri, Dowling, & Taylor, 1991). However, the effect of the level and nature of organizational support is complicated. For example, the support requirements of dual-career couples are very different (Harvey, 1997). In addition, the level of the expatriate's commitment to the organization determines, in part, the effectiveness of support programs (Guzzo, Noonan, & Elron, 1994). Therefore, it is an oversimplification to say that more organizational support is better. Support requirements seem to be related to the needs and expectations of each employee's situation.

Environmental Factors

In addition to job and organizational factors, other factors, external to the expatriate and over which the expatriate has little control, have the opportunity to influence the expatriate's success. Of these, both the novelty and toughness of the new culture and the amount of social support available have been the subject of some research.

Cultural Novelty

The extent to which the host-country culture is different from the expatriate's home culture is theorized to make the adjustment process more difficult (Church, 1982; Mendenhall & Oddou, 1985). Studies of expatriates have found that cultural novelty is negatively related to interaction adjustment, general adjustment, and willingness to accept an assignment and positively related to social difficulty (Thomas, 1998). However, the research support for these negative effects of cultural novelty on outcomes is not universal. Positive relationships between cultural novelty and general adjustment (Black & Gregersen, 1991a; Parker & McEvoy, 1993) and to all three facets of adjustment for Japanese expatriates (Takeuchi & Hannon, 1996) are documented. Similarly, for Europeans on assignment in Europe, North America, and Asia, cultural novelty was found to be positively related to the level of intercultural interaction (Janssens, 1995). These contradictory findings suggest the possibility that cultural novelty can exert its influence differently depending on the characteristics of the individual and the situation. For example, environmental differences encountered by Japanese in the United States might result in over-met expectations about housing that influence their perceptions of adjustment difficulties.

Social Support

The logic behind the effect of social support on the expatriate experience is that being able to draw on social relationships provides a mechanism for dealing with the stress associated with an overseas assignment. Research generally supports the direct positive effect of social support from both host- and home-country nationals on the adjustment of expatriates (Thomas, 1998). However, some differences in the nature of the social support of expatriates and their spouses are documented. For example, at least one study finds that expatriates derived their social support primarily from host-country nationals, whereas spouses interacted primarily with home-country nationals (Briody & Chrisman, 1991).

Repatriation

The notion has long been recognized that reentry to one's home country after a long sojourn requires a process of adjustment similar to that of the initial transfer overseas (Gullahorn & Gullahorn, 1963). Additionally, repatriation is distinct, in both degree and kind, from other types of job-related geographic transfers (Black et al., 1992; Feldman & Thomas, 1992). First, the degree of novelty (cultural, organizational, job, etc.) is higher for a transfer between countries as compared to within a country. Second, in the repatriation situation, the individual is returning to their home country after a period of absence of typically 2 to 5 years for U.S. and British expatriates (Black & Gregersen, 1991b) and potentially longer for German or Japanese expatriates (Peterson et al., 1995). During this time, both the individual and the home country have undergone changes largely independent of each other. Unlike the domestic job changer, the repatriate is likely confronted with these changes simultaneously. In addition, for most expatriates, the repatriate experience is qualitatively different from the expatriate experience. That is, most repatriates (80% according to Black & Gregersen, 1991b) are returning home from an assignment in a country of which they had little or no prior experience. Therefore, their prior knowledge and expectations about the country they are moving to are likely to be substantially different in the case of repatriation versus expatriation.

One of the few studies directly examining repatriation adjustment found that for U.S. expatriates, repatriation adjustment was facilitated by such factors as the amount of clarity and discretion the expatriate had in the new role but negatively affected by the time spent overseas, social status, and housing conditions (Black & Gregersen, 1991b). These results were largely confirmed in a replication with a sample 173 Japanese expatriates who had recently returned from a foreign assignment (Black, 1994).

Results of these studies suggest factors that facilitate expatriate adjustment can in turn inhibit repatriation (Black, 1994; Black & Gregersen, 1991b). For example, the improved housing conditions that most expatriates experience overseas might help them cope while there, but the drop in housing conditions on return has a negative effect. Likewise, the longer employees are overseas, the more difficult is their adjustment on return.

Expatriate Careers

In general, expatriate assignments do not seem to have positive effects on the development of a manager's career. Reports are common that expatriates are often neglected on their return, put in holding patterns, and not valued for their international experience by their firms (e.g., Adler, 1981; Feldman & Thomas, 1992; Harvey, 1989; Tung, 1981). Adler (1981) reports that one out of four expatriates leave the firm upon reentry and that graduating MBAs (Adler, 1987) perceive an international assignment as a risky career move. Although an international assignment might facilitate an individual's movement to a higher career stage, in general, expatriates have reported that their overseas assignment did not have a positive long-term effect on their career, that their firms do not take advantage of the skills they learned overseas, and that their assignments were better for their personal development than for their professional careers (Oddou & Mendenhall, 1991).

However, the extent to which the expatriate assignment fits with employees' career plans influences the effectiveness of expatriates while on assignment. The expatriate's perception of a connection between the expatriate assignment and long-term career has been positively related to their performance on assignment (Feldman & Thomas, 1992) and with their effective repatriation (Gomez-Meija & Balkin, 1987). In addition, the extent to which the assignment was perceived as a promotion was found to be positively related to the intention to remain on assignment (Birdseye & Hill, 1995). It is important to note that the research results of the effects of overseas assignments on careers deal exclusively with U.S. expatriates; therefore, career patterns, career goals, career tactics, and career plans may vary according to the national culture of the individual (Granrose, 1994).

International Assignments: A Double-Edged Sword

The examination of the expatriate experience presented in this chapter suggests that taking on an overseas management role can have both positive and negative consequences. It is managing these contradictory or paradoxical relationships that makes the international assignment challenging both from the standpoint of the firm and the expatriate. The following summarizes the most apparent of these contradictions.

Adjustment-Performance Paradox

The relationship between expatriate adjustment and performance on an international assignment has been assumed to be direct and positive, and this assumption underlies a great deal of research and practice. However, research does not indicate overwhelming support for this assumption. In fact, as stated earlier, it seems possible that the highest-performing expatriates are those who experience the most severe culture shock and have the most difficult time adjusting. That is, the same characteristics that allow individuals to be effective overseas (e.g., others orientation, perceptual skills) can make it more stressful to adjust.

Marital Status Contradiction

A second individual characteristic that has a paradoxical relationship to success on an international assignment is the family situation of the expatriate. Married expatriates adjust better than do single expatriates, and social support (potentially provided by the spouse in some cases) is important to overseas adjustment. However, substantial evidence suggests that the main reason for an expatriate's premature return home is the failure of their family (spouse) to adjust. This apparent paradox suggests that the relationship between the expatriate's family situation and their effectiveness is likely to be much more complex than conceptualized to date.

Selection-Performance Contradiction for Women Expatriates

Very few international assignees are women, and there seems to be a bias against selecting women for overseas assignments. However, women expatriates are likely to be more highly educated and better prepared for international assignments than their male counterparts. In addition, women's management styles are more consistent with the relational and perceptual abilities that some authors suggest are required for overseas effectiveness (Davidson & Cooper, 1987; Freedman & Phillips, 1988). As the presence of women in management roles in general and the expatriate role in particular increases, the need to understand the issues involved in placing women overseas will certainly increase.

Americans-Only Problem

The vast majority of expatriate research has been limited to studying U.S. nationals abroad. However, in the few studies involving other nationalities, cultural differences have had a sometimes contradictory effect on a variety of outcomes. For example, the reasons for staffing with expatriates, selection criteria for expatriates, failure rates as measured by premature return, relationship between adjustment and performance, and antecedents to organizational commitment all vary by nationality (Thomas, 1998).

Selection-Motivation Contradiction

Firms tend to select individuals for overseas assignments based on the individual's ability to fill a technical requirement with little regard for the effect on the individual's career. However, people accept overseas assignments primarily to advance their career and are more effective and satisfied if they see the connection between the expatriate assignment and their long-term career plans. In addition, the clarity of the role expectations that the firm has for the individual has a significant positive relationship on the expatriate experience.

Transfer-of-Knowledge Problem

Individuals report considerable personal development along a wide range of skill and knowledge dimensions because of their overseas assignment. However, upon return to their home country, their newly won skills are rarely used, and the net effect of the overseas assignment is often described as having a neutral to negative effect on their long-term career. In addition, although it can take several years for an individual to become truly effective in an international assignment, longer tenure overseas results in more difficult repatriation. These effects are of considerable concern in the value of an international assignment on an individual's career and for the development of the firm.

Training-Effectiveness Contradiction

Perhaps the most studied organizational factor related to the international assignments is the amount of cross-cultural training provided. The contradiction that cross-cultural training is effective but that firms fail to avail themselves of it is a long-standing issue. Although it seems clear that cross-cultural training can have very positive benefits, the effectiveness of training may have been oversimplified. That is, despite theoretical expositions that suggest that different approaches to cross-cultural training can be effective in different circumstances and questions of predeparture versus in-country training, these issues have not been examined. In addition, it would be naive to suggest that the quality of cross-cultural training was consistent across programs or that quality does not influence effectiveness.

Cultural-Novelty Paradox

The logic of the idea that the greater the differences between one's home and host country, the greater the adjustment difficulties has been supported in a number of studies. However, contradictory results suggest that cultural novelty can facilitate certain types of adjustment. The relationship of cultural novelty to the expatriate experience is clearly not as simple as it is often portrayed. It seems possible that a number of variables, such as the expectation that expatriates have about the foreign environment, might influence the relationship.

Summary

In this chapter, the challenge of overseas assignments was presented from both the point of view of the firm and that of the individual expatriate. These employees are of special concern because of their often-critical role on both organizational and cultural boundaries. Firms might decide to use expatriates for a variety of strategic or developmental reasons, and a significant amount of research identifies individual organizational and environmental factors that contribute to the success or failure of these managers. A review of these findings suggests that an overseas experience can have both positive and negative consequences, for both the individual and the firm. Managing these contradictory or paradoxical effects is a significant challenge for international managers.

Section IV
International
Management
Research

Eleven

The Challenge of Learning More

Evaluating Cross-Cultural Management Studies

The convergence of management will never come.

Hofstede, 1983

The key to a cross-culturally applicable management theory appears to lie in cultural contingency.

Doktor, Tung, & Von Glinow, 1991

The practice of management is anything but static. As globalization increases the amount of intercultural contact in organizational settings, the inadequacy of our present understanding of management to explain and predict behavior in these settings becomes more apparent. For practicing managers and management scholars to continue to enhance their understanding of management in this dynamic environment, it is imperative that systematic study in this field continue to improve. What is needed is effective and functional theory that applies to international settings (Doktor, Tung, & Von Glinow, 1991). It is important to provide international managers with the tools needed to cope with ever more complex jobs. Failure to do so reinforces the lack of relevance of which management research is often accused.

The type of exploration needed is not easy for those conducting international studies, and understanding the findings and their implications is often not straightforward for consumers of this research. In this chapter, general issues about the limitations of current management theory to explaining international management are outlined. Then, studies of international management are classified by the types of questions that they can answer. Finally, key methodological issues regarding cross-national and cross-cultural research are presented, both as a reminder for scholars and a consumer's guide of a sort for practicing managers.

Source of Limitations in Present Management Studies

As noted in this book, it is possible to describe myriad differences that exist among management practices around the world. However, to try to understand what is happening in practice in various countries, management scholars are often relegated to a reliance on theory that has its basis in the United States. As scholars construct theory, they are searching to understand the world that they perceive around them (Doktor et al., 1991). If, as is the case in much management research, that world is the United States, their theory reflects it. This bias in theory development is not the result of an inherent belief in the superiority of U.S. management but of parochialism—a lack of awareness of alternative contexts, models, research, and values (Boyacigiller & Adler, 1991). This parochialism is understandable and can be better considered in our evaluation of management research if we review its origins.

Economic Hegemony

The questions to which management scholars seek answers are a product of the time in which they are studied (Lawrence, 1987). Although some early management thought, emanating from the likes of Henri Fayol, Max Weber, and F. W. Taylor, had its origins outside of North America, much of contemporary management knowledge was defined in the United States during a particular period in history. After World War II, the United States was the only major economic power left intact, and it dominated the world economy for the next 20 years. It was during this period of U.S. economic dominance that the field of management studies began to emerge and was thus imprinted with a U.S. orientation (Boyacigiller & Adler, 1991). Under the assumption that the underlying influence of the economic success of the United States was U.S. management practices, U.S. firms were studied and their practices were held up as models for the world (Beechler & Pucik, 1989). Additionally, many of the most prestigious management journals were founded in the United States during this time (Boyacigiller & Adler, 1991). Whether or not it was actually management practice, or as argued by some (Ouchi, 1984; Thurow, 1984) a benevolent environment that accounted for U.S. success, the study of management has an indelible U.S. imprint.

Institutional Heritage

The legacy of the U.S. origins of management studies is evident in the institutions that perpetuate the way in which management research is done and how it is disseminated. First, it is important to note that the vast majority of scientific knowledge is contained in perhaps as few as 10% of the countries of the world and that the study of organizations is represented in still fewer (Roberts & Boyacigiller, 1984). The United States accounts for the vast majority of published articles in the field of management and organizational studies, and all but a handful of the "key" contributions to the field have come from U.S. researchers (Adler, Doktor, & Redding, 1986; Boyacigiller & Adler, 1991).

It is the responsibility of academic institutions to prepare scholars to create and disseminate knowledge. The record of U.S. academic institutions for fostering an international orientation among their scholars is not particularly notable. For example, the majority of U.S academic institutions do not require a foreign language for a bachelor's degree, and most doctoral programs allow a computer language as credit toward their foreign-language requirement (Boyacigiller & Adler, 1991). The accrediting body for U.S. business schools (American Association of Collegiate Schools of Business—AACSB) has mandated that business schools internationalize their curricula. However, early progress toward that goal was not particularly rapid (Nerht, 1987).

The lack of an international orientation among U.S. management scholars is reflected in the small number of scholarly articles that historically focus on an international or cross-cultural aspect of management. A survey of journals during the early 1980s (Adler, 1983) indicated that less than 5% of published articles focused on international or cross-cultural studies, and more recent surveys have shown little increase (Boyacigiller & Adler, 1991). In summary, the failure of institutions to prepare scholars for international management research, coupled with the increased difficulty, cost, and time involved in conducting these studies, serves to perpetuate parochialism.

Assumed Universality

A U.S. orientation on management theory is important because the activity it purports to describe, management and organizing, does not appear to be universal. The preponderance of evidence, as limited as it is in some areas, indicates substantial cultural variation in management and organizational practices. Therefore, it is important to recognize the unique cultural orientation that a U.S. perspective has brought to the study of management and organizations.

Like all national cultures, the United States has deeply embedded values that influence the way scholars from the United States perceive and think about the world they are investigating. The lack of universality of "made in America" theories is described to some extent in earlier chapters. However, the following examples, drawn from Boyacigiller and Adler (1991), demonstrate three particularly pervasive aspects of the U.S. perspective. Three characteristics of U.S. culture, individualism (Hofstede, 1980), free will (Kluckhohn & Strodtbeck, 1961), and low-context orientation (Hall, 1959), are indicative of the effect of a U.S. cultural orientation on management theory.

The extreme individualism of U.S. people is well-documented (e.g., de Tocqueville, 1899; Hofstede, 1980; Schwartz, 1992). Furthermore, central to U.S. individualism is the importance of individual freedom and choice (Triandis, 1995). Therefore, it is not surprising that management theories that focus on the individual as a rational decision maker with a goal toward maximizing individual utility, such as equity theory (Adams, 1965) or, that emphasize freedom of choice, such as expectancy theory (Vroom, 1964), were U.S. creations.

Another, related characteristic of people from the United States is the belief that individuals are in control of their own circumstances and can, to a great degree, influence their environment and future events (Kluckhohn & Strodtbeck, 1961). This belief manifests itself in conceptions of organizations as being capable of modification, an activity under the control of managers. That is, managers can change them to fit with the environment or even influence the characteristics of the environment itself (Boyacigiller & Adler, 1991). This perspective is in marked contrast to cultures that see the environmental influence on organizations as beyond their control.

As noted in Chapter 6, U.S. culture is classified as low context because of how information is communicated. That is, most of the meaning of a message is contained in the explicit communication as opposed to the context surrounding the information exchange. The relatively low-context orientation of the United States is demonstrated in businesses' reliance on written legal documents (e.g., the United States has the world's highest number of lawyers per capita) as compared to personal relationships in some other cultures (Boyacigiller & Adler, 1991). This low-context orientation may also help to explain the U.S. reliance on "culture-free" rational models of organizations that place little emphasis on the possible influence of contextual factors. As noted in Chapter 10, the consideration of history, culture, and social setting to explaining organizations is a new and far from universally accepted approach.

These three characteristics of U.S. people—individualism, free will, and low-context communication—serve to illustrate the possible limitations in U.S. management theories in explaining organizational phenomenon in cultures with contrasting orientations. However, theories indigenous to other cultures, which might show what is being missed by applying these U.S. approaches abroad, are rare (Smith & Bond, 1999). Box 11.1 provides an example of how a peculiarly U.S. perspective can influence the interpretation of behavior.

In the best case, theoretical relationships could be tested simultaneously in several different cultures based on concepts that are meaningful in each. Then the results are compared for possible convergence. However, this so-called derived-etic approach (Berry, 1989) is not typical, and most cross-cultural research must be carefully evaluated with the recognition of the limitations presented by the cultures involved and of the method used.

Types of International Management Research

There are a number of forms that international management research can take, each with a distinct purpose and characteristic. The types of studies are categorized in a number of ways by different authors. Drenth and Wilpert (1980) focus on the researcher in their categorization of international research as *replication, adaptation,* and *decentralized-collective.* In the first case, a study is repeated in a foreign country; in the second case, a central design is adapted for use in another culture; and in the third case, an international team jointly participates in the design, development,

---

BOX 11.1

Differences in Interpretation of Behavior

In a cross-cultural study of child development (Azuma, 1988), the behavior of U.S. and Japanese mothers in disciplining their children was studied. When a Japanese child refused to eat vegetables, the Japanese mother responded, "All right, then, you don't have to eat them." U.S. researchers coded the mother's behavior as *giving up after a mild attempt at persuasion.* In contrast, Japanese researchers insisted that the response was a *strong threat.* Azuma (1988) explained that the purpose of the Japanese mother's statement was to make the child feel guilty. That is, it implied that the mother was suffering because the child disobeyed and that the very close mother-child bond was in danger of being severed. Although mothers in the United States typically reason with a child, in East Asia, guilt and social relationships are used to socialize children.

SOURCE: Adapted from Kim, Park, & Park, 2000.

---

implementation, and data analysis of the project. Van de Vijver and Leung (1997) focus on the dimensions of exploration versus hypothesis testing and the consideration of context to describe four types of cross- cultural studies. Earley and Singh (1995) also identify four categories of international research, which they labeled as the following:

1. *unitary*—single culture, single phenomenon studies,

2. *gestalt form*—concepts derived from a general principle and tested in other countries,

3. *reduced form*—specific relationships tested regarding the effect of specific aspects of culture, and

4. *hybrid form*—concepts developed in several cultures and used to derive proposed universals that are subsequently tested and refined.

Adler (1983) presented a more general framework that resulted in six categories of studies involving culture. The typology presented in Table 11.1 was influenced by Adler's six categories but incorporates elements of these other approaches.

The six different types of studies described in Table 11.1 differ in terms of the assumptions they make about culture, of the universality of management theory, and in the types of questions they address. As discussed

TABLE 11.1 Types of Cross-Cultural Management Studies

Category	Description	Cultural Assumptions	Research Questions
Domestic	Management studies in a single country	Culture is ignored or universality of theory is assumed	How can we explain and predict the behavior of people in organizations?
Replication	Management study repeated in another country	Universality is questioned, there is not a theory available to predict the effect of culture	Does this theory that applies in culture A also apply in culture B?
Indigenous	Individual management studies conceived and executed in one or many cultures	Cultural differences assumed to exist, indigenous theory required to explain behavior	How can we explain and predict the behavior of people in organizations in country X?
Comparative	Management study conducted in two or more countries	Similarities and differences exist, there may or may not be a theory available to predict the effect of culture	What similarities and differences exist in the behavior of people in organizations? Is this theory universal?
International	Studies of multinational organizations	Similarities and differences exist or culture is ignored	How do organizations that operate in multiple countries function?
Intercultural	Studies of intercultural interactions in organizations	Specific aspects of culture are part of the theoretical framework underlying the study	How is this theory influenced by cultural differences and how is it universal?

later in this chapter, each type also has methodological issues that must be confronted.

Domestic Research

Domestic research is defined here as those management studies designed and conducted within a single country without regard for the boundary conditions set by the cultural orientation of the country. These studies assume the universal applicability of the constructs and relationships they test. The vast majority of this type of research originated in the United States and suffers from the parochialism mentioned earlier. This research, which is confined to a single cultural context, is constrained from both its ability to advance theory and in its practical application. Before it can be applied to a culture other than the one in which it originated, its generalizability across cultures must be proven.

Replication Research

These studies are conceived and managed by a researcher in one country and then repeated in other countries by the originator or by local collaborators. These attempts to replicate studies, typically first conducted in the United States, often use what is called an "imposed etic" design (Berry, 1989). That is, they assume that the concepts being measured and the relationships being studied have the same meaning to the participants in the new culture as they did in the culture in which the study was conceived. Therefore, they also assume that the responses in the two cultures can be compared directly. However, the assumption of equivalence where it may not exist is probably the reason that many studies fail to replicate in other cultures (Smith & Bond, 1999). Many of the studies reported in this book are examples of replication research.

Indigenous Research

Classified as "emic" (Berry, 1989) studies, this research focuses on the different and varied ways in which managers behave and organizations are run in a variety of specific cultural settings. Like domestic research, these studies are conducted within a single country. However, they differ in that they assume cultural differences (and in extreme cases, that cultures are unique, Berry, 1969) and require locally generated theory to explain and predict behavior within a culture. Examples of indigenous approaches are the concept of *sympatia* central to understanding interpersonal interactions in Hispanic cultures (Triandis, Marin, Lisansky, & Betancourt, 1984), *amae* (indulgent dependence) as an important element in superior-subordinate relationships in Japan (Doi, 1973), and *guanxi* (relationships) as a fundamental building block for Chinese businesses (Wu, 1999). Like domestic research, these concepts and the relationships they support are only applicable within their own cultural context until generality is proven. In addition, these types of management studies are rare because of the historical and economic factors mentioned earlier.

Comparative Research

Comparative studies seek to find both the similarities and differences that exist across cultures regarding a particular management issue.

Therefore, the extent to which a theory is universal as well as aspects unique to a particular culture are both key questions. In conducting comparative research, it is important that researchers do not present one cultural perspective as dominant (Adler, 1983). Descriptive comparative studies document the similarities and differences found across cultures, whereas predictive studies test relationships suggested by theory including a theory predicting the expected cross-cultural differences. Numerous examples of comparative research are found in this book, such as Earley's (1989) study of social loafing among U.S. people and Chinese (Chapter 8).

International Research

This category of research was created to capture those studies that focus attention on MNCs. Although these studies recognize that both similarities and differences exist across cultures, the cultural context does not figure prominently in the conceptualization or execution of the study. For example, studies of the human resource policies of MNCs that affect expatriate managers fall into this category, as would studies of how expatiates adjust in their foreign assignment (see Chapter 10). These studies are not concerned with comparing the cultural context in each of the countries the firm might operate, except as it applies to the organization as a whole.

Intercultural Research

Intercultural research seeks to understand the interactions between culturally different individuals in organizational settings. Therefore, the mechanisms responsible for the influence of culture (as discussed in Chapter 4) are an integral part of these studies. Intercultural research considers the culture of both (all) parties in the interaction as well as contextual explanations for observed similarities and differences. These types of studies are a somewhat recent development in management research but are represented in studies of cross-cultural negotiation (e.g., Adler & Graham, 1989; Francis, 1991), in studies of the interactions among members of multicultural work groups (e.g., Thomas, 1999; Thomas et al., 1996), and in studies of leader-follower interactions across cultures (e.g., Thomas & Ravlin, 1995; Ah Chong & Thomas, 1997).

Both managers and researchers can benefit by recognizing the cultural assumptions and purpose of the research on which they depend for theoretical development or practical application. Each of the six categories of studies outlined here has specific characteristics that define the boundaries of its applicability. However, these limitations are not always made explicit in the presentation of the research itself. Therefore, it is important for the consumer of this research to recognize the boundary conditions that might be associated with a cross-cultural study affecting its applicability.

Methodological Issues in Cross-Cultural Research

As noted previously, not all studies that might be of interest to international managers involve more than one culture. For example, descriptions of the characteristics of Chinese family business (Chapter 9) can be very important for managers interested in doing business in China. However, much of the focus of this book is on the behavioral aspects of management, which highlights the similarities and differences in behavior across cultures. Studies that involve two or more cultures share several common methodological issues that are not present in purely domestic research. These are discussed under the broad headings of equivalence, sampling, data collection, and measurement and data analysis.

Equivalence

Perhaps the most important issue in cross-national or cross-cultural research is equivalence. The opportunity for bias because of cultural differences in values, attitudes, and normative behavior is staggering. Cross-cultural equivalence cannot be assumed at any stage of a cross-cultural study, and, in fact, it must be established at three key points: the conceptualization of the theoretical constructs, the study design, and in the data analysis (van de Vijver & Leung, 1997).

Conceptual or construct equivalence relates to the extent to which the concepts examined in cross-cultural research have the same meaning in different countries. Without construct equivalence, comparisons are impossible. An example of lack of construct equivalence is provided by a study of management behavior in China (Adler, Campbell, & Laurent, 1989). In that study, the survey contained items that embodied a Western notion of "truth" nonexistent in the Confucian society. The question of conceptual equivalence can be asked about numerous constructs developed in the management literature as the cartoon in Figure 11.1 suggests.

The involvement of researchers from different cultures in the development of a study is one indication that thought was given to the need for conceptual equivalence.

Figure 11.1. Is the Concept of Surprise Equivalent Across Cultures?

Method equivalence relates to whether the measurement unit is the same in all groups. Threats to this type of equivalence include acquiescence and extremity bias. Acquiesence is the tendency for some cultural groups to agree (or disagree) with all or most questions asked. Extremity bias involves the way different cultures use particular response-scale formats. For example, some cultural groups systematically choose the extreme points on rating scales more often than other groups (e.g., Hui & Triandis, 1989). In addition, different levels of familiarity with the construct being studied, the physical conditions surrounding data collection, and communication between the researcher and participants can contribute to this type of nonequivalence.

Finally, metric equivalence refers to the extent that questions (survey items) have similar measurement properties across different groups. Nonequivalence can result from poor item translation, complex item wording, and culture-specific issues regarding item content. For example, a coping questionnaire that includes the item "watched more television than usual" is meaningless for a population without electricity in their homes (e.g., van de Vijver & Leung, 1997).

Equivalence means that culturally different participants understand equally the concept and its relationship to other concepts in the study. Given cultural differences, unmodified instruments will rarely be equivalent across cultures. This does not mean that replication research or research based on concepts developed in the United States cannot be done. It does mean that the instrument development process and data-collection strategy play a bigger role across national boundaries. In addition, it is much easier to identify the sources of nonequivalence than to solve these problems. More complete discussions of the solutions to these problems are found in books by Brislin et al. (1973) and van de Vijver and Leung (1997). However, one key element of equivalence that merits special mention is the translation of research instruments.

Appropriate translation of research instruments (Brislin, 1970) is a good start toward equivalence. The goal of translation is to produce a research instrument (questionnaire, interview protocol) conceptually equivalent across cultures as opposed to identical (literal translation). Therefore, translators must incorporate both linguistic and cultural differences. They must be fluent in the language of the topic under study as well as the foreign language in general. The issues associated with translation in cross-cultural communication in management practice (Chapter 6) are no less applicable in the research situation. Brislin (1983) suggests four techniques for effective translation, which are outlined in Table 11.2.

Each method has strengths and weaknesses depending on the specific research situation. Combining methods can, of course, help offset the limitations of individual approaches.

Sampling

The goal of sampling is to conduct research with a small number of participants who accurately represent the population about which we wish to make conclusions. In cross-cultural research, selecting an appropriate international research sample is closely tied to conceptual and instrument development. The ability to select a truly representative sample in cross-cultural research is much more difficult, and convenience samples are often used. Therefore, the majority of international studies involve samples of individuals who are readily available, seem intelligent, and are willing to respond (Brislin et al., 1973).

Several unique sampling problems present themselves in cross-national research. First, to prove the universality of a phenomenon would require a random sample of countries. However, it is virtually impossible to collect data from a truly random sample of countries of sufficient size to be meaningful. There are only about 185 countries, and the logistics and statistical requirements of random sampling argue against anything but an approximation of random sampling of countries. The sampling of (now about 50) countries from all regions of the world in the development of the value survey undertaken by Shalom Schwartz (Schwartz, 1992) is an example of one such approximation. Second, because of subcultural variation within countries, any sample selected from a specific geographic region does not necessarily represent the country (Brislin et al., 1973). For example, the representativeness of manufacturing workers in

TABLE 11.2 Basic Translation Techniques

Technique	Issues
Back Translation—material in one language is translated; then a second person independently translates the material back into the original language. Discrepancies are then resolved.	Can result in a literal but not necessarily a conceptually equivalent translation. Some concepts do not have literal equivalents across languages.
Bilingual Method—material is administered to bilingual individuals in the languages in which they are fluent. Differences in responses, or inconsistencies, are identified and corrected.	Bilinguals are a unique group whose reactions to an instrument may not be typical of the culture.
Committee Procedure—a committee formed by bilinguals translates the material from one language to another. Differences in interpretation are discussed and corrected.	A group norm for consensus can develop that overrides criticism of another person's ideas.
Pretest Technique—the material is tested on a group of people similar to the target sample in all cultures represented. Differences associated with translation are identified and corrected.	The availability of a representative sample of participants to participate in a pretest is often an issue.

SOURCE: Adapted from Brislin, 1983.

Cincinnati to all people in the United States and of workers in the same industry in Shenzen to all Chinese is questionable. Finally, inconsistencies in the availability of sampling frames (lists of possible participants) across cultures can affect the sample. This applies not only in developing countries, in which a lack of commonly used devices like telephone books or business directories present problems, but also in developed countries like New Zealand or Canada, in which political or legal agendas dictate the kind of information collected and disseminated.

When random samples are not possible, as is often the case in cross-cultural studies, researchers can use systematic sampling in which selection of participants is based on theoretical considerations. In these cases, the max-min-con principle—which posits that an efficient research design *max*imizes variance on variables of the substantial research hypotheses, *min*imizes random variance, and *con*trols extraneous or unwanted variance—applies (Kerlinger, 1986). This implies that, for cross-national comparison, countries should be selected on dimensions that are as far apart as possible (e.g., New Zealand and China on the dimensions of individualism and collectivism). The problem is that countries that vary on one dimension are likely to differ on other dimensions (e.g., economic, political, legal) that must be controlled. One way to deal with this problem is to test propositions with matched samples in as many countries as possible. Samples are matched according to key dimensions to achieve equivalence. In general, the more countries in which the relationship holds, the more powerful is the result.

In exploratory studies, sampling decisions are less obvious and should be guided by whether the researcher is looking for similarity or difference (van de Vijver & Leung, 1997). Often, practical considerations override some of the conditions of theoretical sampling and convenience samples are used. In these cases, any hint that the samples might be different on a factor should cause the researcher to measure those dimensions of potential difference and assess their effect.

Data Collection

The most common methods of data collection in cross-cultural research are questionnaires, followed by interviews (Peng, Peterson, & Shyi, 1991). This is not surprising because U.S. organizational researchers with similar training conduct most international research. Prior success with these methods may be a reason for the "Safari" or replication research (Drenth & Wilpert, 1980) mentioned previously.

The "have questionnaire, will travel" approach can have negative consequences that often are not apparent in a brief exposure to another culture. For example, people in different cultures differ in how familiar they are with particular research methods and in how ready they are to participate. Such differences come up most strikingly with the self-administered questionnaires so popular in international management research. Some factors, such as variation in literacy rates, are reasonably obvious. However, more subtle effects, such as the following, are typical.

The level of familiarity with questionnaires can dramatically influence responses. For example, Shenkar and Von Glinow (1994) found that the unfamiliarity of Chinese with questionnaires with a multiple-choice response format was a source of bias in responses. Moreover, in many countries, a researcher's purpose is suspect (Napier & Thomas, 2001). Participants can view the researcher as an agent of management, a union, or even the government. This perception can be hard for researchers to avoid if those groups control access to participants. In these cases, concern about response bias emerges. For example, fear of authorities can yield 100% response rates for a "voluntary" survey, a clear signal to question the data.

Raising a sensitive issue and not knowing it can come from using a "standard research approach" (particularly a questionnaire) worldwide. For example, questions related to time off to participate in family activities attract a more emotive response from Pacific Islanders in New Zealand than a researcher unfamiliar with the employment relations of that country would expect (Napier & Thomas, 2001).

Respondents may not have a frame of reference with which to respond to questions. For example, people in the United States are used to responding to hypothetical questions. However, in many cultures, respondents require a concrete example or a detailed explanation of the context to provide a meaningful answer (Shenkar & Von Glinow, 1994). Asking hypothetical questions of respondents who do not think in conditional terms can result in unreliable responses (Bulmer & Warwick, 1983).

Interviews are another commonly used data-collection method in international and cross-cultural research and the most common qualitative method. The advantages of interviews include the ability to give feedback to respondents, probe for clearer answers, and deal with complex topics. However, a key disadvantage is the possible interaction between interviewer and respondent. For example, characteristics of the interviewer (age, gender, personal appearance) can influence respondent answers, the interviewer's technique (e.g., question phrasing, tone of voice) can bias responses, and the interviewer can selectively perceive or anticipate the respondent's answers. When the interviewer and respondent are culturally different, the opportunity for error is heightened. For example, a Chinese person may give very different responses to a Malay than to another Chinese, and Saudis do not feel comfortable with the possibility of having to explain their behavior that an interview suggests (Usunier, 1998). A considerable literature exists regarding improving interview techniques in international settings (e.g., Brislin et al., 1973; Pareek & Rao, 1980). The focus of these techniques is on the recognition of bias introduced by the interview process. A summary of common types of bias that are particularly prevalent in cross-cultural interviews is presented in Table 11.3.

Not all international data contain the kind of "sucker bias" suggested in the cartoon in Figure 11.2. However, the message that emerges from this discussion is that in conducting and evaluating cross-cultural research, it is important to critically evaluate the way in which the data were collected.

TABLE 11.3 Bias in Cross-Cultural Interviews

Capability bias	Giving answers to any question regardless of knowledge
Courtesy bias	Providing the interviewer with the answer the respondent thinks the interviewer wants
Sucker bias	Giving ridiculous answers to make fun of the interviewer
Reticent—loquacious bias	Members of some cultures (also depends on situation) are quiet and reserved in interviews while others are outgoing and verbose
Individual—group bias	Difficulty in obtaining responses from individuals in some group-oriented cultures, or in obtaining different responses when group members are present

SOURCE: Harpaz, 1996. Reprinted with permission of Blackwell Publishers, Inc.

Measurement and Data Analysis

Two measurement and data-handling issues are particularly relevant in conducting or evaluating cross-cultural research. They are also subsets of the equivalence issue mentioned previously. These are the coding of qualitative data and the comparability of multi-item scales.

Often in cross-cultural research, rich descriptions or observations are content analyzed and thereby reduced for further empirical analysis. Multiple coders often conduct this analysis to establish the reliability of the coding. The problem arises in establishing the categories into which observations are tabulated. The categories of a content analysis are rarely neutral and reflect the cultural orientation imposed by the researcher, as suggested in Box 11.1. Obviously, the determinations of categories and the instructions given to coders can have a significant biasing effect on the results of a cross-cultural study (Usunier, 1998).

The second issue involves establishing the comparability of the measurement of psychological constructs across cultures. Nonobservable concepts, such as attitudes, are often measured using multiple-item rating scales. As noted earlier, to make a comparison across cultures, it is important that the underlying concept is understood in the same way in different cultures. The extent to which this was accomplished, through

Figure 11.2. Bias in Survey Research
SOURCE: Calvin and Hobbes. Copyright ©Watterson. Reprinted with permission of Universal Press Syndicate. All rights reserved.

careful instrument design or adaptation and translation, can be assessed after data are collected. Two stages are common. First, the basic psychometric properties of the instrument, such as its internal consistency reliability or item to total correlations, are assessed in the different cultures. Differences in the basic properties of the instrument across the cultures can be closely examined for the influence of culture. Second, the structures of the multiple-item scales can be evaluated simultaneously in the cultures being studied. More similar structures indicate comparability of measurement across cultures. A variety of sophisticated statistical techniques are available to conduct these analyses, as are methods for controlling for cross-cultural dissimilarities discovered. An excellent description of these issues and techniques is found in van de Vijver & Leung (1997). It is inevitable that future cross-cultural research will be more effective in handling these measurement and data-analysis issues because of the availability of new and ever more sophisticated techniques. In examining past research, we must be aware of these issues and recognize the limitations under which the research was conducted.

Summary of Methods Issues

The following is a summary of the major methodological issues associated with cross-national or cross-cultural research, which is adapted from van de Vijver & Leung (1997). The central issue is that when cultural differences are found, they tend to be open to multiple interpretations. For example, when two cultural groups show a difference on a measure of job satisfaction, they may actually be differently satisfied. However, various alternative explanations include the following:

(a) at least some of the items describing satisfaction do not adequately capture the construct of job satisfaction,

(b) differences in social desirability or other response differences are responsible for the difference,

(c) the groups were not matched on some background characteristic such as education or job tenure, or

(d) the physical condition surrounding the administration of the instrument differed across groups.

Consideration of the following factors can aid in preventing such alternative explanations:

- *In cross-cultural studies, the following must be determined in each cultural group:* the appropriateness of the concepts (constructs) examined, the appropriateness of the administration of the instruments, and the operationalization (measurement) of the concepts.

- *A wide variety of techniques are available to improve the validity of cross-cultural comparisons.* Compared to domestic research, cross-cultural studies are subject to more methodological issues. Each study is subject to a different set of threats to its validity. Sophisticated techniques can be employed to combat the threat of bias inherent in cross-cultural research.

- *Equivalence cannot be assumed and must be established at each phase of a cross-cultural study.* Cross-cultural comparisons are meaningful only when construct, method, and metric equivalence are established.

Although the methodological issues associated with cross-cultural research are not insubstantial, this type of research is the only avenue available to establishing the applicability of management theory in more than the cultural context in which it was developed. These issues are indicative of a field of study asking the right questions but as yet does not have all the right answers (Adler, 1984).

Critiques of International and Cross-Cultural Research

A number of critical reviews of the state of international and cross-cultural research have been conducted (e.g., Adler, 1983; Bhagat & McQuaid, 1982;

Peterson, 1993). The following is representative of the types of criticism often leveled at this field of study:

- *Lack of a theoretical base.* Often cross-cultural studies have been concerned with emphasizing the differences among nations as opposed to testing management theory in a cross-cultural context (Sullivan, 1997).

- *Parochialism.* As noted earlier, culture is often ignored in management research, and universality is assumed. However, when an international perspective is included, an assumption that organizations and management behavior in other cultures should be compared to a Western industrial model dominates (Boyacigiller & Adler, 1991).

- *Heavy reliance on convenience samples.* Although understandable and perhaps justifiable in some cases, such samples often do not allow for the kind of comparisons adequate to test theory or inform practice in the future.

- *Lack of relevance.* The critical question consuming scholars and managers in the United States might not be viewed as important at all abroad (Napier & Thomas, 2001). International research puts relevance sharply into focus.

- *Reliance on a single method.* The vast majority of international and cross-cultural research has relied on responses to questionnaires gathered at a single point in time. Both the temporal aspect of cultural influence as well as the richness provided by alternative methods are largely absent from this body of research (Osland & Osland, 2001).

- Bias toward studying large companies. The vast majority of international and cross-cultural studies that have been conducted in an organizational context involved large firms.

- *Reliance on a single organizational level.* Most international or cross-cultural studies rely on responses from a single level (managers or production workers) to draw conclusions about cultural differences. Rarely are samples drawn from multiple positions in the organizational hierarchy (Peterson, 1993).

- *Limited to a small number of locations.* Reviews of cross-cultural research show that most studies were done in a small number of western European countries and Japan. We know very little about the forgotten locations of Eastern Europe, the Middle East, Africa, and Latin America (Thomas, 1996).

Summary

This chapter is not meant as an indictment of cross-cultural research nor is it a comprehensive guide to conducting such research. It is intended to sensitize the reader to methodological issues associated with these complex research projects. Having been so sensitized, it is hoped that instead of accepting the findings of these studies uncritically, readers will interpret studies involving culture with the identified limitations and boundaries in mind. We have learned a great deal from research in this area, yet the field of study is still in its infancy, and much more is to be discovered.

Many of the limitations of the existing body of knowledge about managing across cultures are likely to be remedied because of the increased demand for relevance of research to managers whose jobs are increasingly global in scope. Several trends are already becoming apparent. First, more scholars are extending their domestic work across cultures. The domain of cross-cultural research is no longer restricted to those who study cultural similarities and differences. This movement should improve the generalizability of management theory as well as increase the emphasis on testing management theory in a cross-cultural context. Second, more sophisticated statistical techniques are being developed concurrent with a broader emphasis on richer, more qualitative approaches to cross-cultural management studies. This offers the opportunity for improved understanding through the triangulation of research methods. Finally, the emphasis on traditional geographical areas seems to be waning somewhat in favor of emerging players in the world economy such as Eastern Europe, China, and Southeast Asia.

The field of international management research, like the phenomenon it is concerned with explaining, is complex and rapidly changing. Hopefully, the dynamic and difficult nature of this area of research will not deter researchers from the investigation so obviously needed. The opportunities and challenges presented by extending one's horizons across cultures can be likened to awakening to a new snowfall and realizing that everything familiar has disappeared (M. H. Bond, personal communication, December 31, 1995). To quote Calvin on one such occasion, "It's a magical world, Hobbes ol' buddy . . . Let's go exploring" (Watterson, 1995).

References

Abe, H., & Wiseman, R. L. (1983). A cross-cultural confirmation of the dimensions of intercultural effectiveness. *International Journal of Intercultural Relations, 7,* 53-67.

Abelson, R. P. (1981). Psychological status of the script concept. *American Psychologist, 36,* 715-729.

Adams, J. S. (1965). Inequity in social exchange. In L. Berkowitz (Ed.), *Advances in experimental social psychology* (Vol. 2, pp. 267-299). New York: Academic Press.

Adler, N. J. (1981). Re-entry: Managing cross-cultural transitions. *Group and Organization Studies, 6,* 341-356.

Adler, N. J. (1983). Cross-cultural management research: The ostrich and the trend. *Academy of Management Review, 8,* 226-232.

Adler, N. J. (1984). Women in international management: Where are they? *California Management Review, 26,* 78-89.

Adler, N. J. (1986). Do MBAs want international careers? *International Journal of Intercultural Relations, 10,* 277-300.

Adler, N. J. (1987). Pacific Basin managers: A gaijin, not a woman. *Human Resource Management, 26,* 169-191.

Adler, N. J. (1997). *International dimensions of organizational behavior* (3rd ed.). Cincinnati, OH: South-Western.

Adler, N. J., Campbell, N., & Laurent, A. (1989). In search of appropriate methodology: From outside the People's Republic of China looking in. *Journal of International Business Studies, 20,* 61-74.

Adler, N. J., Doktor, R., & Redding, S. G. (1986). From the Atlantic to the Pacific century: Cross-cultural management reviewed. *Journal of Management, 12,* 295-318.

Adler, N. J., & Graham, J. L. (1989). Cross-cultural interactions: The international comparison fallacy? *Journal of International Business Studies, 20,* 515-537.

Ah Chong, L. M., & Thomas. D. C. (1997). Leadership perceptions in cross-cultural context: Pacific Islanders and Pakeha in New Zealand. *Leadership Quarterly, 8*(3), 275-293.

Aharoni, Y. (1994). How small firms can achieve competitive advantage in an interdependent world. In T. Agmon & R. Drobnick (Eds.), *Small firms in global competition* (pp. 9-18). New York: Oxford University Press.

Albright, L., Malloy, T. E., Dong, Q., Kenny, D. A., & Fang, X. (1997). Cross-cultural consensus in personality judgments. *Journal of Personality and Social Psychology, 73*, 270-280.

Alderfer, C. P. (1977). Group and intergroup relations. In J. R. Hackman & J. L. Suttle (Eds.), *Improving life at work* (pp. 227-296). Santa Monica, CA: Goodyear.

Aldrich, H., & Herker, D. (1977). Boundary spanning roles and organizational structure. *Academy of Management Review, 2*, 217-230.

Ali, A. J. (1990). Management theory in a transitional society: The Arab's experience. *International Studies of Management and Organization, 20*, 7-35.

Al-Kubaisy, A. (1985). A model in the administrative development of Arab Gulf countries. *The Arab Gulf, 17*(2), 29-48.

Allen, T. J., & Hauptman, O. (1990). The substitution of communications technology for organizational structure in research and development. In J. Fulk & C. Stenfield (Eds.), *Organizations and communication technology* (pp. 275-294). Newbury Park, CA: Sage.

Allport, G. W. (1954). *The nature of prejudice.* Reading, MA: Addison-Wesley.

Almaney, A., & Ahwan, A. (1982). *Communicating with the Arabs.* Prospect Heights, IL: Waveland.

Almond, G. A., & Powell, G. B., Jr. (Eds.). (1984). *Comparative politics today: A world view* (pp. 1-9). Boston: Little, Brown.

Al-Zahrani, S. S. A., & Kaplowitz, S. A. (1993). Attributional biases in individualist and collectivists cultures: A comparison of Americans with Saudis. *Social Psychology Quarterly, 56*, 223-233.

Andersen, P. A., & Bowman, L. (1985). *Positions of power: Nonverbal cues of status and dominance in organizational communication.* Paper presented at the annual convention of the international communication association, Honolulu, Hawaii.

Antal, A. B., & Izraeli, D. (1993). A global comparison of women in management: Women managers in their homelands and as expatriates. In E. A. Gagenson (Ed.), *Women in management: Trends, issues, and challenges in managerial diversity* (Vol. 4, pp. 206-223). Newbury Park, CA: Sage.

Argyle, M. (1988). *Bodily communication* (2nd ed.). London: Methuen.

Argyris, C. (1972). *The applicability of organizational sociology.* London: Cambridge University Press.

Aronoff, J., Woike, B. A., & Hyman, L. M. (1992). Which are the stimuli in facial displays of anger and happiness? *Journal of Personality and Social Psychology, 62*, 1050-1066.

Arrow, H., & McGrath, J. E. (1995). Membership dynamics in groups at work: A theoretical framework. *Research in Organizational Behavior, 17*, 373-411.

Arthur, W., & Bennett, W. (1995). The international assignee: The relative importance of factors perceived to contribute to success. *Personnel Psychology, 48,* 99-114.

Asch, S. (1951). Effects of group pressure on the modification and distortion of judgements. In H. Guetzkow (Ed.), *Groups, leadership and men* (pp. 177-190). Pittsburgh, PA: Carnegie.

Ashmore, R. D., & Del Boca, F. K. (1981). Conceptual approaches to stereotypes and stereotyping. In D. L. Hamilton (Ed.), *Cognitive processes in stereotyping and intergroup behavior* (pp. 1-35). Hillsdale, NJ: Lawrence Erlbaum.

Astley, W. G., & Van de Ven, A. H. (1983). Central perspectives and debates in organization theory. *Administrative Science Quarterly, 28,* 245-273.

Au, K. Y. (1999). Intra-cultural variation: Evidence and implications for international business. *Journal of International Business Studies, 30,* 799-812.

Ayman, R., & Chemers, M. M. (1983). Relationship of supervisory behavior ratings to work group effectiveness and subordinate satisfaction among Iranian managers. *Journal of Applied Psychology, 68*(2), 338-341.

Ayman, R., & Chemers, M. M. (1991). The effect of leadership match on subordinate satisfaction in Mexican organizations: Some moderating influences of self-monitoring. *Applied Psychology: An International Review, 40*(3), 299-314.

Azuma, H. (1988, September). *Are Japanese really that different? The concept of development as a key for transformation.* Invited address to the 24th International Congress of Psychology, Sydney, Australia.

Bagby, J. (1957). Dominance in binocular rivalry in Mexico and the United States. *Journal of Abnormal and Social Psychology, 54,* 331-334.

Baliga, B. R., & Jaeger, A. (1984). Multinational corporations: Control systems and delegation issues. *Journal of International Business Studies, 15,* 25-40.

Bandura, A. (1977). *Social learning theory.* Englewood Cliffs, NJ: Prentice Hall.

Barlow, C. (1991). *Tikanga whakaaro: Key concepts in Maori culture.* Auckland, New Zealand: Oxford University Press.

Barnlund, D. C., & Araki, S. (1985). Intercultural encounters: The management of compliments by Japanese and Americans. *Journal of Cross-Cultural Psychology, 16,* 9-26.

Barraclough, R. A., Christophel, D. M., & McCroskey, J. C. (1988). Willingness to communicate: A cross-cultural investigation. *Communication Research Reports, 5,* 187-192.

Barrett, D. B. (Ed.). (1982). *World Christian encyclopedia: A comparative study of churches and religions in the modern world.* New York: Oxford University Press.

Barry, D. (1988). Europe on five vowels a day. In *Dave Barry's greatest hits* (pp. 259-261). New York: Ballantine.

Barry, D. (1991). Managing the bossless team: Lessons in distributed leadership. *Organizational Dynamics, 21*(1), 31-47.

Bartlett, C. A. (1986). Building and managing the transnational: The new organizational challenge. In M. Porter (Ed.), *Competition in global industries* (pp. 367-401). Boston: Harvard Business School Press.

Bartlett, C. A., & Ghoshal, S. (1989). *Managing across borders: The transnational solution.* Boston: Harvard Business School Press.

Bass, B. M. (1985). *Leadership and performance beyond expectation.* New York: Free Press.

Bass, B. M. (1990). *Bass and Stogdill's handbook of leadership: Theory, research and managerial applications* (3rd ed.). New York: Free Press.

Bass, B. M. (1991, August). *In there universality in the full range model of leadership?* Paper presented at the Academy of Management Annual Meeting, Miami, Florida.

Bass, B. M. (1997). Does the transactional-transformational paradigm transcend organizational and national boundaries? *American Psychologist, 52*(2), 130-139.

Bass, B. M., Burger, P. C., Doktor, R., & Barrett, G. V. (1979). *Assessment of managers: An international comparison.* New York: Free Press.

Bazerman, M. (1998). *Judgement in managerial decision making* (4th ed.). New York: John Wiley.

Beamish, P. B., & Killing, J. P. (Eds.). (1997). *Cooperative strategies.* San Francisco: New Lexington Press.

Beaver, W. (1995, March-April). Levis is leaving China. *Business Horizons,* pp. 35-40.

Beechler, S. L. (1992, November). International management control in multinational corporations: The case of Japanese consumer electronics firms in Asia. *OECD Economic Journal,* 20-31.

Beechler, S. L., & Iaquinto, A. L. (1994, August). *A longitudinal study of staffing patterns in U.S. affiliates of Japanese transnational corporations.* Paper presented to the International Management Division of the Academy of Management, Dallas, Texas.

Beechler, S. L., & Pucik, V. (1989). The diffusion of American organizational theory in post war Japan. In C. A. B. Osigweh (Ed.), *Organizational science abroad: Constraints and perspectives* (pp. 119-134). New York: Plenum.

Bennett, M. (1977). Testing management theories cross-culturally. *Journal of Applied Psychology, 62*(5), 578-581.

Bennis, W. (1984). The 4 competencies of leadership. *Training & Development Journal, 38*(8), 14-19.

Benson, P. G. (1978). Measuring cross-cultural adjustment: The problem of criteria. *International Journal of Intercultural Relations, 2*(1), 21-37

Berger, P. L., & Luckman, T. (1966). *The social construction of reality: A treatise in the sociology of knowledge.* Garden City, NY: Doubleday.

Berlo, D. K. (1960). *The process of communication.* New York: Holt, Rinehart & Winston.

Berman, J. J., Murphy-Berman, V., & Singh, P. (1985). Cross-cultural similarities and differences in perceptions of fairness. *Journal of Cross-Cultural Psychology, 16,* 55-67.

Berry, J. W. (1969). On cross-cultural comparability. *International Journal of Psychology, 4,* 119-128.

Berry, J. W. (1989). Imposed etics-emics-derived etics: The operationalisation of a compelling idea. *International Journal of Psychology, 24,* 721-735.

Berry, J. W. (1990). The role of psychology in ethnic studies. *Canadian Ethnic Studies, 22*, 8-21.

Bettenhausen, K. L., & Murnighan, J. K. (1991). The development of intragroup norm and the effects of interpersonal and structural changes. *Administrative Science Quarterly, 36*, 20-35.

Bhagat, R. S., & McQuaid, S. J. (1982). Role of subjective culture in organizations: A review and directions for future research. *Journal of Applied Psychology, 67*(5), 653-685.

Birdseye, M., & Hill, J. S. (1995). Individual, organizational/work and environmental influences on expatriate turnover tendencies: An empirical study. *Journal of International Business Studies, 26*(4), 787-813.

Black, J. S. (1988). Work role transitions: A study of American expatriate managers in Japan. *Journal of International Business Studies, 19*, 277-294.

Black, J. S. (1990). Locus of control, social support, stress and adjustment in international transfers. *Asia Pacific Journal of Management, 7*(1), 1-29.

Black, J. S. (1994). O Kaerinasai: Factors related to Japanese repatriation adjustment. *Human Relations, 47*(12), 1489-1508.

Black, J. S., & Gregersen, H. B. (1990). Expectations, satisfaction and intention to leave of American expatriate managers in Japan. *International Journal of Intercultural Relations, 14*, 485-506.

Black, J. S., & Gregersen, H. B. (1991a). Antecedents to cross-cultural adjustment for expatriates in Pacific Rim assignments. *Human Relations, 44*(5), 497-515.

Black, J. S., & Gregersen, H. B. (1991b). When Yankee comes home: Factors related to expatriate and spouse repatriation adjustment. *Journal of International Business Studies, 21*(4), 671-694.

Black, J. S., Gregersen, H. B., & Mendenhall, M. E. (1992). Toward a theoretical framework of repatriation adjustment. *Journal of International Business Studies, 22*(3), 737-760.

Black, J. S., & Mendenhall, M. E. (1989). A practical but theory-based framework for selecting cross-cultural training methods. *Human Resource Management, 28*(4), 511-539.

Black, J. S., & Mendenhall, M. E. (1990). Cross-cultural training effectiveness: A review and a theoretical framework for future research. *Academy of Management Review, 15*(1), 113-136.

Black, J. S., & Mendenhall, M. E. (1991). The U-curve adjustment hypothesis revisited: A review and theoretical framework. *Journal of International Business Studies, 22*, 225-247.

Black, J. S., Mendenhall, M.E. , & Oddou, G. (1991). Toward a comprehensive model of international adjustment: An integration of multiple theoretical perspectives. *Academy of Management Review, 16*(2), 291-317.

Blake, R. R., & Mouton, J. S. (1964). *The managerial grid: Key orientations for achieving production through people.* Houston, TX: Gulf Publishing.

Blake, R. R., Mouton, J. S., Barnes, L. B., & Greiner, L. E. (1964). Breakthrough in organization development. *Harvard Business Review, 6*, 133-135.

Blau, P. M. (1970). A formal theory of differentiation in organizations. *American Sociological Review, 35,* 201-218.

Blau, P. M., & Schoenherr, R. A. (1971). *The structure of organizations.* New York: Basic Books.

Bochner, S., & Ohsako, T. (1977). Ethnic role salience in racially homogeneous and heterogeneous societies. *Journal of Cross-Cultural Psychology, 8,* 477-492.

Bochner, S., & Perks, R.W. (1971). National role evocation as a function of cross-national interaction. *Journal of Cross-Cultural Psychology, 2,* 157-164.

Boisot, M., & Xing, G. L. (1992). The nature of managerial work in the Chinese enterprise reforms: A study of six directors. *Organization Studies, 13*(2), 161-184.

Bond, M. H. (1985). Language as a carrier of ethnic stereotypes in Hong Kong. *Journal of Social Psychology, 125,* 53-62.

Bond, M. H., & Hwang, K. K. (1986). *The social psychology of the Chinese people.* Hong Kong: Oxford University Press.

Bond, M. H., & King, A. Y. C. (1985). The social psychology of the Chinese people. In M. H. Bond (Ed.), *The psychology of the Chinese people* (pp. 213-264). Hong Kong: Oxford University Press.

Bond, M. H., Leung, K., & Schwartz, S. (1992). Explaining choices in procedural and distributive justice across cultures. *International Journal of Psychology, 27*(2), 211-225.

Bond, M. H., & Yang, K. S. (1982). Ethnic affirmation versus cross-cultural accommodation: The variable impact of questionnaire language on Chinese bilinguals in Hong Kong. *Journal of Cross-Cultural Psychology, 12,* 169-181.

Bontempo, R., Lobel, S. A., & Triandis, H. C. (1990). Compliance and value internalization in Brazil and the U.S.: Effects of allocentrism and anonymity. *Journal of Cross-Cultural Psychology, 21,* 200-213.

Bonvillian, N. (1993). *Language, culture and communication: The meaning of messages.* Englewood Cliffs, NJ: Prentice Hall.

Borchert, D., & Stewart, E. (1986). *Exploring ethics.* New York: Macmillan.

Borrmann, W. A. (1968). The problem of expatriate personnel and their selection in international enterprises. *Management International Review, 8*(4-5), 37-48.

Boski, P. (1991). Remaining a Pole or becoming a Canadian: National self-identity among Polish immigrants to Canada. *Journal of Applied Social Psychology, 21*(1), 41-77.

Bourhis, R. Y., Giles, H., Leyens, J. P., & Tajfel, H. (1979). Psycholinguistic distinctiveness: Language divergence in Belgium. In H. Giles & R. N. St. Clair (Eds.), *Language and social psychology.* Baltimore: University Park Press.

Bowers, D. G., & Seashore S. E. (1966). Predicting organizational effectiveness with a four factor theory of leadership. *Administrative Science Quarterly, 11,* 238-263.

Boyacigiller, N. A. (1990). The role of expatriates in the management of interdependence, complexity and risk in multinational corporations. *Journal of International Business Studies, 21*(4), 357-381.

Boyacigiller, N. A., & Adler, N. J. (1991). The parochial dinosaur: Organizational science in a global context. *Academy of Management Review, 16*(2), 262-290.

Brein, D., & David, K. H. (1971). Intercultural communication and the adjustment of the sojourner. *Psychological Bulletin, 76*(3), 215-230.

Brenner, S. N., & Molander, E. A. (1977). Is the ethics of business changing? *Harvard Business Review, 55*(1), 57-71.

Brett, J. M., & Okumura, T. (1998). Inter- and intracultural negotiation: U.S. and Japanese negotiators. *Academy of Management Journal, 41,* 495-510.

Brett, J. M., Stroh, L. K., & Reilly, A. H. (1993). Pulling up roots in the 1990s: Who's willing to relocate? *Journal of Organizational Behavior, 14,* 49-60.

Briody, E. K., & Chrisman, J. B. (1991). Cultural adaptation on overseas assignments. *Human Organization, 50*(3), 264-282.

Brislin, R. W. (1970). Back-translation for cross-cultural research. *Journal of Cross-Cultural Psychology, 75,* 3-9.

Brislin, R. W. (1983). Cross-cultural research in psychology. *Annual Review of Psychology, 34,* 363-400.

Brislin, R. W., Lonner, W. J., & Thorndike, R. M. (1973). *Cross-cultural research methods.* New York: John Wiley.

Bulmer, M., & Warwick, D. P. (1983). *Social research in developing countries.* New York: John Wiley.

Bunce, D., & West, M. A. (1995). Self perceptions and perceptions of group climate as predictors of individual innovation at work. *Applied Psychology: An International Review, 44*(3), 199-215.

Burns, T. (1978). *Leadership.* New York: Harper & Row.

Burns, T., & Stalker, C. M. (1961). *The management of innovation.* London: Tavistock.

Burris, C. T., Branscombe, N. R., & Jackson, L. M. (2000). For god and country: Religion and the endorsement of national self-stereotypes. *Journal of Cross-Cultural Psychology, 31*(4), 517-527.

Byrne, D. (1971). *The attraction paradigm.* New York: Academic Press.

Campbell, N., Graham, J. L., Jolibert, A., & Meissner, H. G. (1988). Marketing negotiations in France, Germany, the United Kingdom and the United States. *Journal of Marketing, 52,* 49-62.

Campion, M. A., Medsker, G. J., & Higgs, A. C. (1993). Relations between work group characteristics and effectiveness: Implications for designing effective work groups. *Personnel Psychology, 46,* 823-850.

Chandler, A. D., Jr. (1962). *Strategy and structures: Chapters in the history of the industrial enterprise.* Cambridge, MA: MIT Press.

Chen, C., Meindl, J. R., & Hunt, R. (1997). Test effects of horizontal and vertical collectivism: A study of rewards allocation preferences in China. *Journal of Cross-Cultural Psychology, 28,* 44-70.

Chen, M. (1995). *Asian management systems: Chinese, Japanese, and Korean styles of business.* New York: Routledge.

Child, J. (1974, Summer). What determines organizational performance? The universals vs. the it all depends. *Organizational Dynamics,* 2-18.

Child, J. (1981). Culture, contingency and capitalism in the cross-national study of organizations. In L. L. Cummings & B. M. Staw (Eds.), *Research in organizational behavior* (Vol. 3, pp. 303-365). Greenwich, CT: JAI.

Child, J. (1994). *Management in China during the age of reform.* Cambridge, UK: Cambridge University Press.

Child, J., & Kieser, A. (1979). Organization and managerial roles in British and West German companies. In C. J. Lammers & D. J. Hickson (Eds.), *Organizations are alike and unlike* (pp. 251-271). London: Routledge & Kegan Paul.

Chinese Culture Connection. (1987). Chinese values and the search for culture-free dimensions of culture. *Journal of Cross-Cultural Psychology, 18*(2), 143-164.

Choran, I. (1969). *The manager of a small company.* Unpublished master's thesis, Montreal, Quebec, McGill University.

Chung, K. H., & Lee, H. C. (1989). *Korean management dynamics.* NY: Praeger.

Church, A. T. (1982). Sojourner adjustment. *Psychological Bulletin, 91*(3), 540-572.

Churchman, C. W. (1968). *The systems approach.* New York: Dell.

Clark, H. H., & Brennan, S. E. (1991). Grounding in communication. *Perspectives on socially shared communication.* Washington, DC: American Psychological Association.

Clarke, C., & Hammer, M. R. (1995). Predictors of Japanese and American managers job success, personal adjustment, and intercultural interaction effectiveness. *Management International Review, 35*(2), 153-170.

Cleveland, H., Mangone, G., & Adams, J. C. (1960). *The overseas Americans.* New York: McGraw-Hill.

Cohen, S., & Gibson, C. (2000). *Mutual understanding, integration and trust: Creating conditions for virtual team effectiveness.* Unpublished manuscript, University of Southern California, Center for Effective Organizations, Los Angeles, California.

Colby, A., Kohlberg, L., Gibbs, J. C., & Lieberman, M. (1983). A longitudinal study of moral development. *Monographs of the Society for Research in Child Development, 48*, 1-124.

Cole, R. E. (1973). Functional alternatives and economic development: An empirical examination of permanent employment in Japan. *American Sociological Review, 38*, 424-438.

Cole, R. E. (1980). *Work, mobility, and participation: A comparative study of American and Japanese industry.* Berkeley: University of California Press.

Condon, J., & Yousef, F. (1975). *An introduction to intercultural communication.* Indianapolis, IN: Bobbs-Merrill.

Conger, J. A., & Kanungo, R. (1987). Toward a behavioral theory of charismatic leadership in organizational settings. *Academy of Management Review, 12*, 637-647.

Conger, J. A., & Kanungo, R. (1988). *Charismatic leadership: The elusive factor in organizational effectiveness.* San Francisco: Jossey-Bass.

Cox, T. (1993). *Cultural diversity in organizations: Theory, research & practice.* San Francisco: Berrett-Koehler.

Cullen, J. B. (1999). *Multinational management: A strategic approach.* Cincinnati, OH: South-Western.

Cummings, T. G. (1978). Self-regulating work groups: A sociotechnical synthesis. *Academy of Management Review, 3*, 625-634.

Cushner, K., & Brislin, R. W. (1996). *Intercultural interactions: A practical guide.* Thousand Oaks, CA: Sage.

Dacin, M. T., Hitt, M. A., & Levitas, E. (1997). Selecting partners for successful international alliances: Examination of US and Korean firms. *Journal of World Business, 32*(1), 3-15.

D'Andrade, R. (1989). Cultural cognition. In M. I. Posner (Ed.), *Foundations of cognitive science* (pp. 795-830). Cambridge, MA: MIT Press.

Daniels, J. D., & Radebaugh, L. H. (1998). *International business: Environments and operations* (8th ed.). Reading, MA: Addison-Wesley.

Darley, J. M., & Fazio, R. H. (1980). Expectancy confirmation processes arising in the social interaction sequence. *American Psychologist, 35,* 867-881.

Das, G. (1993). Local memoirs of a global manager. *Harvard Business Review, 71*(2), 38-47.

Davidson, M., & Cooper, G. (1987). Female managers in Britain: A comparative perspective. *Human Resource Management, 26*(2), 217-242.

Davis, F. (1971). *Inside intuition: What we know about nonverbal communication.* New York: McGraw-Hill.

Davis, M. A., Johnson, N. B., & Ohmer, D. G. (1998). Issue-contingent effects on ethical decision making: A cross-cultural comparison. *Journal of Business Ethics, 17,* 373-389.

Davis, S. M. (1992). Managing and organizing multinational corporations. In C. A. Bartlett & S. Ghoshal (Eds.), *Transnational management* (pp. 607-620). Homewood, IL: Richard D. Irwin.

Dawes, R. M. (1980). Social dilemmas. *Annual Review of Psychology, 31,* 169-193.

Dawes, R. M. (1988). *Rational choice in an uncertain world.* New York: Harcourt Brace.

de Tocqueville, A. (1899). *Democracy in America* (H. Reeve, Trans.). New York: Colonial Press.

Deal, T., & Kennedy, A. (1982). *Corporate culture: The rites and rituals of corporate life.* Reading, MA: Addison-Wesley.

Dearborn, D. C., & Simon, H. A. (1958, June). Selective perception: A note on the departmental identification of executives. *Sociometry,* 140-144.

DeCieri, H., Dowling, P. J., & Taylor, K. F. (1991). The psychological impact of expatriate relocation on partners. *International Journal of Human Resource Management, 2*(3), 377-414.

DeMeyer, A. (1993). Management of an international network of industrial R & D laboratories. *R & D Management, 23,* 109-120.

DePaulo, B. M. (1992). Nonverbal behavior and self-presentation. *Psychological Bulletin, 111,* 230-243.

Der-Karabetian, A. (1992). World-mindedness and the nuclear threat: A multi-national study. *Journal of Social Behavior and Personality, 7,* 293-308.

Deshpande, S. P. ,& Viswesvaran, C. (1992). Is cross-cultural training of expatriate managers effective: A meta-analysis. *International Journal of Intercultural Relations, 16,* 295-310.

Dill, W. R. (1958). Environment as an influence on managerial autonomy. *Administrative Science Quarterly, 2,* 409-443.

DiMaggio, P. J., & Powell, W. W. (1983). The iron cage revisited: Institutional isomorphism and collective rationality in organizational fields. *American Sociological Review, 48,* 147-160.

Dobbins, G. H., Long, W. S., Dedrick, E. J., & Clemons, T. C. (1990). The role of self-monitoring and gender on leader emergence: A laboratory and field study. *Journal of Management, 16*(3), 609-618.

Doi, T. (1973). *The anatomy of dependence.* New York: Harper Row.

Doi, T. (1986). *The anatomy of self: The individual versus society.* Tokyo: Kodansha.

Doktor, R. H. (1983). Culture and the management of time: A comparison of Japanese and American top management practice. *Asia Pacific Journal of Management, 1,* 65-71.

Doktor, R. H. (1990). Asian and American CEOs: A comparative study. *Organizational Dynamics, 19*(3), 46-56.

Doktor, R. H., Tung, R., & Von Glinow, M. (1991). Incorporating international dimensions in management theory building. *Academy of Management Review, 16*(2), 259-261.

Donaldson, L. (1986). Size and bureaucracy in East and West: A preliminary meta-analysis. In S. Clegg, D. C. Dunphy, and S. G. Redding (Eds.), *The enterprise and management in South-East Asia* (pp. n.p.). Hong Kong: Hong Kong University, Centre for Asian Studies.

Donaldson, T. (1989). *The ethics of international business.* New York: Oxford University Press.

Donaldson, T. (1993). When in Rome, do . . . what? International business and cultural relativism. In P. M. Minus (Ed.), *The ethics of business in a global economy* (pp. 67-78). Boston: Kluwer Academic.

Dorfman, P. W. (1996). International and cross-cultural leadership. In J. Punnett & O. Shenkar (Eds.), *Handbook for international management research* (pp. 276-349). Cambridge, MA: Blackwell.

Dorfman, P. W., & Howell, J. P. (1988). Dimensions of national culture and effective leadership patterns: Hofstede revisited. *Advances in International Comparative Management, 3,* 127-150.

Drenth, P. J. D., & Wilpert, B. (1980). The role of "social contracts" in cross-cultural research. *International Review of Applied Psychology, 29* (3), 293-306.

Druckman, D., Benton, A. A., Ali, F., & Bagur, J. S. (1976). Cultural differences in bargaining behavior. *Journal of Conflict Resolution, 20,* 413-449.

Dunbar, E. (1992). Adjustment and satisfaction of expatriate U.S. personnel. *International Journal of Intercultural Relations, 16,* 1-16.

Dunbar, E. (1994). The German executive in the U.S. work and social environment: Exploring role demands. *International Journal of Intercultural Relations, 18,* 277-291.

Duncan, R. B. (1972). Characteristics of organizational environments and perceived environmental uncertainty. *Administrative Science Quarterly, 17*(3), 313-327.

Dunphy, D. (1987). Convergence/divergence: A temporal review of the Japanese enterprise and its management. *Academy of Management Review, 12,* 445-459.

Earley, P. C. (1987). Intercultural training for managers: A comparison of documentary and interpersonal methods. *Academy of Management Journal, 30*(4), 685-698.

Earley, P. C. (1989). Social loafing and collectivism: A comparison of the U.S. and the People's Republic of China. *Administrative Science Quarterly, 34,* 565-581.

Earley, P. C. (1999). Playing follow the leader: Status determining traits in relation to collective efficacy across cultures. *Organizational Behavior and Human Decision Processes, 80*(3), 192-212.

Earley, P. C., & Gibson, C. B. (1998). Taking stock in our progress on individualism-collectivism: 100 years of solidarity and community. *Journal of Management, 24,* 265-304.

Earley, P. C., & Mosakowski, E. (2000). Creating hybrid team cultures: An empirical test of transnational team functioning. *Academy of Management Journal, 43*(1), 26-49.

Earley, P. C., & Singh, H. (1995). International and intercultural management research: What's next? *Academy of Management Journal, 38*(2), 327-340.

Echavarria, N. U., & Davis, D. D. (1994, July). *A test of Bass's Model of transformational and transactional leadership in the Dominican Republic.* Paper presented at the 23rd International Congress of Applied Psychology, Madrid, Spain.

Edstrom, A., & Galbraith, J. R. (1977). Transfer of managers as a coordination and control strategy in multinational organizations. *Administrative Science Quarterly, 22,* 248-263.

Eisenberg, A. M., & Smith, R. R. (1971). *Nonverbal communication.* Indianapolis, IN: Bobbs-Merrill.

Eisenhardt, S. N. (1973). *Tradition, change and modernity.* New York: John Wiley.

Ekman, P. W. (1982). *Emotion in the human face* (2nd ed.). Cambridge, UK: Cambridge University Press.

Ekman, P. W., Friesen, V., & Ellsworth, P. (1972). *Emotions in the human face: Guidelines for research and an intergration of the findings.* Elmsford, NY: Pergamon.

Elron, E. (1997). Top management teams within multinational corporations: Effects of cultural heterogeneity. *Leadership Quarterly, 8,* 393-412.

Ellegard, K., Jonsson, D., Enstrom, T., Johansson, M., Medbo, L., & Johansson, B. (1992). Reflective production in the final assembly of motor vehicles: An emerging Swedish challenge. *International Journal of Operations and Production Management, 12*(7-8), 117-133.

Elliott, G. C., & Meeker, B. F. (1984). Modifiers of the equity effect: Group outcome and causes for individual performance. *Journal of Personality and Social Psychology, 46,* 586-597.

Ellis, S., Rogoff, B., & Cramer, C. C. (1981). Age segregation in children's social interactions. *Developmental Psychology, 17,* 399-407.

Ellsworth, P. C., & Carlsmith, J. M. (1973). Eye contact and gaze aversion in aggressive encounter. *Journal of Personality and Social Psychology, 33,* 117-122.

Emery, F. E., & Trist, E. L. (1965). The causal texture of organizational environments. *Human Relations, 17*(1), 21-32.

Enderwick, P., & Hodgson, D. (1993). Expatriate management practices of New Zealand businesses. *International Journal of Human Resource Management, 4*(2), 407-423.

Engholm, C. (1991). *When business East meets business West: The guide to practice and protocol in the Pacific Rim.* New York: John Wiley.

England, G. W. (1983). Japanese and American management: Theory Z and beyond. *Journal of International Business Studies, 14,* 131-141.

English, H. B. (1958). *A comprehensive dictionary of psychological and psychoanalytical terms.* New York: David McKay.

Erez, M. (1997). A culture-based model of work motivation. In P. C. Earley & M. Erez, (Eds.), *New perspectives on international industrial/organizational psychology* (pp. 193-242). San Francisco: New Lexington Press.

Erez, M., & Earley, P. C. (1993). *Culture, self-identity and work.* New York: Oxford University Press.

Farnham, A. (1994, June 27). Global—or just globaloney? *Fortune,* 97-100.

Fayweather, J., & Kapoor, A. (1972). Simulated international business negotiations. *Journal of International Business Studies, 3,* 19-31.

Feign, L. (1988). *The world of Lily Wong.* Hong Kong: Macmillan.

Feldman, D. C. (1976). A contingency theory of socialization. *Administrative Science Quarterly, 21,* 433-451.

Feldman, D. C. (1984). The development and enforcement of group norms. *Academy of Management Journal, 27,* 47-53.

Feldman, D. C., & Brett, J. M. (1983). Coping with new jobs: A comparative study of new hires and job changers. *Academy of Management Journal, 26,* 258-272.

Feldman, D. C., & Thomas, D. C. (1992). Career management issues facing expatriates. *Journal of International Business Studies, 23*(2), 271-293.

Feldman, D. C., & Tompson, H. B. (1993). Expatriation, repatriation, and domestic geographical relocation: An empirical investigation of adjustment to new job assignments. *Journal of International Business Studies, 24*(2), 507-529.

Ferraro, G. P. (1994). *The cultural dimension of international business.* Englewood Cliffs, NJ: Prentice Hall.

Ferrell, O., & Fraedrich, J. (1994). *Business ethics: Ethical decision making and cases* (2nd ed.). Boston: Houghton Mifflin.

Ferris, G. R., & Wagner, J. A. (1985). Quality circles in the United States: A conceptual re-evaluation. *Journal of Applied Behavioral Science, 21,* 155-167.

Festinger, L. (1957). *A theory of cognitive dissonance.* Stanford, CA: Stanford University Press.

Fiedler, F. E. (1966). The effect of leadership and cultural heterogeneity on group performance: A test of the contingency model. *Journal of Experimental Social Psychology, 2,* 237-264.

Fiedler, F. E. (1967). *A theory of leadership effectiveness.* New York: McGraw-Hill.

Fiedler, F. E. (1993). The leadership situation and the black box in contingency theories. In M. M. Chemers & R. Ayman (Eds.), *Leadership theory and research: Perspectives and directions* (pp. 2-28). San Diego, CA: Academic Press.

Fiske, A. P. (1990). *Structures of social life: The four elementary forms of human relations.* New York: Free Press.

Fiske, S., & Taylor, S. (1984). *Social cognition.* Reading, MA: Addison-Wesley.

Fleishman, E. A. (1953). The description of supervisory behavior. *Personnel Psychology, 37,* 1-6.

Fortune Global 500. (2000, July 24). *Fortune.*

Francis, J. N. P. (1991). When in Rome? The effects of cultural adaptation on intercultural business negotiations. *Journal of International Business Studies, 22*(3), 403-428.

Franko, L. (1973). Who manages multinational enterprises? *Columbia Journal of World Business, 8,* 30-42.

Frederick, W. C. (1991). The moral authority of transnational corporate codes. *Journal of Business Ethics, 10,* 165-177.

Freedman, S., & Phillips, J. (1988). The changing nature of research on women at work. *Journal of Management, 14*(2), 231-251.

Freedom House. (1999). *Freedom in the world: The annual survey of political rights and civil liberties.* Washington, DC: Authoruse.

Friedlander, F. (1989). The ecology of work groups. In J. W. Lorsch (Ed.), *Handbook of organizational behavior* (pp. 301-314). Englewood Cliffs, NJ: Prentice Hall.

Fritzsche, D. J., & Becker, H. (1984). Linking management behavior to ethical philosophy: An empirical investigation. *Academy of Management Journal, 27*(1), 166-175.

Furnham, A., & Bochner, S. (1986). *Culture shock: Psychological reactions to unfamiliar environments.* New York: Methuen.

Gabrielidis, C., Stephen, W. G., Ybarra, O., Dos Santos Pearson, V. M., & Villareal, L. (1997). Preferred styles of conflict resolution: Mexico and the United States. *Journal of Cross-Cultural Psychology, 28*(6), 661-677.

Gallois, C., & Callan, V. (1997). *Communication and culture: A guide for practice.* Chichester, UK: Wiley.

Gass, S. M., & Varonis, E. M. (1985). Variation in native speaker speech modification to nonnative speakers. *Studies in Second Language Acquisition, 7,* 37-58.

George, J. M. (1990). Personality, affect, and behavior in groups. *Journal of Applied Psychology, 75*(2), 107-116.

Geringer, M. J. (1988, Summer). Partner selection criteria for developed country joint alliances. *Business Quarterly,* pp. 54-61.

Geringer, M. J., & Hebert, L. (1991). Measuring performance of international joint ventures. *Journal of International Business Studies, 22*(2), 249-264.

Gersick, C. J. G. (1988). Time and transition in work team: Toward a new model of group development. *Academy of Management Journal, 31,* 9-41.

Gersick, C. J. G. (1989). Marking time: Predictable transitions in task groups. *Academy of Management Journal, 32,* 274-309.

Ghauri, P. N., & Prasad, S. B. (1995). A network approach to probing Asia's interfirm linkages. *Advances in International Comparative Management, 10,* 63-77.

Ghoshal, S. (1997). Of cakes, clothes, emperors, and obituaries. In B. Toyne & D. Nigh (Eds.), *International business: An emerging vision* (pp. 361-366). Columbia: University of South Carolina Press.

Ghoshal, S., & Bartlett, C. A. (1990). The multinational corporation as an inter-organizational network. *Academy of Managment Review, 15,* 603-625.

Gibbs, B. (1994). The effects of environment and technology on managerial roles. *Journal of Management, 20*(3), 581-604.

Gibson, C. B. (1994). The implications of national culture for organization structure: An investigation of three perspectives. *Advances in International Comparative Management, 9,* 3-38.

Giles, H., Bourhis, R. Y., & Taylor, D. M. (1977). Toward a theory of language in ethnic group relations. In H. Giles (comp.), *Language, ethnicity, and intergroup relations* (pp. 307-348). London: Academic Press.

Giles, H., Coupland, N., & Wiemann, J. M. (1992). Talk is cheap . . . but my word is my bond: Beliefs about talk. In K. Boulton & H. Kwok (Eds.), *Sociolinguistics today: Eastern and Western perspectives* (pp. 218-243). London: Routledge.

Giles, H., & Smith, P. (1979). Accommodation theory: Optimal levels of convergence. In H. Giles & R. N. St.Clair (Eds.), *Language and social psychology* (pp. 45-63). Baltimore: University Park Press.

Gioa, D. A., & Poole, P. P. (1984). Scripts in organizational behaviour. *Academy of Management Review, 9,* 449-459.

Glenn, E. S., Witmeyer, D., & Stevenson, K. A. (1977). Cultural styles of persuasion. *International Journal of Intercultural Relations, 1,* 52-66.

Gomez-Mejia, L., & Balkin, D. (1987). The determinants of managerial satisfaction with the expatriation and repatriation process. *Journal of Management Development, 6*(1), 7-17.

Goodman, P. S. (1986). Impact of task and technology on group performance. In P. S. Goodman & Associates (Eds.), *Designing effective work groups* (pp. 120-167). San Francisco: Jossey-Bass.

Goodman, P. S., Ravlin, E. C., & Schminke, M. (1987). Understanding groups in organizations. In B. Staw & L. Cummings (Eds.), *Research in organizational behavior* (Vol. 9, pp. 124-128). Greenwich, CT: JAI.

Graen, G. (1976). Role-making processes within complex organizations. In M. D. Dunnette (Ed.), *Handbook of industrial and organizational psychology* (pp. 1201-1246). Chicago: Rand McNally.

Graham, J. L. (1983, Spring/Summer). Brazilian, Japanese and American business negotiations. *Journal of International Business Studies,* 47-61.

Graham, J. L. (1985). The influence of culture on the process of business negotiations: An exploratory study. *Journal of International Business Studies, 16,* 81-96.

Graham, J. L. (1986). The problem solving approach to interorganizational negotiations: A laboratory experiment. *Journal of Business Research, 14,* 271-286.

Graham, J. L. (1987). A theory of interorganizational negotiations. *Research in Marketing, 9,* 163-183.

Graham, J. L., Kim, D. K., Lin, C. Y., & Robinson, M. (1988). Buyer-seller negotiations around the Pacific Rim: Differences in fundamental exchange processes. *Journal of Consumer Research, 15,* 48-54.

Graham, J. L., Mintu, A. T., & Rodgers, W. (1994). Explorations of negotiation behaviors in ten foreign cultures using a model developed in the United States. *Management Science, 40*(1), 72-95.

Graham, J. L., & Sanyo, Y. (1984). *Smart bargaining: Doing business with the Japanese.* Cambridge, MA: Ballinger.

Granrose, C. (1994). Careers of Japanese and Chinese expatriate managers in U.S. multinational firms. *Journal of Asian Business, 10,* 59-79.

Gray, I. (1987). *Henri Fayol's classic: General and industrial management.* Belmont, CA: Lake Publishers.

Gregersen, H. B., & Black, J. S. (1990). A multifaceted approach to expatriate retention in international assignments. *Group and Organization Studies, 15*(4), 461-485.

Gregersen, H. B., Hite, J. M., & Black, J. S. (1996). Expatriate performance appraisal in U.S. multinational firms. *Journal of International Business Studies, 27*(4), 711-738.

Gregory, A. (1989). Political risk management. In A. Rugman (Ed.), *International business in Canada* (pp. 310-329). Scarborough, Ontario: Prentice Hall.

Greiner, R., & Metes, G. (1995). *Going virtual.* Upper Saddle River, NJ: Prentice Hall.

Gudykunst, W. B., Gao, G., & Franklyn-Stokes, A. (1996). Self-monitoring and concern for social appropriateness in China and England. In J. Pandey & D. Sinha (Eds.), *Asian contributions to cross-cultural psychology* (pp. 255-267). New Delhi, India: Sage India.

Gudykunst, W. B., Ting-Toomey, S., & Chua, E. (1988). *Culture and interpersonal communication.* Newbury Park, CA: Sage.

Gullahorn, J. T., & Gullahorn, J. E. (1963). An extension of the U-curve hypothesis. *Journal of Social Issues, 19,* 33-47.

Gulliver, P. H. (1979). *Disputes and negotiations.* New York: Academic Press.

Guthrie, G. M., & Azores, F. M. (1968). Philippine interpersonal behavior patterns. *Ateneo de Manila University IPC Papers, 6,* 3-63.

Guthrie, G. M., & Zektrick, I. (1967). Predicting performance in the Peace Corps. *Journal of Social Psychology, 71,* 11-21.

Guzzo, R. A., Noonan, K. A., & Elron, E. (1994). Expatriate managers and the psychological contract. *Journal of Applied Psychology, 79*(4), 617-626.

Hackman, J. R. (1987). The design of work teams. In J. W. Lorsch (Ed.), *Handbook of organizational behavior* (pp. 315-342). Englewood Cliffs, NJ: Prentice Hall.

Hackman, J. R. (1991). *Groups that work (and those that don't).* San Francisco: Jossey Bass.

Hackman, J. R., & Morris, C. G. (1978). Group process and group effectiveness: A reappraisal. In L. Berkowitz (Ed.), *Group process* (pp. 57-66). Reading, MA: Addison-Wesley.

Hackman, J. R., & Oldham, G. R. (1980). *Work redesign.* Reading, MA: Addison-Wesley.

Hage, J., & Aiken, M. (1969). Routine technology, social structure, and organizational goals. *Administrative Science Quarterly, 14,* 366-377.

Haire, M., Ghiselli, E. E., & Porter, L. W. (1966). *Management thinking: An international study.* New York: John Wiley.

Hales, C., & Tamangani, Z. (1996). An investigation of the relationship between organizational structure, managerial role expectations and managers' work activities. *Journal of Management Studies, 33*(6), 731-756.

Hales, C. P. (1986). What managers do? A critical review of the evidence. *Journal of Management Studies, 23*(1), 88-115.

Hall, E. T. (1959). *The silent language*. New York: Doubleday.

Hall, E. T. (1966). *The hidden dimension*. New York: Doubleday.

Hall, E. T. (1976). *Beyond culture*. New York: Doubleday.

Hall, E. T., & Hall, M. R. (1987). *Hidden differences*. New York: Doubleday.

Hall, R. H., Haas, J. E., & Johnson, N. J. (1967). Organizational size, complexity, and formalization. *Administrative Science Quarterly, 12*, 903-912.

Hallowell, A. I. (1955). *Culture and experience*. Philadelphia: University of Pennsylvania Press.

Hamaguchi, E. (1985). A contextual model of the Japanese: Toward a methodological innovation in Japan studies. *Journal of Japanese Studies, 11*, 289-321.

Hamilton, D. L. (1979). A cognitive-attributional analysis of stereotyping. In L. Berkowitz (Ed.), *Advances in experimental social psychology* (Vol. 12, pp. 53-84). New York: Academic Press.

Hammer, M. R. (1987). Behavioral dimensions of intercultural effectiveness: A replication and extension. *International Journal of Intercultural Relations, 11*, 65-87.

Hammer, M. R., Gudykunst, W. B., & Wiseman, R. L. (1978). Dimensions of intercultural effectiveness: An exploratory study. *International Journal of Intercultural Relations, 8*, 1-10.

Hannan, M. T., & Freeman, J. (1977). The population ecology of organizations. *American Journal of Sociology, 82*, 929-946.

Hannan, M. T., & Freeman, J. (1984). Structural inertia and organizational change. *American Sociological Review, 49*, 149-164.

Harpaz, I. (1990). The importance of work goals: An international perspective. *Journal of International Business Studies, 21*(1), 75-93.

Harpaz, I. (1996). International management survey research. In B. J. Punnett & O. Shenkar (Eds.), *Handbook for international management research* (pp. 37-62). Cambridge, MA: Blackwell.

Hartog, D. N., Van Muijen, J. J., & Koopman, P. L. (1994, July). *Transactional versus transformational leadership: An analysis of the MLQ in the Netherlands*. Paper presented at the 23rd International Congress of Applied Psychology, Madrid, Spain.

Harvey, M. C. (1989). Repatriation of corporate executives: An empirical study. *Journal of International Business Studies, 20*, 131-144.

Harvey, M. C. (1997). Dual career expatriates: Expectations, adjustment and satisfaction with international relocation. *Journal of International Business Studies, 28*(3), 627-658.

Haselberger, A., & Stroh, L. K. (1992). Development and selection of multinational expatriates. *Human Resource Development Quarterly, 3*, 287-293.

Hays, R. D. (1971). Ascribed behavioral determinants of success-failure among U.S. expatriate managers. *Journal of International Business Studies, 2*(1), 25-37.

Hays, R. D. (1974). Expatriate selection: Insuring success and avoiding failure. *Journal of International Business Studies, 5*(1), 25-37.

Hecht, M. L., Andersen, P. A., & Ribeau, S. A. (1989). The cultural dimensions of nonverbal communication. In M. Kasante & W. B. Gudykunst (Eds.), *Handbook of international and intercultural communication* (pp. 163-185). Newbury Park, CA: Sage.

Heine, S. J., & Lehman, D. R. (1995). Cultural variation in unrealistic optimism: Does the West feel more invulnerable than the East? *Journal of Personality and Social Psychology, 68,* 595-607.

Heller, F., & Wilpert, B. (1981). *Competence and power in managerial decision-making.* Chichester, UK: Wiley.

Helmreich, R. L., & Schaefer, H. (1994) Team performance in the operating room. In M. S. Bogner (Ed.), *Human error in medicine* (pp. 225-253). Hillsdale, NJ: Lawrence Erlbaum.

Henley, N. M. (1977). *Body politics: Power, sex, and nonverbal communication.* Englewood Cliffs, NJ: Prentice Hall.

Hewstone, M. (1990). The "ultimate attribution error"? A review of the literature on intergroup causal attribution. *European Journal of Social Psychology, 20,* 614-623.

Hickson, D. J., Hinings, C. R., McMillan, C. J., & Schwitter, J. P. (1991). The culture-free context of organizational structure: A tri-national comparison. *Sociology, 8,* 59-80.

Hickson, D. J., & McMillan, C. J. (1981). *Organization and nation: The Aston programme IV.* Farnborough, UK: Gower Publishing.

Hickson, D. J., & Pugh, D. S. (1995). *Management worldwide: The impact of societal culture on organizations around the globe.* London: Penguin Books.

Hill, C. W. L. (2001). *International business: Competing in the global market place, Postcript 2001.* New York: Irwin-McGraw Hill.

Hill, G. W. (1982). Group versus individual performance: Are N+1 heads better than one? *Psychological Bulletin, 91,* 517-539.

Hinkle, S., & Brown, R. (1990). Intergroup comparisons and social identity: Some links and lacunae. In D. Abrams & M. Hogg (Eds.), *Social identity theory: Constructive and critical advances* (n.p.). Hemel Hempstead, UK: Harvester Wheatsheaf.

Hoerr, J. (1989, July 10). The payoff from teamwork. *Business Week,* 55-62.

Hofstede, G. (1980). *Culture's consequences: International differences in work related values.* Beverly Hills, CA: Sage.

Hofstede, G. (1983). The cultural relativity of organizational practices and theories. *Journal of International Business Studies, 14*(2), 75-89.

Hofstede, G. (1991). *Culture and organisations: Software of the mind.* London: McGraw-Hill.

Hofstede, G., Neuijen, B., Ohayv, D. D., & Sanders, G. (1990). Measuring organizational cultures: A qualitative/quantitative study across twenty cases. *Administrative Science Quarterly, 35,* 286-316.

Hofstede, G., & Usunier, J. C. (1996). Hofstede's dimensions of culture and their influence on international business negotiations. In P. Ghauri & J. C. Usunier (Eds.), *International business negotiations* (pp. 119-129). Oxford, UK: Pergamon.

House, R. J. (1971). A path-goal theory of leader effectiveness. *Administrative Science Quarterly, 16,* 556-571.

House, R. J. (1977). A 1976 theory of charismatic leadership. In J. G. Hunt & L. L. Larson (Eds.), *Leadership: The cutting edge* (pp. 189-207). Carbondale: Southern Illinois University Press.

House, R. J. (1991, August). *The universality of charismatic leadership.* Paper presented at the Academy of Management Annual Meeting, Miami, Florida.

House, R. J., & Aditya, R. N. (1997). The social scientific study of leadership: Quo Vadis? *Journal of Management, 23*(3), 409-473.

House, R. J., & Mitchell, T. R. (1974, Fall). Path-goal theory of leadership. *Contemporary Business, 3*, 81-98.

House, R. J., Wright, N. S., & Aditya, R. N. (1997). Cross-cultural research on organizational leadership: A critical analysis and a proposed theory. In P. C. Earley & M. Erez (Eds.), *New perspectives on international industrial/organizational psychology* (pp. 535-625). San Francisco: New Lexington Press.

Howard, C. G. (1974, March-April). Model for the design of a selection program for multinational executives. *Public Personnel Management,* 138-145.

Howard, G. (1991). Culture tales: A narrative approach to thinking, cross-cultural psychology and psychotherapy. *American Psychologist, 46,* 187-197.

Howell, J. P., & Dorfman, P. W. (1988, April). *A comparative study of leadership and its substitutes in a mixed cultural work settings.* Paper presented at the Western Academy of Management Meeting, Big Sky, Montana.

Howell, J. P., Dorfman, P. W., Hibino, S., Lee, J. K., & Tate, U. (1994). *Leadership in Western and Asian countries: Commonalties and differences in effective leadership processes and substitutes across cultures.* Las Cruces: New Mexico State University Center for Business Research.

Howell, J. P., Dorfman, P. W., & Kerr, S. (1986). Moderator variables in leadership research. *Academy of Management Review, 11,* 88-102.

Hoyle, R. H., & Crawford, A. M. (1994). Use of individual-level data to investigate group phenomena: Issues and strategies. *Small Group Research, 25*(4), 464-485.

Hui, C. H. (1990). Work attitudes, leadership styles, and managerial behaviors in different cultures. In R. W. Brislin (Ed.), *Cross-cultural research and methodology series: Applied cross-cultural psychology* (Vol. 14, pp. 186-208). Newbury Park, CA: Sage.

Hui, C. H., & Triandis, H. C. (1989). Effects of culture and response format on extreme response styles. *Journal of Cross-Cultural Psychology, 20,* 296-309.

Hui, H. C., & Cheng, I. W. M. (1987). Effects of second language proficiency of speakers and listeners on person perception and behavioural intention: A study of Chinese bilinguals. *International Journal of Psychology, 22,* 421-430.

Huo, Y. P., & Von Glinow, M. A. (1995). On transplanting human resource practices to China: A culture-driven approach. *International Journal of Manpower, 16*(9), 3-13.

IDE Research Group. (1993). *Industrial democracy in Europe revisited.* New York: Oxford University Press.

Indvik, J. (1986). Path-goal theory of leadership: A meta-analysis. *Proceedings of the Academy of Management Meeting* (pp. 189-192).

Inglehart, R. (1977). *The silent revolution: Changing values and political styles among Western publics.* Princeton, NJ: Princeton University Press.

Inglehart, R. (1990). *Cultural shift in advanced industrial society.* Princeton, NJ: Princeton University Press.

nzerilli, G., & Laurent, A. (1983). Managerial views of organization structure in France and the USA. *International Studies of Management and Organization, 13*(1-2), 97-118.

vancevich, J. M. (1969, March). Selection of American managers for overseas assignments. *Personnel Journal,* 189-193.

zard, C. (1991). *Human emotions* (2nd ed.). New York: Plenum.

zraeli, D. (1988). Ethical beliefs and behavior among managers: A cross-cultural perspective. *Journal of Business Ethics, 7,* 263-271.

zraeli, D. N., Banai, M., & Zeira, Y. (1980). Women expatriates in subsidiaries of multinational corporations. *California Management Review, 23*(1), 53-63.

ackofsky, E. F., Slocum, J. W., Jr., & McQuaid, S. J. (1988). Cultural values and the CEO: Alluring companions? *The Academy of Management Executive, 2*(1), 39-49.

ackson, S. E. (1992). Team composition in organizational settings: Issues in managing an increasingly diverse work force. In S. Worchel, W. Wood, & J. A. Simpson (Eds.), *Group process and productivity* (pp. 138-173). Newbury Park, CA: Sage.

ackson, S. E., & Schuler, R. S. (1985). A meta-analysis and conceptual critique of research on role ambiguity and role conflict in work settings. *Organizational Behavior and Human Decision Processes, 36,* 16-78.

anis, I. L. (1982). *Groupthink.* Boston: Houghton Mifflin.

anis, I. L., & Mann, L. (1977). *Decision making.* New York: Free Press.

anssens, M. (1995). Intercultural interaction: A burden on international managers? *Journal of Organizational Behavior, 16,* 155-167.

arillo, J. (1988). On strategic networks. *Strategic Management Journal, 9,* 31-41.

arvenpaa, S., & Leidner, D. (1999). Communication and trust in global virtual teams. *Organization Science, 10,* 791-815.

ehn, K. A., Northcraft, G. B., & Neale, M. A. (1999). Why differences make a difference: A field study of diversity, conflict and performance in workgroups. *Administrative Science Quarterly, 44,* 741-763.

ensen, J. V. (1982). Perspective on nonverbal intercultural communication. In L. A. Samovar & R. E. Porter (Eds.), *Intercultural communication: A reader.* (pp. 260-276). Belmont, CA: Wadsworth.

ohnston, W. B. (1991). Global workforce 2000: The new world labor market. *Harvard Business Review, 69,* 115-127.

Kahl, J. A. (1968). *The measurement of modernism: A study of values in Brazil and Mexico.* Austin: University of Texas Press.

Kahn, R., Wolfe, D., Quinn, R., Snoek, J., & Rosenthal, R. (1964). *Organizational stress: Studies in role conflict and ambiguity.* New York: John Wiley.

Kakar, S. (1971). Authority patterns and subordinate behavior in Indian organizations. *Administrative Science Quarterly, 16,* 298-307.

Kandel, D. B. (1978). Similarity in real-life adolescent friendship pairs. *Journal of Personality and Social Psychology, 36,* 306-312.

Katriel, T. (1986). *Talking straight: Dugri speech in Israeli Sabra culture.* Cambridge, UK: Cambridge University Press.

Katz, D., & Braly, K. W. (1933). Verbal stereotypes and racial prejudice. *Journal o Abnormal and Social Psychology, 28,* 280-290.

Katz, D., & Kahn, R. L. (1978). *The social psychology of organizations.* New York John Wiley.

Katz, R. (1982). The effects of group longevity on project communication and performance. *Administrative Science Quarterly, 27,* 81-104.

Katzner, K. (1975). *The languages of the world.* New York: Funk & Wagnalls.

Kavanaugh, K. H. (1991). Invisibility and selective avoidance: Gender and ethnicity in psychiatry and psychiatric nursing staff interaction. *Culture, Medicine and Psychiatry, 15*(2), 245-274.

Kayany, J. M., Wotring, C. E., & Forrest, E. J. (1996). Relational control and interactive media choice in technology-mediated communication situations. *Human Communication Research, 22,* 371-398.

Kealey, D. J. (1989). A study of cross-cultural effectiveness: Theoretical issues practical applications. *International Journal of Intercultural Relations, 13,* 387-428.

Kelley, H. H. (1972). Attribution in social interaction. In E. E. Jones, D. E. Kanouse, H. H. Kelley, R. E. Nisbett, S. Valins, & B. Weiner (Eds.), *Attribution: Perceiving the causes of behavior* (pp. 1-26). Morristown, NJ: General Learning Press.

Kenis, I. (1977). A cross-cultural study of personality and leadership. *Group and Organization Studies, 2*(1), 49-60.

Kerlinger, F. N. (1986). *Foundations of behavioral research* (3rd ed.). Chicago: Holt, Rinehart & Winston.

Kerr, C., Dunlop, J. T., Harbison, F. H., & Myers, C. A. (1960). *Industrialism and industrial man: The problems of labor and management in economic growth.* London: Heineman.

Kerr, S., & Jermier, J. M. (1978). Substitutes for leadership: Their meaning and measurement. *Organizational Behavior and Human Performance, 22,* 375-403.

Khadra, B. (1990). The Prophetic-Caliphal model of leadership: An empirical study. *International Studies of Management and Organization, 20*(3), 37-51.

Kim, K. I., Park, H. J., & Suzuki, N. (1990). Reward allocations in the United States, Japan, and Korea: A comparison of individualistic and collectivistic cultures. *Academy of Management Journal, 33*(1), 188-198.

Kim, M. S. (1994). Cross-cultural comparisons of the perceived importance of interactive constraints. *Human Communication Research, 21,* 128-151.

Kim, U., Park, Y., & Park, D. (2000). The challenge of cross-cultural psychology: The role of indigenous psychologies. *Journal of Cross-Cultural Psychology, 31*(1), 63-75.

Kirkman, B. L., & Rosen, B. (1999). Beyond self-management. Antecedents and consequences of team empowerment. *Academy of Management Journal, 42*(1), 58-74.

Kirkman, B. L., & Shapiro, D. L. (1997). The impact of cultural values on employee resitance to teams: Toward a model of globalized self-managing work team effectiveness. *Academy of Management Review, 22*(3), 730-757.

Kirkpatrick, S. A., & Locke, E. A. (1991). Leadership: Do traits matter? *The Academy of Management Executive, 5*(2), 48-60.

Kleinke, C. L. (1986). Gaze and eye contact: A research review. *Psychological Bulletin, 100,* 78-100.

Kluckhohn, C. (1954). *Culture and behavior.* New York: Free Press.

Kluckhohn, C., & Strodtbeck, K. (1961). *Variations in value orientations.* Westport, CT: Greenwood.

Knoke, W. (1996). *Bad new world.* New York: Kodansha International.

Kobrin, S. J. (1979). Political risk: A review and reconsideration. *Journal of International Business Studies, 10*(1), 67-80.

Kobrin, S. J. (1988). Expatriate reduction and strategic control in American multinational corporations. *Human Resource Management, 27*(1), 63-75.

Kobrin, S. J., Basek, J., Blank, S., & La Palombra, J. (1980). The assessment and evaluation of non-economic environment by American firms: A preliminary report. *Journal of International Business Studies, 11*(1), 32-47.

Kogut, B. (1989). A note on global strategy. *Strategic Management Journal, 10,* 383-389.

Kogut, B., & Singh, H. (1988). The effect of national culture on the choice of entry mode. *Journal of International Business Studies, 19*(3), 411-432.

Koh, W. L. (1990). *An empirical validation of the theory of transformational leadership in secondary schools in Singapore.* Unpublished doctoral dissertation, University of Oregon, Eugene, Oregon.

Kohlberg, L. (1969). Stage and sequence: The cognitive-developmental approach to socialization. In D. A. Goslin (Ed.), *Handbook of socialization theory and research* (pp. 347-480). New York: Rand Mcnally.

Kohlberg, L. (1984). *Philosophy of moral development.* New York: Harper & Row.

Kopp, R. (1994). International human resource policies and practices in Japanese, European and United States multinationals. *Human Resource Management, 33*(4), 581-599.

Kotter, J. P., & Heskitt, J. L. (1992). *Corporate culture and performance.* New York: Free Press.

Kraut, R. E., Egido, C., & Galegher, J. (1990). Patterns of contact and communication in scientific research collaborations. In J. Galegher, R. E. Kraut, & C. Egido (Eds.), *Intellectual teamwork: Social and technological foundations of cooperative work* (pp. 23-62). Hillsdale, NJ: Lawrence Erlbaum.

Kroeber, A. L., & Kluckhohn, F. (1952). Culture: A critical review of concepts and definitions. *Peabody museum papers* (Vol. 47, No. 1). Cambridge, MA: Harvard University Press.

Lachman, R., Nedd, A., & Hinings, B. (1994). Analyzing cross-national management and organizations: A theoretical framework. *Management Science, 40*(1), 40-55.

Lalonde, R. N., & Cameron, J. E. (1993). An intergroup perspective on immigrant acculturation with a focus on collective strategies. *International Journal of Psychology, 28,* 57-74.

Landis, D., & Brislin, R. W. (Eds.). (1983). *Handbook of intercultural training.* Elmsford, NY: Pergamon.

Larson, L. L., Hunt, J. G., & Osborn, R. N. (1974). Correlates of leadership and demographic variables in three organizational settings. *Journal of Business Research, 64*(2), 151-156.

Laurent, A. (1983). The cultural diversity of western conceptions of management. *International Studies of Management and Organization, 13*(1), 75-96.

Lawrence, P. R. (1987). Historical development of organizational behavior. In J. W. Lorsch (Ed.), *Handbook of organizational behavior* (pp. 1-9). Englewood Cliffs, NJ: Prentice Hall.

Lawrence, P., & Lorsch, J. (1967). Differentiation and integration in complex organizations. *Administrative Science Quarterly, 12*, 1-47.

Lazerson, M. (1995). A new phoenix? Modern putting-out in the Modena knitwear industry. *Administrative Science Quarterly, 40*, 34-59.

Lee, Y.-T., & Duenas, G. (1995). Stereotype accuracy in multicultural business. In Y.-T. Lee, L. J. Jussim, & C. R. McCauly (Eds.), *Stereotype accuracy: Toward appreciating group differences* (pp. 157-186). Washington, DC: American Psychological Association.

Leifer, R., & Huber, G. (1977). Relations among perceived environmental uncertainty, organizational structure, and boundary spanning behavior. *Administrative Science Quarterly, 22*, 235-247.

Leksell, L. (1981). *Headquarter-subsidiary relationships in multinational corporations.* Stockholm: Stockholm School of Economics.

Leung, K. (1987). Some determinants of reactions to procedural models of conflict resolution: A cross-national study. *Journal of Personality and Social Psychology, 53*(5), 898-908.

Leung, K. (1997). Negotiation and reward allocation across cultures. In P. C. Earley & M. Erez (Eds.), *New perspectives on international industrial/organizational psychology* (pp. 640-675). San Francisco: Jossey-Bass.

Leung, K., & Bond, M. H. (1982). How Chinese and Americans reward task-related contributions: A preliminary study. *Psychology, 25*, 32-39.

Leung, K., & Bond, M. H. (1984). The impact of cultural collectivism on reward allocation. *Journal of Personality and Social Psychology, 47*, 793-804.

Leung, K., Bond, M. H., & Schwartz, S. H. (1995). How to explain cross-cultural differences: Values, valences and expectancies? *Asian Journal of Psychology, 1*, 70-75.

Leung, K., & Lind, E. A. (1986). Procedural justice and culture: Effects of culture, gender, and investigator status on procedural preferences. *Journal of Personality and Social Psychology, 50*(6), 1134-1140.

Leung, K., & Wu, P.-G. (1990). Dispute processing: A cross-cultural analysis. In R. Brislin (Ed.), *Applied cross-cultural psychology* (Vol. 14, pp. 209-231). Newbury Park, CA: Sage.

Levenson, R. W., Ekman, P., Heider, K., & Friesen, W. V. (1992). Emotion and autonomic nervous system activity in the Minangkabau of West Sumatra. *Journal of Personality and Social Psychology, 62*, 972-988.

Levine, D. N. (1985). *The flight from ambiguity.* Chicago: University of Chicago Press.

Lewis, S. A., & Fry, W. R. (1977). Effects of visual access and orientation on the discovery of integrative bargaining activities. *Organizational Behavior and Human Performance, 20*, 75-92.

Li, H. Z. (1994). *Inter- and intra-cultural information transmission.* Unpublished doctoral dissertation, University of Victoria, British Columbia, Canada.

Lincoln, J. R., & Miller, J. (1979). Work and friendship ties in organizations: A comparative analysis of related networks. *Administrative Science Quarterly, 24,* 181-199.

Lincoln, J. R., Olson, J., & Hanada, M. (1978). Cultural effects of organizational structures: The case of Japanese firms in the United States. *American Sociological Review, 43,* 829-847.

Linville, P. W., Fischer, O. W., & Salovey, P. (1989). Perceived distributions of the characteristics of in-group and out-group members: Empirical evidence and a computer simulation. *Journal of Personality and Social Psychology, 57,* 165-188.

Linville, P. W., & Jones, E. E. (1980). Polarized appraisals of out-group members. *Journal of Personality and Social Psychology, 38*(5), 689-703.

Litka, M. (1988). *International dimensions of the legal environment of business.* Boston: PWS-Kent.

Little, K. B. (1968). Cultural variations in social schemata. *Journal of Personality and Social Psychology, 10,* 1-7.

Liu, I. (1986). Chinese cognition. In M. H. Bond (Ed.), *The psychology of the Chinese people* (pp. 73-105). New York: Oxford University Press.

Loh, T. W. C. (1993). *Responses to compliments across languages and cultures: A comparative study of British and Hong Kong Chinese.* (Research Rep. No. 30). Hong Kong: City University of Hong Kong.

Loher, B. T., Noe, R. A., Moeller, N. L., & Fitzgerald, M. P. (1980). A meta-analysis of the relation of job characteristics to job satisfaction. *Journal of Applied Psychology, 65,* 280-289.

Lorange, P., & Roos, J. (1992). *Strategic alliances.* Cambridge, MA: Blackwell.

Lord, R. G., & Maher, K. J. (1991). *Leadership and information processing: Linking perceptions and performance.* Boston: Unwin-Everyman.

Lord, R. G., Foti, R. J., & DeVader, C. L. (1984). A test of leadership categorization theory: Internal structure, information processing, and leadership perceptions. *Organizational Behavior and Human Performance, 34,* 343-378.

Lord, R. G., & Kernan, M. C. (1987). Scripts as determinants of purposeful behaviour in organizations. *Academy of Management Review, 12,* 265-277.

Lydon, J. E., Jamieson, E. W., & Zanna, M. P. (1988). Interpersonal similarity and the social and intellectual dimensions of first impressions. *Social Cognition, 6*(4), 269-286.

Lysgaard, S. (1955). Adjustment in a foreign society: Norwegian Fulbright grantees visiting the United States. *International Social Science Bulletin, 7,* 45-51.

Mann, L., Burnett, P., Radford, M., & Ford, S. (1997). The Melbourne decision making questionnaire: An instrument for measuring patterns for coping with decisional conflict. *Journal of Behavioral Decision Making, 10,* 1-19.

March, J., & Simon, H. (1958). *Organizations.* New York: John Wiley.

Markus, H. R., & Kitayama, S. (1991). Culture and the self: Implications for cognition, emotion, and motivation. *Psychological Review, 98*(2), 224-253.

Markus, H. R., & Zajonc, R. B. (1985). The cognitive perspective in social psychology. In G. Lindzey & E. Aronson (Eds.), *Handbook of social psychology* (Vol. 1, pp. 139-230). New York: Random House.

Marschan, R. (1996). *New structural forms and inter-unit communication in multinationals.* Helsinki, Finland: Helsinki School of Economics.

Matsumoto, D., & Kudoh, T. (1993). American-Japanese cultural differences in attributions of personality based on smiles. *Journal of Nonverbal Behavior, 17,* 231-244.

Mayer, D., & Cava, A. (1993). Ethics and the gender equality dilemma for U.S. multinationals. *Journal of Business Ethics, 12, 701-708.*

Maxwell, G., & Schmitt, D. R. (1975). *Cooperation: An experimental analysis.* New York: Academic Press.

Maznevski, M. L., DiStefano, J. J., & Nason, S. W. (1993, October). *The cultural perspectives questionnaire: Summary of results using CPQ3.* Paper presented at the annual meeting of the Academy of International Business, Kihei, Hawaii.

McCall, J. B., & Warrington, M. B. (1990). *Marketing by agreement: A cross-cultural approach to business negotiations* (2nd ed.). Chichester, UK: Wiley.

McCall, M. W., Jr., & Segrist, C. A. (1980). *In pursuit of the manager's job: Building on Mintzberg.* (Tech. Rep. No. 14). Greensboro, NC: Center for Creative Leadership.

McGuire, W. J., & Padawer-Singer, A. (1976). Trait salience in the spontaneous self-concept. *Journal of Personality and Social Psychology, 33,* 743-754.

McLeod, P. L., Lobel, S. A., & Cox, T. H. (1996). Ethnic diversity and creativity in small groups. *Small Group Research, 27*(2), 248-264.

Mead, M. (1937). *Cooperation and competition among primitive peoples.* New York: McGraw-Hill.

Meaning of Work International Research Team. (1987). *The meaning of working: An international view.* New York: Academic Press.

Meglino, B. M., & DeNisi, A. (1987). Realistic job previews: Some thoughts on their more effective use in managing the flow of human resources. *Human Resource Planning, 10,* 157-167.

Mendenhall, M. E., & Oddou, G. (1985). The dimensions of expatriate acculturation. *Academy of Management Review, 10,* 39-47.

Mendenhall, M. E., Punnett, B. J., & Ricks, D. (1995). *Global management.* Cambridge, MA: Blackwell.

Merritt, A. C., & Helmreich, R. L. (1996). Human factors on the flight deck. *Journal of Cross-Cultural Psychology, 27,* 5-24.

Miles, R. E., & Snow, C. C. (1978). *Organizational strategy, structure, and process.* New York: McGraw-Hill.

Mileti, D. S., Gillespie, D. F., & Haas, J. E. (1977, September). Size and structure in complex organizations. *Social Forces,* 208-217.

Mill, J. (1863). *Utilitarianism*. Indianapolis, IN: Bobbs-Merrill.

Miller, E. L. (1975). The job satisfaction of expatriate American managers: A function of regional location and previous work experience. *Journal of International Business Studies, 6*(2), 65-73.

Miller, E. L., & Cheng, J. L. (1978). A closer look at the decision to accept an overseas position. *Management International Review, 18,* 25-33.

Miller, G. A. (1956). The magical number seven plus or minus two. Some limits on our capacity for processing information. *Psychological Review, 63,* 81-97.

Miller, J. G. (1994). Cultural diversity in the morality of caring: Individually-oriented versus duty-oriented interpersonal codes. *Cross-Cultural Research, 28,* 3-39.

Miller, J. G., Bersoff, D. M., & Harwood, R. L. (1990). Perceptions of social responsibilities in India and the United States: Moral imperatives or personal decisions. *Journal of Personality and Social Psychology, 58,* 33-47.

Miller, L. (1995). Two aspects of Japanese and American co-worker interaction: Giving instructions and creating rapport. *Journal of Applied Behavioral Science, 2,* 212-221.

Milliken, F. J., & Martins, L. L. (1996). Searching for common threads: Understanding the multiple effects of diversity in organizational groups. *Academy of Management Review, 21*(2), 402-433.

Mintzberg, H. (1973). *The nature of managerial work*. New York: Harper & Row.

Mintzberg, H. (1993). *Structure in fives: Designing effective organizations*. Englewood Cliffs, NJ: Prentice Hall.

Misumi, J. (1984). Decision making in Japanese groups and organizations. In B. Wilpert & A. Sorge (Eds.), *International perspectives on organizational democracy,* (pp. 92-123). New York: John Wiley.

Misumi, J. (1985). *The behavioral science of leadership: An interdisciplinary Japanese research program*. Ann Arbor: University of Michigan Press.

Misumi, J., & Peterson, M. F. (1985). The performance-maintenance theory of leadership: Review of a Japanese research program. *Administrative Science Quarterly, 30,* 198-223.

Misumi, J., & Peterson, M. F. (1987). Supervision and leadership. In B. M. Bass, P. J. D. Drenth, & P. Weissenberg (Eds.), *Advances in organizational psychology: An international review* (pp. 220-231). Newbury Park, CA: Sage.

Montagu, A. (1972). *Touching: The human significance of the skin*. New York: Harper & Row.

Moreland, R. L., & Levine, J. M. (1982). Socialization in small groups: Temporal changes in individual-group relations. *Advances in Experimental Social Psychology, 15,* 137-192.

Morris, D. (1977). *Manwatching: A field guide to human behavior*. New York: Abrams.

Morris, D., Collett, P., Marsh, P., & O'Shaugnessy, M. (1979). *Gestures: Their origins and distribution*. Briarcliff Manor, NY: Stein & Day.

Morrison, E. W., & Robinson, S. L. (1997). When employees feel betrayed: A model of how psychological contract violation develops. *Academy of Management Review, 22,* 226-256.

Morrison, T., Conaway, W. A., & Borden, G. A. (1994). *Kiss, bow, or shake hands: How to do business in sixty countries.* Holbrook, MA: Bob Adams.

Morsbach, H. (1982). Aspects of nonverbal communication in Japan. In L. A. Samovar & R. E. Porter (Eds.), *Intercultural communication: A reader* (pp. 300-316). Belmont, CA: Wadsworth.

Mottram, R. (Ed.). (1963). *The selection of personnel for international service.* New York: World Federation for Mental Health.

Mullen, B. (1987). Self-attention theory: The effects of group composition on the individual. In B. Mullen & G. R. Goethals (Eds.), *Theories of group behaviour* (pp. 125-146). New York: Springer-Verlag.

Mullen, B., & Baumeister, R. F. (1987). Groups effects on self-attention and performance: Social loafing, social facilitation, and social impairment. In C. Hendrick (Ed.), *Review of personality and social psychology* (pp. 189-206). Newbury Park, CA: Sage.

Naisbitt, J. (1994). *Global paradox.* New York: William Morrow.

Naisbitt, J., & Aburdene, P. (1990). *Megatrends 2000: Ten new directions for the 1990's.* New York: Avon.

Nakane, C. (1970). *Japanese society.* Berkeley: University of California Press.

Napier, N. K., & Thomas, D. C. (2001). Some things you may not have learned in graduate school: A rough guide to collecting primary data overseas. In B. Toyne, Z. Martinez, & R. Menger (Eds.), *International business scholarship: Mastering intellectual, institutional, and research design challenges,* Westport, CT: Quorum Books.

Naumann, E. (1993). Organizational predictors of expatriate job satisfaction. *Journal of International Business Studies, 24*(1), 61-80.

Neale, M. A., & Northcraft, G. B. (1991). Behavioral negotiation theory: A framework for conceptualising dyadic bargaining. In L. L. Cummings & B. M. Staw (Eds.), *Research in organizational behavior* (Vol. 13, pp. 147-190). Greenwich, CT: JAI.

Nelson, G. L., El Bakary, W., & Al Batal, M. (1993). Egyptian and American compliments: A cross-cultural study. *International Journal of Intercultural Relations, 17,* 293-314.

Nemeth, C. J. (1992). Minority dissent as a stimulant to group performance. In S. Worchel, W. Wood, & J. A. Simpson (Eds.), *Group process and productivity* (pp. 95-111). Newbury Park, CA: Sage.

Nerht, L. C. (1987). The international studies curriculum. *Journal of International Business Studies, 18*(1), 83-90.

Nicholson, N., & Imaizumi, A. (1993). The adjustment of Japanese expatriates to living and working in Britain. *British Journal of Management, 4,* 119-134.

Noller, P. (1984). *Nonverbal communication and marital interaction.* Oxford, UK: Pergamon.

Nonaka, I. (1994). A dynamic theory of knowledge creation. *Organization Science, 5*(1), 14-38.

Oberg, K. (1960). Cultural shock: Adjustment to new cultural environments. *Practical Anthropology, 7,* 177-182.

O'Connell, M. S., Lord, R. G., & O'Connell, M. K. (1990, August). *An empirical comparison of Japanese and American leadership prototypes: Implications for overseas assignment of managers.* Paper presented at the 1990 meeting of the Academy of Management, San Francisco, California.

Oddou, G. R., & Mendenhall, M. (1991). Succession planning for the 21st century: How well are we grooming our future business leaders? *Business Horizons, 34,* 26-34.

Offerman, L. R., & Gowing, M. K. (1990). Organizations of the future: Changes and challenges. *American Psychologist, 45,* 95-108.

Ohmae, K. (1995). *The end of the nation state.* Cambridge, MA: Free Press.

Onglatco, M. L. U. (1988). *Japanese quality control circles: Features, effects and problems.* Tokyo: Asian Productivity Center.

Osland, J. S., & Bird, A. (2000). Beyond sophisticated stereotypes: Cultural sense-making in context. *Academy of Management Executive, 14,* 65-79.

Osland, J. S., & Osland, A. (2001). Mastering international qualitative research. In B. Toyne, Z. Martinez, & R. Menger (Eds.), *International business scholarship: Mastering intellectual, institutional, and research design challenges.* Westport, CT: Quorum Books.

Ott, J. S. (1989). *The organizational culture perspective.* Belmont, CA: Dorsey Press.

Ouchi, W. (1981). *Theory Z: How American business can meet the Japanese challenge.* Reading, MA: Addison-Wesley.

Ouchi, W. (1984). *The M-form society.* Reading, MA: Addison-Wesley.

Pareek, U., & Rao, T. V. (1980). Cross-cultural survey and interviewing. In H. C. Triandis & W. W. Lambert (Eds.), *Handbook of cross-cultural psychology, methodology* (Vol. 2, pp. 127-180). Boston: Allyn & Bacon.

Park, H., Sun, D. H., & David, J. M. (1993). Local manager selection for U.S. firms in Korea. *Multinational Business Review, 1*(2), 57-65.

Parker, B. (1998). *Globalization: Managing across boundaries.* London: Sage Ltd.

Parker, B., & McEvoy, G. M. (1993). Initial examination of a model of intercultural adjustment. *International Journal of Intercultural Relations, 17,* 355-379.

Parsons, T., & Shils, E. A. (1951). *Toward a general theory of action.* Cambridge, MA: Harvard University Press.

Patterson, M. L. (1991). A functional approach to nonverbal exchange. In R. S. Feldman & B. Rime (Eds.), *Fundamentals of nonverbal behavior* (pp. 458-495). New York: Cambridge University Press.

Pearce, J. A., & Ravlin, E. C. (1987). The design and activation of self regulating work groups. *Human Relations, 11,* 751-782.

Pekerti, A. A. (2001). *Influence of culture on communication: An empirical test and theoretical refinement of the high- and low-context dimension.* Unpublished doctoral dissertation, The University of Auckland, New Zealand.

Pelto, P. J. (1968, April). The difference between tight and loose societies. *Transaction, 37-40.*

Pelz, D. C. (1956). Some social factors related to performance in a research organization. *Administrative Science Quarterly, 1,* 310-325.

Peng, T. K., Peterson. M. F., & Shyi, Y. P. (1991). Quantitative methods in cross national management research: Trends and equivalence issues. *Journal of Organizational Behavior, 12,* 87-107.

Penn, W., & Collier, B. (1985). Current research in moral development as a decision support system. *Journal of Business Ethics, 4,* 131-136.

Perlmutter, H. (1969). The tortuous evolution of the multinational corporation. *Columbia Journal of World Business, 4,* 39-41.

Perrewe, P. L., Ralston, D. A., & Fernandez, D. R. (1995). A model depicting the relations among perceived stressors, role conflict and organizational commitment: A comparative anaysis of Hong Kong and the United States. *Asia Pacific Journal of Management, 12*(2), 1-21.

Perrow, C. (1967). A framework for the comparative analysis of organizations. *American Sociological Review, 32*(2), 194-208.

Peters, T. J., & Waterman, R. H. (1982). *In search of excellence.* New York: Harper & Row.

Peterson, M. B., Smith, P. B., Akande, A., Ayestaran, S., Bochner, S., Callan, V., Cho, N., Jesuino, J., D'Amorim, M., Francois, P., Hofmann, K., Koopman, P., Leung, K., Lim, T., Mortazavi, S., Muene, J., Radford, M., Ropo, A., Savage, G., Setiadi, B., Sinha, T., Sorenson, R., & Viedge, C. (1995). Role conflict, ambiguity, and overload: A 21-nation study. *Academy of Management Journal, 38*(2), 429-452.

Peterson, M. F. (1988). PM theory in Japan and China: What's in it for the United States? *Organizational Dynamics, 16,* 22-38.

Peterson, M. F., Brannen, M. Y., & Smith, P. B. (1994). Japanese and U.S. leadership: Issues in current research. In S. B. Prasad (Ed.), *Advances in international comparative management* (Vol. 9, pp. 57-82). Greenwich, CT: JAI.

Peterson, M. F., Smith, P. B., & Tayeb, M. H. (1993). Development and use of English version of Japanese PM leadership measures in electronics plants. *Journal of Organizational Behavior, 14,* 251-267.

Peterson, R. A., & Jolibert, A. J. P. (1995). A meta-analysis of country of origin effects. *Journal of international Business Studies, 26,* 883-900.

Peterson, R. B. (1993). Future directions in international comparative management research. In D. Wong-Reiger & F. Reiger (Eds.), *International management research: Looking to the future* (pp. 13-25). New York: de Gruyter.

Peterson, R. B., Napier, N., & Won, S. S. (1995, November). *Expatriate management: The differential role on multinational corporation ownership.* Paper presented to the annual meeting of the Academy of International Business, Seoul, Korea.

Pettigrew, T. F. (1979). The ultimate attribution error: Extending Allport's cognitive analysis of prejudice. *Personality and Social Psychology Bulletin, 5,* 461-476.

Phatak, A., & Habib, M. (1998). How should managers treat ethics in international business? *Thunderbird International Business Review, 40*(2), 101-117.

Pinker, S. (1994). *The language instinct*. London: Penguin.

Pittman, J. (1994). *Voice in social interaction: An interdisciplinary approach*. Thousand Oaks, CA: Sage.

Porat, A. (1970). Cross-cultural differences in resolving union management conflict through negotiation. *Journal of Applied Psychology, 54*, 441-451.

Porter, M. E. (1980). *Competitive strategy*. New York: Free Press.

Porter, M. E. (1986). Changing patterns of international competition. *California Management Review, 28*(2), 9-40.

Privatisation. (1997, March). *Economist, 143.*

Prokofiev, Sergei. (1982). *Peter and The Wolf* (1st ed.). (Maria Carlson, trans., Charles Mikolaycak, illus.). New York: Viking Press.

Prothro, E. T. (1955). Arab-American differences in the judgement of written messages. *Journal of Social Psychology, 42*, 3-11.

Pugh, D. S., & Hickson, D. J. (1976) *Organizational structure in its context: The Aston programme I*. Farnborough, UK: Gower Publishing.

Pugh, D. S., Hickson, D. J., Hinings, C. R., MacDonald, K. M., & Turner, C. (1963). Dimensions of organization structure. *Administrative Science Quarterly, 13*, 65-105.

Putnam, R. (1993). *Making democracy work: Civic traditions in modern Italy*. Princeton, NJ: Princeton University Press.

Pye, L. (1982). *Chinese commercial negotiating style*. Cambridge, MA: Oelgeschlager, Gunn, and Hain.

Radford, M. H. B., Mann, L., Ohta, Y., & Nakane, Y. (1989). Individual decision making behavior and personality: A preliminary study using a Japanese university sample. *Japanese Journal of Experimental Social Psychology, 28*, 115-122.

Radford, M. H. B., Mann, L., Ohta, Y., & Nakane, Y. (1991). Differences between Australian and Japanese students in reported use of decision processes. *International Journal of Psychology, 26*, 284-297.

Ralston, D. A. (1993). Differences in managerial values: A study of the U.S., Hong Kong, and PRC managers. *Journal of International Business Studies, 24*(2), 249-275.

Ralston, D. A., Holt, D. H., Terpstra, R. H., & Yu, K. (1997). The impact of national culture and economic ideology on managerial work values: A study of the United States, Russia, Japan, and China. *Journal of International Business Studies, 28*(1), 177-207.

Rao, A., & Hashimoto, K. (1996). Intercultural influence: A study of Japanese expatriate managers in Canada. *Journal of International Business Studies, 27*, 443-466.

Ravlin, E. C., Thomas, D. C., & Ilsev, A. (2000). Beliefs about values, status, and legitimacy in multicultural groups. In P. C. Earley & H. Singh (Eds.), *Innovations in international and cross-cultural management* (pp. 17-51). Thousand Oaks, CA: Sage.

Redding, S. G., Norman, A., & Schlander, A. (1994). The nature of individual attachment to the organization: A review of East Asian variations. In H. C. Triandis (Ed.), *Handbook of industrial/organizational psychology* (2nd ed., Vol. 4, pp. 647-688). Palo Alto, CA: Consulting Psychologists Press.

Reichers, A. (1986). Conflict and organizational commitments. *Journal of Applied Psychology, 71*, 508-514.

Renesch, J. (Ed.). (1992). *New traditions in business.* San Francisco: Berrett-Koehler.

Ricks, D. A. (1993). *Blunders in international business.* Cambridge, MA: Blackwell.

Robbins, S. P. (1992). *Essentials of organizational behavior* (3rd ed.). Englewood Cliffs, NJ: Prentice Hall.

Roberts, K. H., & Boyacigiller, N. A. (1984). Cross national organizational research: The grasp of the blind men. In B. M. Staw & L. L. Cummings (Eds.), *Research in organizational behavior* (Vol. 6, pp. 423-475). Greenwich, CT: JAI.

Robertson, R. (1995). Glocalization: Time-space and homogeneity-heterogeneity. In M. Featherstone, S. Lash, & R. Robertson (Eds.), *Global modernities* (pp. 25-44). London: Sage Ltd.

Robertson, C., & Fadil, P. A. (1999). Ethical decision making in multinational organizations: A culture-based model. *Journal of Business Ethics, 19*, 385-392.

Robinson, R. D. (1984). *The internationalization of business: An introduction.* Chicago: Dryden Press.

Rohner, R. (1984). Toward a conception of culture for cross-cultural psychology. *Journal of Cross-Cultural Psychology, 15*, 111-138.

Rokeach, M. (1973). *The nature of human values.* New York: Free Press.

Rosenzweig, P. M., & Nohria, N. (1994). Influences on human resource management practices in multinational corporations. *Journal of International Business Studies, 25*(2), 229-251.

Rosenzweig, P. M., & Singh, J. V. (1991). Organizational environments and the multinational enterprise. *Academy of Management Review, 16*(2), 340-361.

Ross, S., & Shortreed, I. M. (1990). Japanese foreigner talk: Convergence or divergence. *Journal of Asian Pacific Communication, 1*, 134-145.

Roth, K., Schweiger, D., & Morrison, A. J. (1991). Global strategy implementation at the business unit level: Operational capabilities and administrative mechanisms. *Journal of International Business Studies, 22*, 369-402.

Rotter, J. B. (1966). Generalized expectancies for internal versus external control of reinforcement. *Psychological Monographs: General and Applied, 80*(1), 609.

Rousseau, D. M. (1989). Psychological and implied contracts in organizations. *Employee Responsibilities and Rights Journal, 2*, 121-139.

Ruben, B. D., & Kealey, D. J. (1979). Behavioral assessment of communication competency and the prediction of cross-cultural adaptation. *International Journal of Intercultural Relations, 3*, 15-47.

Rubin, E. (1915). *Synsoplevede figurer.* Kobenhaven: Gyldendalske Boghandel.

Ruedi, A., & Lawrence, P. R. (1970). Organization in two cultures. In J. W. Lorsch & P. R. Lawrence (Eds.), *Studies in organizational design* (pp. 54-83). Homewood, IL: R. D. Irwin.

Rusbult, C. E., Insko, C. A., & Lin, Y.-H. W. (1993). Seniority-based reward allocation in the US and Taiwan. *Social Psychology Quarterly, 58*, 13-30.

Rushton, J. P. (1989). Genetic similarity, human altruism, and group selection. *Behavioral and Brain Sciences, 12*, 503-559.

Russia's State Sell Off: "It's sink or swim time." (1994, July 7). *Business Week,* 46.

Russo, J. E., & Shoemaker, P. J. H. (1989). *Decision traps.* New York: Doubleday.

Sack, R. (1973). The impact of education on individual modernity in Tunisia. *International Journal of Comparative Sociology, 14,* 245-272.

Sagiv, L., & Schwartz, S. H. (1995). Value priorities and readiness for outgroup social contact. *Journal of Personality and Social Psychology, 69,* 437-448.

Sagiv, L., & Schwartz, S. H. (2000). A new look at national culture: Illustrative applications to role stress and managerial behavior. In N. N. Ashkanasy, C. Wilderom, & M. F. Peterson (Eds.), *The handbook of organizational culture and climate* (pp. 417-435). Thousand Oaks, CA: Sage.

Salacuse, J. (1991). *Making global deals.* Boston: Houghton Mifflin.

Salancik, G. R., & Pfeffer, J. (1978). A social information processing approach to job attitudes and task design. *Administrative Science Quarterly, 23,* 224-253.

Sanderson, S. W., & Hayes, R. H. (1990). Mexico—Opening ahead of Eastern Europe. *Harvard Business Review, 68,* 32-43.

Sayles, L. R. (1964). *Managerial behavior.* New York: McGraw-Hill.

Schein, E. H. (1985). *Organizational culture and leadership.* San Francisco: Jossey-Bass.

Scherer, K. R. (1979). Personality markers in speech. In K. R. Scherer & H. Giles (Eds.), *Social markers in speech* (pp. 147-209). Cambridge, UK: Cambridge University Press.

Schmidt, D. A. (1986). Analyzing political risk. *Business Horizons, 29*(2), 43-50.

Schneider, S. C., & Barsoux, J. L. (1997). *Managing across cultures.* London: Prentice Hall–Europe.

Schramm, W. (1980). How communication works. In S. B. Weinberg (Ed.), *Message: A reader in human communication.* New York: Random House.

Schriesheim, C. A., & Kerr, S. (1977). Theories and measures of leadership: A critical appraisal. In J. C. Hunt & L. L. Larson (Eds.), *Leadership: The cutting edge* (pp. 9-44). Carbondale: Southern Illinois University Press.

Schuster, B., Fosterlung, F., & Weiner, B. (1989). Perceiving the causes of success and failure. *Journal of Cross-Cultural Psychology, 20*(2), 191-213.

Schwartz, S. H. (1992). Universals in the content and structure of values: Theoretical advances and empirical tests in 20 countries. In M. P. Zanna (Ed.), *Advances in experimental social psychology* (pp. 1-65). San Diego, CA: Academic Press.

Schwartz, S. H. (1994). Beyond individulism/collectivism: New dimensions of values. In U. Kim, H. C. Triandis, C. Kagitçibasi, S. C. Choi, & G. Yoon (Eds.), *Individualism and collectivism: Theory, applications, and methods* (pp. 85-119). Thousand Oaks, CA: Sage.

Schwartz, S. H., & Bilsky, W. (1990). Toward a universal psychological structure of human values. *Journal of Personality and Social Psychology, 53,* 550-562.

Schwartz, S. H., & Sagie, G. (2000). Value consensus and importance: A cross-national study. *Journal of Cross-Cultural Psychology, 31*(4), 465-497.

Scullion, H. (1991, November). Why companies prefer to use expatriates. *Personnel Management,* 32-35.

Sewell, W. H., & Davidson, O. M. (1956). The adjustment of Scandinavian students. *Journal of Social Issues, 12,* 9-19.

Shackleton, V., & Newell, S. (1994). European management selection methods: A comparison of five countries. *International Journal of Selection and Assessment, 2*, 91-102.

Shapira, Z., & Dunbar, R. L. M. (1980). Testing Mintzberg's managerial roles classification using an in-basket simulation. *Journal of Applied Psychology, 65*(1), 87-95.

Shaw, J. B. (1990). A cognitive categorization model for the study of intercultural management. *Academy of Management Review, 15*(4), 626-645.

Shaw, W. (1996). *Business ethics* (2nd ed.). Belmont, CA: Wadsworth.

Shenkar, O., & Von Glinow, M. (1994). Paradoxes of organizational theory and research: Using the case of China to illustrate national contingency. *Management Science, 40*(1), 56-71.

Sherif, M., Harvey, O. J., White, B. J., Hood, W. R., & Sherif, C. W. (1961). *Intergroup conflict and cooperation.* Norman: University of Oklahoma, Institute of Group Relations.

Shimoda, K., Argyle, M., & Ricci-Bitti, P. (1984). The intercultural recognition of emotional expressions by three national racial groups: English, Italian, and Japanese. *European Journal of Social Psychology, 8*(2), 169-179.

Shuter, R. (1977). A field study of non-verbal communication in Germany, Italy and the United States. *Communication Monographs, 44*(3), 298-305.

Sidanius, J. (1993). The psychology of group conflict and the dynamics of oppression: A social dominance perspective. In S. Iyenger & W. McGuire (Eds.), *Explorations in political psychology* (pp. 183-219). Durham, NC: Duke University Press.

Simon, H. A. (1955). A behavioral model of rational choice. *Quarterly Journal of Economics, 69*, 129-138.

Singelis, T. M., & Brown, W. J. (1995). Culture, self, and collectivist communication: Linking culture to individual behavior. *Human Communication Research, 21*, 354-389.

Smircich, L. (1983). Concepts of culture in organizational analysis. *Administrative Science Quarterly, 28*, 339-358.

Smircich, L., & Calas, M. B. (1986). Organizational culture: A critical assessment. *Annual Review of Sociology, 2*, 228-263.

Smith, P. B., & Bond, M. H. (1999). *Social psychology across cultures.* Boston: Allyn & Bacon.

Smith P. B., Dugan, S., & Trompenaars, F. (1996). National culture and the values of organizational employees: A dimensional analysis across 43 nations. *Journal of Cross-Cultural Psychology, 27*(2), 231-264.

Smith, P. B., Misumi, J., Tayeb, M. H., Peterson, M., & Bond, M. (1989). On the generality of leadership styles across cultures. *Journal of Occupational Psychology, 62*, 97-109.

Smith, P. B., & Peterson, M. F. (1994, July). *Leadership in event management: A cross-cultural survey based upon middle managers from 25 nations.* Paper presented at the 23rd International Congress of Applied Psychology, Madrid, Spain.

Smith, P. B., Peterson, M. F., Bond, M., & Misumi, J. (1992). Leader style and leader behavior in individualist and collectivist cultures. In S. Iwawaki, Y. Kashima

& K. Leung (Eds.), *Innovations in cross-cultural psychology* (pp. 76-85). Amsterdam: Swets & Zeitlinger.

Smith, P. B., Peterson, M. F., & Wang, Z. M. (1996). The manager as mediator of alternative meanings: A pilot study from China, the USA and U.K. *Journal of International Business Studies, 27*(1), 115-137.

Smith, P. B., Trompenaars, F., & Dugan, S. (1995). The Rotter locus of control scale in 43 countries: A test of cultural relativity. *International Journal of Psychology, 30*, 377-400.

Snarey, J. R. (1985). Cross-cultural universality of social-moral development: A critical review of Kohlbergian research. *Psychological Bulletin, 97*, 202-232.

Snyder, M. (1981). On the self-perpetuating nature of social stereotypes. In D. L. Hamilton (Ed.), *Cognitive processes in stereotyping and intergroup behavior* (pp. 183-212). Hillsdale, NJ: Lawrence Erlbaum.

Solomon, C. M. (1998, May). Women expats: Shattering myths. *Workforce*, 5-10.

Steers, R. M., Shin, Y. K., & Ungson, G. R. (1989). *The chaebol*. New York: Harper-Business.

Stein, M. I. (1966). *Volunteers for peace*. New York: John Wiley.

Steiner, I. D. (1972). *Group process and productivity*. New York: Academic Press.

Stening, B. W. (1979). Problems in cross-cultural contact: A literature review. *International Journal of Intercultural Relations, 3*, 269-313.

Stening, B. W., & Hammer, M. R. (1992). Cultural baggage and the adaptation of expatriate Japanese managers. *Management International Review, 32*(1), 77-89.

Stewart, R. (1976). *Contrasts in management*. Maidenhead, UK: McGraw-Hill.

Stewart, R. (1982). *Choices for the manager*. Englewood Cliffs, NJ: Prentice Hall.

Stewart, R. (1991). *Managing today and tomorrow*. Basingstoke, UK: Macmillan.

Stewart, R., Barsoux, J. L., Kieser, A., Ganter, H. D., & Walgenbach, P. (1994). *Managing in Britain and Germany*. Basingstoke, UK: Macmillan.

Stogdill, R. M. (1974). *Handbook of leadership: A survey of theory and research*. New York: Free Press.

Stone, R. J. (1991). Expatriate selection and failure. *Human Resource Planning, 29*(1), 9-17.

Stopford, J. M., & Wells, L. T. (1972). *Strategy and structure in multinational enterprise*. New York: Basic Books.

Stroh, L. K., Dennis, L. E., & Cramer, T. C. (1994). Predictors of expatriate adjustment. *International Journal of Organizational Analysis, 2*, 176-192.

Sullivan, J. (1997). Theory development in international business research: The decline of culture. In B. Toyne & D. Nigh (Eds.), *International business: An emerging vision* (pp. 380-395). Columbia: University of South Carolina Press.

Sumner, W. G. (1940). *Folkways*. Boston: Ginn.

Sundaram, A. K., & Black, J. S. (1995). *The international business environment*. Englewood Cliffs, NJ: Prentice Hall.

Szilagyi, A. D., & Wallace, M. J., Jr. (1987). *Organizational behavior and performance* (4th ed.). Glenview, IL: Scott, Foresman.

Tajfel, H. (1981). *Human groups and social categories*. Cambridge, UK: Cambridge University Press.

Tajfel, H., & Turner, J. C. (1986). The social identity theory of intergroup behavior. In S. Worchel & W. G. Wood (Eds.), *Psychology of intergroup relations* (pp. 7-24). Chicago: Nelson-Hall.

Takeuchi, R., & Hannon, J. M. (1996). *The antecedents of adjustment for Japanese expatriates in the United States*. Paper presented to the annual meeting of the Academy of International Business, Banff, Canada.

Tannenbaum, A. S. (1980). Organizational psychology. In H. C. Triandis & W. W. Lambert (Eds.), *Handbook of cross-cultural psychology* (pp. 281-334). Boston: Allyn & Bacon.

Tayeb, M. H. (1987). Contingency theory and culture: A study of matched English and the Indian manufacturing firms. *Organization Studies, 8*(3), 241-261.

Taylor, D. M., & Jaggi, V. (1974). Ethnocentrism and causal attribution in a South Indian context. *Journal of Cross-Cultural Psychology, 5,* 162-171.

Taylor, F. W. (1911). *The principles of scientific management*. New York: Harper & Row.

Taylor, S. (1981). A categorization approach to stereotyping. In D. Hamilton (Ed.), *Cognitive processes in stereotyping and intergroup behavior* (pp. 83-114). Hillsdale, NJ: Lawrence Erlbaum.

Taylor, S., & Napier, N. (1996). Working in Japan: Lessons from women expatriates. *Sloan Management Review, 37,* 76-84.

Taylor, S. E. (1989). *Positive illusions*. New York: Basic Books.

Taylor, W. (1991, March-April). The logic of global business: An interview with Abb's Percy Barnevik. *Harvard Business Review*, pp. 91-105.

Terpstra, V., & David, K. (1985). *The cultural environment of international business*. Dallas, TX: South-Western Publishing.

Thal, N. L., & Cateora, P. R. (1979). Opportunities for women in international business. *Business Horizons, 22*(6), 21-27.

The world's richest people. (1998, July 6) *Forbes, 162,* 190-250.

Thibaut, J. W., & Kelley, H. H. (1959). *The social psychology of groups*. New York: John Wiley.

Thomas, A. (1996). A call for research in forgotten locations. In B. J.Punnett & O. Shenkar (Eds.), *Handbook for international management research* (pp. 485-506). Cambridge, MA: Blackwell.

Thomas, D. C. (1992). *Subordinates' responses to cultural adaptation by managers: The effect of stereotypic expectation*. Unpublished doctoral dissertation, The University of South Carolina, Columbia, South Carolina.

Thomas, D. C. (1994). The boundary-spanning role of expatriates in the multinational corporation. *Advances in International Comparative Management, 9,* 145-170.

Thomas, D. C. (1998). The expatriate experience: A critical review and synthesis. *Advances in International Comparative Management, 12,* 237-273.

Thomas, D. C. (1999). Cultural diversity and work group effectiveness: An experimental study. *Journal of Cross-Cultural Psychology, 30*(3), 242-263.

Thomas, D. C., & Au, K. (1999, August). *Effect of cultural variation on the behavioral response to declining job satisfaction.* Paper presented at the annual meeting of The Academy of Management, Chicago, Illinois.

Thomas, D. C., & Au, K. (2000). Cultural variation in the psychological contract. *Academy of Management Best Paper Proceedings* (pp. IM F1-F6). Toronto, Canada.

Thomas, D. C., & Ravlin, E. C. (1995). Responses of employees to cultural adaptation by a foreign manager. *Journal of Applied Psychology, 80,* 133-146.

Thomas, D. C., Ravlin, E, C., & Barry, D. (2000). Creating effective multicultural teams. *University of Auckland Business Review, 2*(1), 10-25.

Thomas, D. C., Ravlin, E. C., & Wallace, A. W. (1996). Cultural diversity in work teams. *Research in the Sociology of Organizations, 14,* 1-13.

Thomas, E. J., & Fink, C. F. (1963). Effects of group size. *Psychological Bulletin, 60,* 371-384.

Thurow, L. (1984). Revitalizing American industry: Managing in a competitive world economy. *California Management Review, 27*(1), 9-41.

Tinsley, C. (1998). Models of conflict resolution in Japanese, German, and American cultures. *Journal of Applied Psychology, 83*(6), 316-323.

Torbiorn, I. (1982). *Living abroad: Personal adjustment and personnel policy in the overseas setting.* New York: John Wiley.

Torrence, E. P. (1980). Lessons about giftedness and creativity from a nation of 115 million achievers. *Gifted Child Quarterly, 24,* 10-14.

Townsend, A. M., DeMarie, S. M., & Hendrickson, A. R. (1998). Virtual teams: Technology and the workplace of the future. *Academy of Management Executive, 12,* 17-29.

Trafimow, D., & Finlay, K. A. (1996). The importance of subjective norms for a minority of people: Between-subjects and within-subjects analyses. *Personality and Social Psychology Bulletin, 60,* 820-828.

Trevino, L. K. (1986). Ethical decision making in organizations. *Academy of Management Review, 11,* 601-617.

Trevino, L. K., Lengel, R. H., & Daft, R. L. (1987). Media symbolism, media richness, and media choice in organizations. A symbolic interactionist perspective. *Communication Research, 14,* 553-574.

Triandis, H. C. (1972). *The analysis of subjective culture.* New York: John Wiley.

Triandis, H. C. (1978). Some universals of social behavior. *Personality and Social Psychology Bulletin, 4,* 1-16.

Triandis, H. C. (1989). Cross-cultural studies of individualism and collectivism. In J. Berman (Ed.), *Nebraska symposium on motivation* (pp. 41-133). Lincoln: University of Nebraska Press.

Triandis, H. C. (1993). The contingency model in cross-cultural perspective. In M. M. Chemers & R. Ayman (Eds.), *Leadership theory and research: Perspectives and directions* (pp. 167-188). San Diego, CA: Academic Press.

Triandis, H. C. (1994). *Culture and social behavior.* New York: McGraw-Hill.

Triandis, H. C. (1995). *Individualism and collectivism.* Boulder, CO: Westview.

Triandis, H. C., Marin, G., Lisansky, J., & Betancourt, H. (1984). Simpatia as a cultural script for Hispanics. *Journal of Personality and Social Psychology, 47*, 1363-1375.

Trist, E. L. (1981). *The evolution of a socio-technical system.* Toronto, Canada: Quality of Working Life Center.

Trompenaars, F. (1993). *Riding the waves of culture.* Burr Ridge, IL: Irwin.

Trope, Y. (1986). Identification and inferential processes in dispositional attribution. *Psychological Review, 93*, 239-257.

Tscheulin, D. (1973). Leader behaviors in German industry. *Journal of Applied Psychology, 57*, 28-31.

Tse, D. K., Francis, J., & Walls, J. (1994). Cultural differences in conducting intra- and inter-cultural negotiations: A Sino-Canadian comparison. *Journal of International Business Studies, 25*(3), 537-555.

Tuckman, B. W. (1965) Developmental sequence in small groups. *Psychological Bulletin, 63*(6), 384-399.

Tung, R. L. (1981). Selection and training of personnel for overseas assignments. *Columbia Journal of World Business, 16*, 68-78.

Tung, R. L. (1984). *Business negotiations with the Japanese.* Lexington, MA: Lexington Books.

Tung, R. L. (1988). Toward a conceptual paradigm of international business negotiations. *Advances in International Comparative Management, 3*, 203-219.

Turner, J. C. (1987). *Rediscovering the social group.* Oxford, UK: Basil Blackwell.

Turnley, W. H., & Feldman, D. C. (1999). The impact of psychological contract violations on exit, voice, loyalty and neglect. *Human Relations, 52*, 895-922.

Tversky, A., & Kahneman, D. (1973). Availability: A heuristic for judging frequency and probability. *Cognitive Psychology, 5*, 207-232.

Tversky, A., & Kahneman, D. (1974). Judgment under uncertainty: Heuristics and biases. *Science, 185*, 1124-1131.

UN Conference on Trade and Investment (1994). *World Investment Report.* New York and Geneva: United Nations.

UN Conference on Trade and Investment (1999). *World Investment Report 1999.* New York and Geneva: United Nations.

UN Conference on Trade and Investment (2000). *World Investment Report 2000.* New York and Geneva: United Nations.

United Nations Development Program (2000). *Human development report 1999.* New York: Oxford University Press.

Usunier, J. C. (1996). Cultural aspects of international business negotiations. In P. Ghauri & J. C. Usunier (Eds.), *International business negotiations* (pp. 91-118). Oxford, UK: Pergamon.

Usunier, J. C. (1998). *International and cross-cultural management research.* London: Sage Ltd.

van de Vijver, F., & Leung, K. (1997). *Methods and data analysis for cross-cultural research.* Thousand Oaks, CA: Sage.

Vroom, V. H. (1964). *Work and motivation.* New York: John Wiley.

Wageman, R. (1995). Interdependence and group effectiveness. *Administrative Science Quarterly, 40,* 145-180.

Wagner, H., Hibbits, N., Rosenblatt, R. D., & Schulz, R. (1977). *Team training and evaluation strategies: State of the art.* (Tech. Rep. No. 771-1). Alexandria, VA: Human Resources Research Organization.

Warren, W., Black, S., & Rangsit, S. (Eds.). (1985). *Thailand.* Englewood Cliffs, NJ: Prentice Hall.

Watson, O. M. (1970). *Proxemic behavior : A cross cultural study.* The Hague, Netherlands: Mouton.

Watson, O. M., & Graves, T. D. (1966). Quantitative research in proxemic behavior. *American Anthropologist, 68,* 971-985.

Watson, W. E., Johnson, L., & Merritt, D. (1998). Team orientation, self orientation, and diversity in task groups. *Group and Organization Management, 23*(2), 161-188.

Watson, W. E., Kumar, K., & Michaelson, L. K. (1993). Cultural diversity's impact on interaction process and performance: Comparing homogeneous and diverse task groups. *Academy of Management Journal, 36*(3), 590-602.

Watterson, B. (1995, December 31). Calvin and Hobbes. *South China Morning Post,* p. 6.

Webber, R. H. (1969). Convergence or divergence? *Columbia Journal of World Business, 4*(3), 75-83.

Weick, K. E. (1974). Henry Mintzberg, *The nature of managerial work* [Review of the book *The nature of managerial work*]. *Administrative Science Quarterly, 19,* 111-118.

Weiss, S. E. (1993). Analysis of complex negotiations in international business: The RBC Perspective. *Organization Science, 2,* 269-300.

Weiss, S. E. (1994). Negotiating with Romans, No 2. *Sloan Management Review, 35*(3), 85-89.

Westney, D. E. (1993). Institutionalization theory and the multinational corporation. In S. Ghoshal & E. Westney (Eds.), *Organization theory and the multinational corporation* (pp. 53-76). New York: St. Martin's.

Westney, D. E. (1997). Organization theory perspectives and international business. In B. Toyne & D. Nigh (Eds.), *International business: An emerging vision* (pp. 296-312). Columbia: University of South Carolina Press.

Westwood, R. I., & Leung, S. M. (1994). The female expatriate manager experience: Coping with gender and culture. *International Studies of Management and Organization, 24,* 64-85.

Whitehill, A. M., & Takezawa, S. (1978). Workplace harmony: Another Japanese "miracle"? *Columbia Journal of World Business, 13*(3), 25-39.

Whorf, B. L. (1956). A linguistic consideration of thinking in primitive communities. In J. B. Carroll (Ed.), *Language, thought and reality: Selected readings of Benjamin Lee Whorf* (pp. 65-86). Cambridge, MA: MIT Press.

Wiemann, J., Chen, V., & Giles, H. (1986, n.m.). *Beliefs about talk and silence in a cultural context.* Paper presented to the Speech Communication Association, Chicago, Illinois.

Wilder, D. A. (1978). Perceiving persons as a group: Effects on attribution of causality and beliefs. *Social Psychology, 41*(1), 13-23.

Wilder, D. A. (1986). Social categorization: Implications for creation and reduction of intergroup bias. In L. Berkowitz (Ed.), *Advances in experimental social psychology* (Vol. 19, pp. 291-355). New York: Academic Press.

Witkin, H. A., & Goodenough, D. R. (1977). Field dependence and interpersonal behavior. *Psychological Bulletin, 84,* 661-689.

Wood, D. J. (1991). Corporate social performance revisited. *Academy of Management Review, 16,* 693-718.

Woodward, J. (1965). *Industrial organization: Theory and practice.* London: Oxford University Press.

World Almanac and Book of Facts. (2000). New York: Author.

World Bank. (2000). *World development indicators.* Washington, DC: Author.

World Trade Organization. (1999). *WTO annual report.* Geneva: Author.

Wright, G. N., & Phillips, L. D. (1980). Cultural variation in probabilistic thinking: An alternative way of dealing with uncertainty. *International Journal of Psychology, 15,* 239-257.

Wu, L. (1999). *Guanxi: A cross-cultural comparative study.* Unpublished master's thesis, University of Auckland, New Zealand.

Yang, K. S. (1988). Will societal modernization eventually eliminate cross-cultural pychological difference? In M. H. Bond (Ed.), *The cross-cultural challenge to social psychology* (pp. 67-85). Newbury Park, CA: Sage.

Yates, J. F., Lee, J. W., & Shinotsuka, H. (1996). Beliefs about overconfidence, including its cross-national variation. *Organizational Behavior and Human Decision Processes, 65,* 138-147.

Yates, J. F., Zhu, Y., Ronis, D. L., Wang, D., Shinostsuka, H., & Toda, M.(1989). Probability judgment accuracy: China, Japan and the United States. *Organizational Behavior and Human Decision Processes, 43,* 147-171.

Yukl, G. (1989). *Leadership in organizations* (2nd ed.). Englewood Cliffs, NJ: Prentice Hall.

Yukl, G. (1994a). *Leadership in organizations* (3rd ed.). Upper Saddle River, NJ: Prentice Hall.

Yukl, G. (1994b). A retrospective on Robert House's 1976 theory of charismatic leadership and recent revisions. *Leadership Quarterly, 4*(3-4), 367-373.

Yukl, G. A., & Van Fleet, D. (1992). Theory and research on leadership in organizations. *Handbook of industrial and organizational psychology* (pp. 147-197). Palo Alto, CA: Consulting Psychologists Press.

Zeira, Y., & Banai, M. (1985). Selection of expatriate managers in MNCs: The host environment point of view. *International Studies of Management and Organization, 15*(1), 33-51.

Zenger, T. R., & Lawrence, B. S. (1989). Organizational demography: The differential effects of age and tenure on technical communication. *Academy of Management Journal, 32,* 353-376.

Zimbardo, P. G. (1977). *Shyness: What it is and what we can do about it.* Reading, MA: Addison-Wesley.

Author Index

Subject Index

About the Author

David C. Thomas is Associate Professor and Area Coordinator of International Business at Simon Fraser University, Canada. A naturalized New Zealander, Thomas was born and educated in the United States and received his Ph.D. from the University of South Carolina in Organizational Behavior and International Business.

His interest in the interaction of individuals from different cultures in organizational settings has prompted him to conduct research studies in more than a dozen different countries. His research has appeared in such journals as the *Journal of International Business Studies, Journal of Applied Psychology, Journal of Cross-Cultural Psychology, Journal of Business Research, Advances in International Comparative Management, Research in the Sociology of Organizations, Leadership Quarterly,* and *Organizational Dynamics.* He serves on the editorial boards of the *Journal of World Business, Advances in International Management,* and the *International Journal of Organizational Analysis* and is a reviewer for numerous other journals.

Before returning to academia in 1988, he was a Vice President with the bank holding company NationsBank (now Bank of America). His previous academic postings have included positions at the Pennsylvania State University and The University of Auckland, New Zealand, where he was also Director of the Master of International Business Program. He has held visiting positions at The Chinese University of Hong Kong and the University of Hawaii. In addition to his teaching at both undergraduate and postgraduate level, he has developed Executive Education programs in Australia, New Zealand, Canada, and the United States and has served as a consultant to a number of multinational firms.